Günter Bischof/Jason Dawsey

The Life and Work of Günther Anders

TRANSATLANTICA
Günter Bischof, Editor

Volume 8: Günter Bischof/Jason Dawsey/Bernhard Fetz (Eds.)
The Life and Work of Günther Anders

Günter Bischof/Jason Dawsey/Bernhard Fetz (Eds.)

The Life and Work of Günther Anders

Émigré, Iconoclast, Philosopher, Man of Letters

StudienVerlag

Innsbruck
Wien
Bozen

 Gefördert von

This publication is supported by: University of New Orleans, International Relations Office, Universität Innsbruck, Amt der Vorarlberger Landesregierung, Abt. IIb – Wissenschaft und Weiterbildung, Kulturabteilung der Tiroler Landesregierung, Wissenschaftsfonds FWF (Fonds zur Förderung der wissenschaftlichen Forschung) and Kulturabteilung der Stadt Wien, Wissenschafts- und Forschungsförderung and Zukunftsfonds der Republik Österreich.
It is the result of a cooperation between the Literature Archives of the Austrian National Library which holds the Anders Papers, the FWF-research project P 24012: "Günther Anders: Editing und Contextualization of Selected Writings from the Estate" und Center Austria of the University of New Orleans.

© 2014 by Studienverlag Ges.m.b.H., Erlerstraße 10, A-6020 Innsbruck
E-Mail: order@studienverlag.at
Internet: www.studienverlag.at

Corporate design by Kurt Höretzeder
Layout: Studienverlag/Roland Kubanda, www.rolandkubanda.com
Cover: Studienverlag/Karin Berner
Photo: Anders in New York, 1945
Photo Credit for all pictures in this volume: Anders Papers, Literature Archives, Austrian National Library, Vienna (Sign. ÖLA 237/04). With kind permission of Gerhard Oberschlick.

Distributed in North America and South America and the rest of the world excluding Austria, Germany and Switzerland by: Transaction Publishers, Rutgers – the State University, 35 Berrue Circle, Piscataway, New Jersey, 08854-8042, USA, www.transactionpub.com

This book is printed on acid-free paper.

Bibliographic information published by Die Deutsche Bibliothek
Die Deutsche Bibliothek lists this publication in the Deutsche Nationalbibliographie; detailed bibliographic data is available in the Internet at http://dnb.ddb.de

ISBN 978-3-7065-5352-0

Table of Contents

Anders—The Literary Figure

Anders—In His Own Words

Günter Bischof

Preface

The time is ripe to reevaluate the rich and fertile contributions of Günther Anders (1902–1992) to twentieth century thought and letters. The time has come to (re)-introduce Anders' œuvre to Anglo-American audiences. As the essays and a selection of his own writings show, Anders' contribution to twentieth century thought were wide-ranging. Anders personally experienced the high and low points of the troubled century he lived through. Born Günther Stern in Breslau/Wrocław, he studied with Heidegger and Husserl in Freiburg, Germany. He married Hannah Arendt and lived in Berlin. Germany's descent into National Socialism and Hitler's totalitarianism and anti-Semitism forced him into exile, first in Paris, then in Los Angeles and New York City. He returned to Europe with his Austrian wife Elisabeth Freundlich in 1950 and settled in Vienna. As a Jew living in (now more subtly) anti-Semitic Vienna, he got exasperated with the Austrians' failure to confront their role in the genocidal holocaust and their murderous World War II past. Anders lived in Vienna to the end of his life in 1992 but never felt at home in the provincial and anti-intellectual climate of the Austrian capital. He lived the role of the *Aussenseiter* and burr in the saddle of Austrian politicians, academics, and intellectuals high on their horses.

His role as an arch-critic of ever more advancing technological mass society in general and the nuclear age in particular defined him as a public intellectual *par excellence* of the Cold War era. Anders felt mankind lived on borrowed time with the advent of nuclear weapons in Hiroshima and Nagasaki in 1945. The detonation of a Soviet bomb in 1949 unleashed a nuclear arms race in the Cold War. During the 1950s both superpowers built every more powerful nuclear arsenals and produced the potential for "nuclear overkill." MAD—"mutual assured destruction"—defined the prospect for the destruction of the planet and mankind. By the early 1960s these anxieties about both genocide and ecocide, produced an outpouring in American popular culture (film, literature, music) on nuclear fears in "Dr. Strangelove's America." While Günther Anders (and his friend Robert Jungk) were often lonely voices in the desert warning about the nuclear apocalypse, in the United States popular culture made these discourses part of mainstream debates. Anders was often prescient in his critiques. Here was also a very creative mind and addressed many of these issues as a prolific writer of essays, poetry, and even a novel.

Center Austria of the University of New Orleans (UNO) and the University of Innsbruck have been organizing annual scholarly symposia since 1982. On March 14–15, 2013, they organized a conference on the philosopher and critical man of letters Günther Anders in New Orleans. Many people and institutions were instrumental in helping us to put the symposium together and finance the meeting. I got the initial idea for organizing such a symposium from Jason Dawsey, who at the time was finishing his University of Chicago dissertation on Günther Anders. In conversations with both Bernhard Fetz, the director of the Literature Archives of the Austrian National Library in Vienna, and Johann Holzner, the director of the

Brenner Archives in Innsbruck, ideas were refined of what areas needed to be covered. Fetz suggested Konrad Paul Liessmann from the Department of Philosophy at the University of Vienna as keynoter. Fetz and Liessmann had a research project going on Anders funded by the Austrian Research Fund (*Fonds zur Förderung der wissenschaftlichen Forschung, FWF*), which was funding Kerstin Putz' and Reinhard Ellensohn's research. Holzner identified University of Innsbruck specialists on Anders' philosophy Wolfgang Palaver and Andreas Oberprantacher. Palaver in turn led us to the Jean-Pierre Dupuy at Stanford, who was also on a mission to familiarize both French and American academia with this important European twentieth century contrarian thinker. I was in contact with Elisabeth Röhrlich, a young historian at the University of Vienna, who was working on the early history of the International Atomic Energy Agency in Vienna and a rare specialist on the nuclear age in Austria. Berthold Molden, who served as the Austrian Marshall Plan Chair at UNO during that time, offered his expertise on Anders as a prominent critic of the Vietnam War in the 1960s.

Once the symposium program was designed and agreed upon, UNO's Center Austria team sprang into action to execute arrangements for the planned conference. Gertraud Griessner, my associate and office manager at Center Austria, was instrumental as always in helping with hotel arrangements, conference meals, transportation, and logistics. Christian Riml, a fellow at Center Austria from the University of Innsbruck, assisted Gertraud with all these chores and also designed the conference program brochure. We are also grateful at UNO to President Peter Fos for opening the conference and welcoming our international visitors as well as Professor Frank Schalow from the Philosophy Department for chairing a session.

Piecing together the financing of such a meeting is always a challenge. Center Austria's conference budget is supported by the University of New Orleans, the Austrian Ministry of Science and Research in Vienna, as well as the Austrian Marshall Plan Foundation in Vienna. We would like to thank Barbara Weitgruber, Christoph Ramoser, and Josef Leidenfrost at the Ministry, as well as Florian Gerhardus at the Austrian Academic Exchange Service for their support. In the offices of the Marshall Plan Foundation Eugen Stark and Markus Schweiger, as well as Anton Fink and Ambassador Wolfgang Petritsch on the Foundation Board kept the UNO connection going. The Austrian Cultural Forum in New York and its director and deputy director Andreas Stadler and Hannah Liko supported the conference by paying the transatlantic flights of two participants. Hannah Liko also graced the conference with her presence. We would also like to thank Ambassador Martin Eichtinger, the chief of the cultural section at the Austrian Ministry for European and International Affairs, for his ongoing support of Center Austria activities. The University of Innsbruck Office of Foreign Affairs (*Auslandsamt*) financed the flights of Austrian participants as did the Literature Archives of the National Library through its Günther Anders project. In Innsbruck we would like to express our thanks specifically to Andreas Schennach at the *Auslandsamt*, as well as Barbara Tasser, Klaus Frantz, Christina Antenhofer and Marion Wieser. The *Wissenschaftsfonds FWF (Fonds zur Förderung der wissenschaftlichen Forschung)* in Vienna supported the conference, as well as the translation of "*Der Emigrant*", with their funds for the Anders project at the Austrian Literature Archives. Center Austria financed the reprinting fees paid to the *Massachusetts Review*.

Finally, we are very grateful to Kerstin Putz at the Literature Archives for her unusually quick and unstinting help when it was needed. She selected and provided the illustrations for us from the Anders Papers (*Nachlass*) at the Literature Archives. She was particularly helpful in selecting the Anders texts reprinted in the final section of this book and also helped us secure the rights to reprint these texts. "The Pathology of Freedom" is reprinted with the permission of the translator of the text Katharine Wolfe. "The Émigré", expertly translated by Otmar Binder (Vienna), is reprinted with the permission of Gerhard Oberschlick, the executor (*Nachlassverwalter*) of the Anders estate. The "Theses for the Atomic Age" are reprinted here with the permission of the *Massachusetts Review* and its Managing Editor Emily Wojcik. We are most grateful to all of them for allowing us to reprint these texts and thereby giving Anglo-American readers a flavor of Anders' compelling and complex thoughts on major issues of twentieth century pathologies.

Lauren Capone of the University of New Orleans copy-edited the entire manuscript and brought her usual discerning skills of the English language to bear on often complex Andersian language in the translations. All authors were most agreeable in proof-reading their chapters on short notice while I taught summer school in August 2014 in Innsbruck. In the final stage of proof-reading the entire manuscript Kerstin Putz, Bernhard Fetz and Jason Dawsey made invaluable suggestions, particularly with regard to the original Anders texts.

The team of the StudienVerlag in Innsbruck has helped the project along to final publication every step of the way. We would like to thank particularly Ruth Mayr for her unfailing support.

Günter Bischof   New Orleans, June 2014

Jason Dawsey

Introduction

If one accepts Eric Hobsbawm's designation of the twentieth century as an "Age of Extremes," then the German-Jewish intellectual Günther Anders (1902–1992) should be regarded as one of its chief witnesses and interpreters.[1] Although he is still not well known in the Anglophone world, Anders, during a career as a writer stretching almost seventy years, lived through and explored most of the crucial events in twentieth-century European and world history. His works, including his multi-volume *magnum opus*, *Die Antiquiertheit des Menschen* (The Obsolescence of Human Beings), illuminate the lasting effects of industrialism, the psychological and political implications of mass media, the legacy of the Holocaust and the invention of the atomic bomb for history and memory, the Vietnam War, ecological devastation, and new forms of internationalism and collective political action.[2]

The philosophical outlook Anders applied to these "extremes" drew upon central currents in contemporary European thought: his dissertation director Edmund Husserl's phenomenology, his teacher Martin Heidegger's fundamental ontology, which Anders later sharply criticized, and the philosophical anthropology of Max Scheler and Helmuth Plessner, both of whom he knew. Moreover, Anders' thinking was shaped by his extensive contacts with Marxist intellectuals, including Bertolt Brecht, Georg Lukács, and the Frankfurt School of Critical Theory. Concerned about the rapid mechanization of all spheres of life and, most importantly, the creation of nuclear weapons, he eventually developed an original and powerful "philosophy of discrepancy" organized around the argument about a rapidly expanding cleft between our ability to produce and our ability to imagine.[3] As an extension of this critique of the growing autonomy of technology, he authored a pathbreaking book on the Soviet and American space voyages and the photographs of Earth that resulted from them.[4]

Beyond his noted analyses of the growing predominance of technology and the nuclear danger, Anders, who spent seventeen years in exile (1933–36 in France, 1936–50 in the United States) after fleeing Germany in the wake of the Reichstag Fire, also wrote movingly and perceptively of exile, statelessness, and homesickness.[5] After he settled in Vienna in 1950 (where he lived until his death in 1992), Anders penned fierce criticisms of the failure to confront the Nazi past in West Germany and Austria.[6] His penetrating critique of his former teacher Martin

---

1   Eric Hobsbawm, The Age of Extremes: A History of the World 1914–1991, New York 1994.
2   For Anders' most important philosophical work, see Die Antiquiertheit des Menschen, Volume 1: Über die Seele im Zeitalter der zweiten industriellen Revolution, Munich 1956; Die Antiquiertheit des Menschen, Volume 2: Über die Zerstörung des Lebens im Zeitalter der dritten industriellen Revolution, Munich 1980. Anders planned a third volume that was not published in its entirety.
3   For his most salient analyses of the nuclear threat, see, in addition to Die Antiquiertheit des Menschen, Volume 1, see Endzeit und Zeitenende: Gedanken über die atomare Situation, Munich 1972; Hiroshima ist überall, Munich 1982.
4   Der Blick vom Mond: Reflexionen über Weltraumflüge, Munich 1970.
5   See his Tagebücher und Gedichte, Munich 1985.
6   In addition to the section titled Wiedersehen und Vergessen in Tagebücher und Gedichte, see Wir Eichmannsöhne: Offener Brief an Klaus Eichmann, Munich 1964; Besuch im Hades, Munich 1979.

Heidegger's involvement with National Socialism has not yet won the recognition it deserves.[7] Anders' anti-fascism carried over into his other political commitments. Like many other left-wing intellectuals during the 1960s, he also supported the New Left's condemnation of the Vietnam War and served as as juror on the Bertrand Russell Peace Foundation War Crimes Tribunal, which indicted the United States for crimes against humanity in Southeast Asia.[8]

A sophisticated critic of modern literature, Anders wrote exegeses of Brecht, Franz Kafka, Rainer Maria Rilke, Alfred Döblin, Hermann Broch, and Samuel Beckett.[9] Not content to interpret the works of others, he produced hundreds of poems, numerous fables, several works of short fiction, and a dystopian novel about a quasi-mythical dictatorship, *Die molussiche Katakombe* (The Catacombs of Molussia).[10] The extraordinary life he lived and the breadth and depth of the philosophical, political, and aesthetic writings he published easily justify careful and protracted scrutiny. The present volume, a collection of essays that grew out of a March 2013 international symposium on Anders at the University of New Orleans organized by Günter Bischof and Bernhard Fetz, furthers a process of critical engagement with his impressive writings by academics that began twenty-five years ago.[11]

In the opening pages of his 1982 *Ketzereien* (Heresies), Günther Anders, reflecting on his career as a politically-engaged writer, insisted that the "*Kampfthesen* (militant theses or battle-theses)" he had devised at least "deserved to be attacked."[12] Thus far, this honor had been denied him, he claimed. Seven years later, Gabriele Althaus complained that "one can read much *by* Günther Anders but little *about* him."[13] Long overshadowed by other intellectual luminaries (e.g. Martin Heidegger, his first wife Hannah Arendt, his distant cousin Walter Benjamin, his friends Herbert Marcuse and Ernst Bloch), his work had received minimal attention from academics. Since that time, a massive literature about Anders, most of it produced by German and Austrian scholars in philosophy and literature departments, has corrected the deficiency Althaus identified.[14] Within that literature, several impres-

---

7   Über Heidegger, ed. Gerhard Oberschlick in association with Werner Reimann, Munich 2001.

8   For example, see his Nürnberg und Vietnam: Synoptisches Mosaik, Frankfurt am Main 1967; Visit Beautiful Vietnam: ABC der Aggressionen heute, Cologne 1968.

9   Many of these works are reproduced in Anders' Mensch ohne Welt: Schriften zur Kunst und Literatur, Munich 1984.

10   For these works, see Tagebücher und Gedichte; Der Blick vom Turm: Fabeln, Munich 1968; Kosmologische Humoreske und andere Erzählungen, Frankfurt am Main 1978; Mariechen, Munich 1987, Die molussische Katakombe: Roman, 2nd ed., Munich 2012.

11   I would like to express my thanks to Günter Bischof and Bernhard Fetz for the opportunity to be one of the editors of this book.

12   Ketzereien, Munich 1982, 5.

13   Gabriele Althaus, Leben zwischen Sein und Nichts: Drei Studien zu Günther Anders, Berlin 1989, 7. Italics in the original.

14   In addition to Althaus' book cited above, see Micha Brumlik, Günther Anders: Zur Existenzialontologie der Emigration, in: Dan Diner, ed., Zivilisationsbruch: Denken nach Auschwitz, Frankfurt am Main 1988, 111–149; Jürgen Langenbach, Günther Anders: Eine Monographie, Munich 1988; Konrad Paul Liessmann, Günther Anders zur Einführung, Hamburg 1988; Eckhard Wittulski, Kein Ort, Nirgends: Zur Gesellschaftskritik Günther Anders', Frankfurt am Main 1989; Werner Reimann, Verweigerte Versöhnung: Zur Philosophie von Günther Anders, Vienna 1990; Oliver G'schrey, Günther Anders: "Endzeit" Diskurs und Pessimismus, Cuxhaven 1991; Elke Schubert, Günther Anders: Mit Selbstzeugnissen und Bilddokumenten, Reinbek bei Hamburg 1992; Ludger Lütkehaus, Philosophieren nach Hiroshima: Über Günther Anders, Frankfurt am Main 1992; Konrad Paul Liessmann, ed., Günther Anders kontrovers, Munich 1992; Margret Lohmann, Philosophieren in der Endzeit: Zur Gegenwartsanalyse von Günther Anders, Munich 1996; Sabine Palandt, Die Kunst der Vorausschau: Günther Anders' methodische und psychologische Ansätze zur Technikkritik, Berlin 1999.

sive comparative works have appeared.[15] In the last decade, another wave of Germano-phone publications has greatly expanded the purview of research on Anders' philosophical thought.[16]

Recently, an intensive discussion of Anders' work in France has begun.[17] A burgeoning Italian literature has followed.[18] This level of interest in Anders has yet to be matched in the Anglophone world. For more than a decade, the 2001 translation of the Dutch philosopher Paul van Dijk's book has been the only available monograph on him in English.[19] During this period, historian Harold Marcuse maintained a detailed webpage about new studies of Anders but, for several years, had little to report with respect to English-language publica-tions.[20] In the last five years, however, a nascent body of work, much of it by historians, has

---

15 Helmut Hildebrandt, Weltzustand Technik: Ein Vergleich der Technikphilosophien von Günther Anders und Martin Heidegger, Berlin 1990; Wolfgang Kramer, Technokratie als Entmaterialisierung der Welt: Zur Aktualität der Philosophien von Günther Anders und Jean Baudrillard, Münster 1998; Volker Kempf, Günther Anders: Anschlusstheoretiker an Georg Simmel?, Frankfurt am Main 2000; Berthold Wiesenberger, Enzyklopädie der apokalyptischen Welt: Kulturphilosophie, Gesellschaftstheorie und Zeitdiagnose bei Günther Anders und Theo-dor W. Adorno, Munich 2003; Konrad Paul Liessmann, Verzweiflung und Verantwortung: Koinzidenz und Differenz im Denken von Hans Jonas und Günther Anders, in: Christian Wiese/Eric Jacobson, eds., Weiter-wohnlichkeit der Welt: Zur Aktualität von Hans Jonas, Berlin 2003, 53–70; Bernhard Fetz, Attacke von zwei Seiten: Über Dichten und Philosophieren bei Günther Anders, in: Klaus Kastberger/Konrad Paul Liessmann, eds., Die Dichter und das Denken: Wechselspiele zwischen Literatur und Philosophie, Vienna 2004, 264–273; idem, Anthropologie im Exil: Das Archiv des Schriftstellers und Philosophen Günther Anders, in: Stéphanie Cudré-Mauroux/Irmgard Wirtz, eds., Literaturarchiv-Literarisches Archiv, Göttingen 2013, 51–74; Christian Dries, Die Welt als Vernichtungslager: Eine kritische Theorie der Moderne im Anschluss an Günther Anders, Hannah Arendt und Hans Jonas, Bielefeld 2012; Babette Babich, O Superman! Or Being Towards Transhu-manism: Martin Heidegger, Günther Anders, and Media Aesthetics, Divinatio 36 (Autumn-Winter 2012–2013): 41–99.
16 For a selection of some of these works, see Dirk Röpcke and Raimund Bahr, ed., Geheimagent der Massenere-miten: Günther Anders, St. Wolfgang 2002. See also two collections edited by Raimund Bahr, Urlaub vom Nichts: Dokumentation des gleichnamigen Symposiums zum 100. Geburtstag von Günther Anders im Juni 2002 in Wien, St. Wolfgang 2004, and Zugänge: Günther Anders: Leben und Werk, St. Wolfgang 2007. In addition, see Daniel Morat, Die Aktualität der Antiquiertheit: Günther Anders' Anthropologie des industriellen Zeitalters, Zeithistorische Forschungen/Studies in Contemporary History, Online Ausgabe, 3 (2006): 2; Reinhard Ellen-sohn, Der andere Anders: Günther Anders als Musikphilosoph, Frankfurt am Main 2008; Christian Dries, Gün-ther Anders, Paderborn 2009; idem, Marcel Müller, Von der Weltfremdheit zur Antiquiertheit: Philosophische Anthropologie bei Günther Anders, Marburg 2012; Ann-Kathrin Pollmann, Die Rückkehr von Günther Anders nach Europa: Eine doppelte Nach-Geschichte, Jahrbuch des Simon Dubnow-Instituts XI (2012): 389–409; idem, Ein offener Brief an Eichmanns Söhne: Günther Anders schreibt Klaus Eichmann, in: Werner Renz, ed., Interes-sen um Eichmann: Israelische Justiz, deutsche Strafverfolgung und alte Kameradschaften, Frankfurt am Main 2012, 241–258; Kerstin Putz, … unter Ihrem Applaus aus dem Lokal geführt: Günther Anders be-und entgegnet Salvador Dali, Sichtungen, 14/15(2014): 294–297.
17 Andreas Pfersmann and Jacques le Rider, ed., Günther Anders, Rouen 1993; Thierry Simonelli, Günther Anders: De la désuétude de l'homme, Paris 2004; Christophe David and Karin Parienti-Maire, ed., Günther Anders: Agir pour repousser la fin du monde, Paris 2007; Édouard Jolly, Nihilisme et Technique: Étude sur Günther Anders, Lille 2010.
18 For example, see Pier Paolo Portinaro, Il principio disperazione: Tre studi su Günther Anders, Turin 2003; Val-lori Rossini, ed., Potere e violenza nel pensiero di Günther Anders/Power and Violence in Günther Anders' Thinking, Etica & Politica/Ethics & Politics XV, no. 2 (2013).
19 Paul van Dijk, Anthropology in the Age of Technology: The Philosophical Contribution of Günther Anders, trans. Frans Kooymans, Atlanta 2000. The Dutch original was published in 1998.
20 See Marcuse's informative webpage, <http://www.history.ucsb.edu/faculty/marcuse/anders.htm>.

13

emerged in the United Kingdom and United States.[21] After years of neglect by academics, the analysis of Anders' life and thought has become a transnational phenomenon.

∗ ∗ ∗ ∗

Divided into four parts, *The Life and Work of Günther Anders* exhibits the research of established figures as well as more recent scholarship. Also thematically diverse, the essays in this volume, in some cases, place Anders' ideas into dialogue with those of other thinkers (e.g. Theodor W. Adorno, Ernst Bloch, Martin Heidegger, Hannah Arendt). Other pieces scrutinize texts often overlooked in the secondary literature, including Anders' fables, his poetry, published and unpublished, his scattered essays, and his private correspondence.

The contributors to Part I examine how Anders responded to central phenomena of twentieth-century history. Jason Dawsey's "Fragile Apprehension: Günther Anders and the Poetics of Destruction" reviews a selection of the poetry Anders produced in American exile in the 1940s as he learned about and responded to the monstrous news of the annihilation of European Jews. These astonishing poems, Dawsey argues, bear witness to Anders' efforts to devise a poetics capable of imagining and communicating to others such dreadful events while remaining self-critically aware of its own limits. Moreover, Anders and his poetry about the Holocaust should be considered as a vital part of a broader "culture of resistance" (Jost Hermand) against Nazism that crystallized among German intellectuals in the United States during the war.

As a translator and commentator, Jean-Pierre Dupuy has asserted the salience of Anders' apocalypticism for contemporary French debates. In "An Andersian Approach to Nuclear Deterrence," he utilizes Anders' insights about the nuclear peril and applies them to the doctrine of nuclear deterrence, a subject that, he claims, Anders neglected. Subtly probing the "logic" of deterrence theory, Dupuy finds that Anders' pronouncements about the fundamental irreversibility of the Atomic Age are not only relevant but resoundingly confirmed.

Elisabeth Röhrlich and Berthold Molden's contributions contextualize Anders' post-1945 career as a politically-engaged writer. Röhrlich's "'To Make the End Time Endless': The Early Years of Günther Anders' Fight against Nuclear Weapons" fleshes out the Austrian context— in 1955 the country declared its neutrality in the Cold War—for Anders' passionate involvement in peace politics. In addition, she details the very productive yet frequently contentious association with his chief comrade in Austrian anti-nuclear campaigns, the formidable Robert Jungk, and his polemics with his arch-nemesis in Vienna, Friedrich Torberg, the fiercely anti-communist and anti-neutralist editor of the journal *Forum*. Her important research indi-

---

21 See Holger Nehring, "Cold War, Apocalypse and Peaceful Atoms: Interpretations of Nuclear Energy in the British and West German Anti-Nuclear Weapons Movements, 1955–1964," *Historical Social Research* 29, no. 3 (2004): 150–170; Benjamin Ziemann, "The Code of Protest: Images of Peace in the West German Peace Movements, 1945–1990," Contemporary European History 17, no. 2 (2008): 237–261; idem, Introduction, in: Ziemann, ed., Peace Movements in Western Europe, Japan and the USA during the Cold War (Essen: Klartext, 2007); Jason Dawsey, Where Hitler's Name is Never Spoken: Günther Anders in 1950s Vienna, in: Günter Bischof/ Fritz Plasser/Eva Maltschnig, eds. Austrian Lives (Contemporary Austrian Studies=CAS 21), New Orleans 2012, 212–239; idem, The Limits of the Human: Günther Anders, Post-Marxism, and the Emergence of Technology Critique, Phil. Diss. University of Chicago 2013. See also Dawsey, After Hiroshima: Günther Anders and the History of Anti-Nuclear Critique, in: Benjamin Ziemann and Matthew Grant, eds., Unthinking the Imaginary War: Intellectual Reflections of the Nuclear Age, 1945–1990, Stanford in preparation, and Daniel Costello's forthcoming dissertation.

cates that the emergence of the Ban-the-Bomb movement in Austria and elsewhere after 1955 pushed Anders to both develop and deepen his critique of the Atomic Age and to link the theory to this burgeoning international anti-nuclear politics.

Berthold Molden's piece provides much-needed analysis of Anders' political activities beyond his participation in the struggle against nuclear weapons. Through an examination of Anders' writings from the late 1960s and early 1970s about the Vietnam War and decolonization, especially his 1968 *Visit Beautiful Vietnam*, he asks about the nature of Anders' self-conception as an independent critic and thinker on the Left, i.e. whether the term "transnational intellectual" is a fair classification for Anders' stance as a militant opponent of the war waged by the Americans in Vietnam. In so doing, Molden raises several crucial questions that merit further consideration. Among them, Anders' recourse to Holocaust analogies as part of his denunciation of American policy in Southeast Asia and his comments about the repression of the black freedom struggle in the United States should not be overlooked by scholars interested in his ideas and his admirable dedication to the ideal of the critical intellectual.

Since the early 1980s, Konrad Paul Liessmann has tirelessly promoted the philosophical importance of Anders' œuvre. Drawing on an extensive series of previous studies, his "Between the Chairs: Günther Anders—Philosophy's Outsider" introduces the volume's second part and surveys the major themes and transitions in Anders' intellectual biography. Throughout Anders' life as a politically-engaged writer, Liessmann discerns a deep continuity—an identification with the role of the outsider, the maverick, and the non-conformist, a role from which, he suggests, academic philosophy could learn a great deal, if it is to be more than a seminar phenomenon.

In his "The Respite: Günther Anders' Apocalyptic Vision in Light of the Christian Virtue of Hope," theologian Wolfgang Palaver finds that the current state of our world (e.g. the constant threat of terrorism, economic crisis, the dangers posed by climate change) warrants "to a certain degree an apocalyptic perspective." His piece sympathetically explores Anders' fully secular apocalypticism, especially his incisive concepts of post-Hiroshima history as *die Endzeit* (time of the end) and *die Frist* (the respite). Also a critical rejoinder to Anders' extremely harsh comments on the notion of hope, Palaver's essay draws on the work of the Catholic theologian Josef Pieper to reformulate a theology of hope that can answer Anders' equation of hoping with passivity. For Palaver, such a theological position could critically appropriate insights from Anders' philosophy of Atomic Age within a framework that remains theistic yet is resolutely committed to preserving our world.

Anders' complex and evocative concept of *Weltlosigkeit* (worldlessness) is the subject of Andreas Oberprantacher's essay. He considers the transition in Anders' thinking from an early concern with *Mensch ohne Welt* (Man without World) to his later goal, to prevent the advent of a *Welt ohne Mensch* (World without Man) through nuclear cataclysm. Basing his claims on a close reading of Anders' 1931 essay on Alfred Döblin's novel *Berlin Alexanderplatz* and its protagonist, Franz Biberkopf, Oberprantacher argues, suggestively, Anders' discussions of "worldlessness" and the condition of human "being-in-the-world" already move sharply away from Heidegger, his former teacher, and closer to Marx's theory of alienation. For Oberprantacher, this early commentary on *Weltlosigkeit* and its reformulation in later works, is one of Anders' most vital legacies for a twenty-first century where social marginalization is no longer a marginal phenomenon at all.

More than any other scholar, Reinhard Ellensohn has reconstructed and evaluated the philosophy of music Anders worked out in the 1920s before his proposal for a *Habilitations-*

schrift on the topic at the University of Frankfurt was blocked by Theodor W. Adorno. In his "The Art of Listening: On a Central Motif in Günther Anders' Early Philosophy of Music," Ellensohn distills central elements from this research. Ranging over Anders' numerous texts on music, including his detailed unpublished manuscript, *Philosophische Untersuchungen über musikalische Situationen* (Philosophical Investigations on Musical Situations), he presents a portrait of Anders as a major theorist of the transformation of music and listening in the twentieth century.

In Part III, Bernhard Fetz and Kerstin Putz examine Anders' literary aspirations. Fetz, Director of the Austrian Literature Archive of the Austrian National Library, contends that any approach to Anders, the author of numerous poems, works of fiction, and impressive critiques of modernist literature, that neglects the literary aspects of his thought or crudely separates the philosophical from the literary in his case gravely misunderstands him. Questions of style, genre, and technique always informed Anders' approach to philosophy. According to Fetz, Anders is best understood as one of those "hybrid thinkers" or "hybrid writers" who labored "between literature and philosophy."

Putz's essay scrutinizes Anders, the (quite literal) "man of letters," pointing out that he was both a prolific writer of letters and, moreover, a perceptive commentator on the increasing obsolescence of letter-writing. She focuses on Anders' correspondence with his first wife Hannah Arendt, an equally ardent letter-writer. These missives, she shows, reveal the fascinating connection between the two, long after their 1937 divorce, but also illustrate a mode of communication that, in retrospect, has largely vanished in the so-called Digital Age.

Any serious work about a thinker should lead the curious to that thinker's own writings. With this in mind, the editors have designed this volume to double as a reader. For Part IV, we have chosen three texts that represent different but essential dimensions of Anders' thought. The first, "The Pathology of Freedom: An Essay on Non-Identification," presents a substantial part of his early philosophical anthropology. Originally published in the mid-1930s in the important French journal *Recherches Philosophiques* (associated with Alexander Koyré and Emmanuel Levinas), the essay's treatments of ontological freedom, of nihilism and history, and its affinities with and direct influence on Jean-Paul Sartre's Existentialism will be of great value to those interested in philosophical debates about it what means to be human.[22] "The Émigré," translated into English here for the first time by Otmar Binder, is one of the most trenchant analyses of the Central European exile experience in the twentieth century and should invite comparison with Theodor W. Adorno's *Minima Moralia* and W.G. Sebald's *Die Ausgewanderten (The Emigrants)*.[23] The third of the original texts, "Theses for the Atomic Age," is perhaps the most concise and accessible presentation of Anders' conception of the Atomic Age as a distinct—and final—epoch of world history.[24] In this case, we have utilized the English translation Anders himself prepared for an issue of *The Massachusetts Review*.[25]

---

22 Pathologie de la liberté: Essai sur la non-identification, trans. P.-A. Stéphanopoli, Recherches Philosophiques no. 6 (1936–37): 22–54. The English translation first appeared as The Pathology of Freedom: An Essay on Non-Identification, trans. Katherine Wolfe, Deleuze Studies 3, no. 2 (2009): 278–310. We gratefully reprint Wolfe's fine translation.

23 For the original, see Der Emigrant, Merkur 16, no. 7 (July 1962): 601–622.

24 Thesen zum Atomzeitalter, Das Argument, no. 17 (1960): 226–234. The piece is also available in Die atomare Drohung: Radikale Überlegungen, Munich 1981, 93–105.

25 "Theses for the Atomic Age," trans. Günther Anders, The Massachusetts Review, 3, no. 3 (Spring 1962): 493–505.

This volume will be judged a success if it stimulates further inquiry and critical reflection. It is an opportune time to consider and debate the life and thought of Anders. Gerhard Oberschlick, the editor of the Vienna journal *Forum* and executor of Anders' *Nachlass*, turned the latter over in 2004 to the Austrian Literature Archive of the Austrian National Library where it is open to scholars. Massive bibliographic labors have already been undertaken to organize Anders' sprawling œuvre.[26] Although no comprehensive biography of him yet exists, students of Anders' work have had detailed, archivally-rooted, biographical descriptions available since 2010.[27] Thanks to Konrad Paul Liessmann, Christian Dries, and Bernhard Fetz, an International Günther Anders Society was founded in 2012 that coordinates the latest research. As part of this larger constellation of ongoing inquiries, this collection of essays makes a compelling case that Anders' ideas are quite fruitful, if not indispensable points of reference for critical philosophical, literary, and historical studies dedicated to rethinking the legacy of the twentieth century and to imagining and shaping what kind of future may unfold for human beings in the twenty-first.

26 For extensive bibliographies of primary and secondary sources, see Jan Stümpel, Bibliographie Günther Anders, in the special issue on Anders of Text + Kritik 115 (July 1992): 89–101; Raimund Bahr, ed., Günther Anders: Werkbibliographie, St. Wolfgang 2008; Heinz Scheffelmeier's invaluable Bibliographie, first compiled in 1995 and recently updated before his untimely death in 2012, is available at http://www.forvm.at/texte/ga_bibliographie.html (accessed May 26, 2014).

27 See Raimund Bahr, Günther Anders: Leben und Denken im Wort, St. Wolfgang 2010; Dawsey, The Limits of the Human, Ch. 1.

Historical Contexts

Historical Notes

Jason Dawsey

Fragile Apprehension:
Günther Anders and the Poetics of Destruction

In his recent critical study, *Culture in Dark Times*, Jost Hermand enjoins his readers not to overlook how, among the "Hitler refugees," the writers, "despite everything," "did contribute to a culture of resistance, which is remarkable and deserves lasting appreciation."[1] Hermand's important plea covers a broad range of German authors, including the familiar names of Thomas Mann, Bertolt Brecht, and Theodor W. Adorno, but also extends to Arnold Zweig, Anna Seghers, Lion Feuchtwanger, and Ernst Toller, who have largely been forgotten in the Anglophone world. Given his extensive contacts with many of these writers and his own remarkable body of work about the experience of exile, Günther Anders' contribution to this "culture of resistance" is a surprisingly understudied area of his life and thought. The long period of exile Anders endured (1933–1950) was a crucial aspect of his identity as a writer and deserves further investigation, especially in light of the texts (correspondence, unpublished manuscripts) that have been found in the Anders *Nachlass*.

As Micha Brumlik has noted, Anders' philosophy permanently carried the imprint of these years of expulsion. His philosophy was so "obviously coined by the circumstances of the time, of the emigration, of Hiroshima and Auschwitz, that an attempt to explain his thinking outside of these circumstances could end scarcely differently than in tautology (*kaum anders als tautologisch enden könnte*)."[2] This critical essay initiates an assessment of Anders' place within the anti-Nazi resistance. I leave aside Anders' earlier time in Paris (1933–36) and concentrate on the fourteen years he spent in the United States (1936–1950). My emphasis is on the remarkable poetry Anders wrote during his exile in America about the persecution and consequent destruction of European Jewry, while these horrors unfolded and in their immediate aftermath.

Through an examination of these poems, most of them produced between 1940 and 1949, we can discern Anders' hard-won, if quite fragile apprehension of the Shoah.[3] By "fragile apprehension," a concept indebted to the field of Holocaust literature, I understand a didactic poetics that responds with imagination and empathy in order to depict the plight of victims

---

1   Jost Hermand, Culture in Dark Times: Nazi Fascism, Inner Emigration, and Exile, trans. Victoria W. Hill, New York 2013, 211.

2   One of the first scholars to examine Anders' œuvre, Micha Brumlik designated Anders' philosophy as an "existential ontology of emigration." See his Günther Anders: Zur Existenzialontologie der Emigration, in: Dan Diner, ed., Zivilisationsbruch: Denken nach Auschwitz, Frankfurt am Main 1988, 113.

3   Lawrence Langer, The Holocaust and the Literary Imagination (New Haven, 1975); Alvin Rosenfeld, A Double Dying: Reflections on Holocaust Literature, Bloomington 1980; James Young, Writing and Rewriting the Holocaust: Narrative and the Consequences of Interpretation, Bloomington 1988; Sarah Horowitz, Voicing the Void: Muteness and Memory in Holocaust Fiction, Albany 1997; Harold Bloom, ed., Literature of the Holocaust, Broomall 2004; Alan Rosen, ed., Literature of the Holocaust, Cambridge 2013. It was Michael Geyer who first pushed me to explore the topic of this piece.

of the genocide when precise information about the mass killing of European Jews was often fragmentary and when the benefit of hindsight was not available. Much of Anders' poetic output from these years has gone largely unnoticed in the secondary literature.[4] Neglect of these works has hindered a fair, historically rigorous assessment of when and to what degree the Nazi genocide imprinted his thinking. I argue that Anders' poems from the 1940s disclose what he knew and how he reacted to one of world history's greatest crimes before his later philosophy (including his impressive critique of technology), coalesced around the primary signifiers "Auschwitz" and "Hiroshima," and before he fervently endorsed Adorno's pronouncement about the barbarity of writing poetry after the former.[5]

This essay complements my earlier piece on Anders' critical impressionistic ethnography of post-Nazi Vienna.[6] Together, these works, I hope, provide a more complete understanding of Anders' response to two of the principal "caesuras" in his remarkable life: the Third Reich and Auschwitz.[7]

* * * *

Recalling his time in California (1939–1943), Anders told an interviewer how he kept company with "The Other Germany (das andere Deutschland)" during those years.[8] The extraordinary "Other Germany" Anders remembered included the Frankfurt School theorists Max Horkheimer, Theodor W. Adorno, and Herbert Marcuse (with whom he lived briefly), the writers Bertolt Brecht, Thomas Mann, and Alfred Döblin, and the composers Arnold Schoenberg and Hanns Eisler. "Is it not absurd," he mused in the interview, "that there was on the stillness of the ocean such a politically, sociologically, and philosophically conversant group,

---

4   Ludger Lütkehaus and Johann Holzner are among the few researchers who have written about Anders' poetry from this period. See Lütkehaus, Antiquiertheit des Menschen—Antiquiertheit der Kunst? Über Günther Anders' ästhetische Theorie und literarische Praxis, in: Klaus Kastberger/Konrad Paul Liessmann, eds., Die Dichter und das Denken: Wechselspiele zwischen Literatur und Philosophie, Vienna 2004, 255–256, 258–259; Johann Holzner, Philippika im Lärm der Sterbenden: Zum lyrischen Werk von Günther Anders, in: Helmut Pfanner, ed., Der Zweite Weltkrieg und die Exilanten: Eine literarische Antwort, Bonn 1991, 37–42 (my thanks to Kerstin Putz for bringing Holzner's piece to my attention). Lütkehaus and Holzner do not devote much space, however, to looking at the poetry Anders wrote specifically about the Nazi genocide.

5   For Anders' interpretation of and support for Adorno's statements on poetry-writing after Auschwitz, see his 1985 interview with Fritz Raddatz, Brecht konnte mich nicht riechen, in: Elke Schubert, ed., Günther Anders antwortet: Interviews & Erklärungen, Berlin 1987, 111 (hereafter GAa). For Adorno's much disputed pronouncements, see his "Cultural Criticism and Society," in: Samuel and Shierry Weber, trans., Prisms, Cambridge 1981, 34. For more on Adorno, see Horowitz, Voicing the Void, 8, 16; Jack Zipes, On the Necessity of Writing Poetry After Auschwitz: A Reassessment of Adorno's Cultural Critique, in: John McCarthy/Walter Grünzweig/Thomas Koebner, eds., The Many Faces of Germany: Transformations in the Study of German Culture, New York 2004, 34–42; Josh Cohen, Interrupting Auschwitz: Art, Religion, Philosophy, New York 2005, Ch.2; Gerhard Richter, Thought-Images: Frankfurt School Writers' Reflections from Damaged Life, Stanford 2007, 183.

6   Jason Dawsey, Where Hitler's Name is Never Spoken: Günther Anders in 1950s Vienna, in: Günter Bischof/Fritz Plasser/Eva Maltschnig, eds. Austrian Lives (Contemporary Austrian Studies=CAS 21), New Orleans 2012, 212–239.

7   I refer here too Anders' discussion of the four "caesuras" in his 1979 interview with Mathias Greffrath of the four "caesuras" in his life. Hitler's assumption of power in 1933 and "Auschwitz" were the second and third of these. See Wenn ich verzweifelt bin, was geht's mich an? GAa, 41–42.

8   The term is derived from the book by Thomas Mann's daughter and son, Erika Mann and Klaus Mann, The Other Germany, New York 1940.

Anders in exile in California in the 1940s.
Photo: Anders Papers, Literature Archives, Austrian
National Library

while Hitler raged in Europe and millions were burned to ashes in Auschwitz?"[9] Anders' corpus contains incredibly rich information about this group and his participation in it.[10]

Yet Anders' connections with these men and others during his years of exile, both in southern California and in New York, were quite aysmmetrical. Lacking an established reputation as an academic or as a writer, he frequently depended on his contacts with the aristocracy of the émigrés for work opportunities and for favorable reviews of his writings.[11] Anders' discomfort with English and determination to continue working in his native German compounded his marginality. In a letter to Thomas Mann, he admitted that his decision to primarily write in German "was for an unknown writer," like himself, "the first hindrance."[12] This combination of factors sealed Anders' status as an outsider.[13]

Despite his marginality, Anders wrote dozens of works in America, including screenplays, essays, and book-length manuscripts, most of which were never published. When interviewed about his activities during these years, he stressed that his fellow émigrés actually knew him best for his poetry.[14] Poems, Anders said, made up half of his total output as a writer.[15] His love for poetry had flowered long before his time in the United States. During

---

9   See Wenn ich verzweifelt bin, in GAa, 36. For more about this group, see Erhard Bahr, Weimar on the Pacific: German Exile Culture in Los Angeles and the Crisis of Modernism, Berkeley 2007.

10 A good place to start are Anders' writings about Döblin, Brecht, and the artist George Grosz, as well as the Austrian novelist and émigré Hermann Broch, in Mensch ohne Welt: Schriften zur Kunst und Literatur, Munich 1984.

11 These contacts sometimes aided him in finding work. In a letter to Heinrich Mann, Anders mentioned that the Hollywood Press Syndicate had assigned him the task of interviewing prominent Europeans for American papers. See Günther Anders to Heinrich Mann, November 12, 1941, Heinrich Mann Papers, Feuchtwanger Memorial Library, Specialized Libraries and Archival Collections, University of Southern California (hereafter FML-USC).

12 Günther Anders to Thomas Mann, October 14, 1945, Österreichisches Literaturarchiv der Österreichischen Nationalbibliothek, Vienna, Nachlass Günther Anders 237/04 (hereafter ÖLA-ÖNB, NGA 237/04).

13 For a longer view of Anders' status as an outsider, see Konrad Paul Liessmann, Between the Chairs: Günther Anders—Philosophy's Outsider, in this volume.

14 Wenn ich verzweifelt bin, in GAa, 36–37.

15 See the 1982 interview with Mathias Greffrath, Den Tod der Welt vor Augen, in ibid., 61.

the Weimar period, he placed a poem in the important arts periodical *Das Dreieck*.[16] The following year, three of his poems appeared in an anthology that featured the poetry of Bertolt Brecht, Johannes Becher, Max Hermann-Neisse, Ernst Toller, and Georg Kaiser.[17] In 1930, Anders co-authored an impressive essay on Rainer Rilke's famed *Duino Elegies* with his then wife Hannah Arendt.[18]

During this early period of Anders' interest in poetry, itself part of a broader curiosity about the arts, including music, and the history of art, purely philosophical and aesthetic concerns predominated.[19] After 1933 and, especially, 1939, a major, if unsurprising turn occurred in the content of his poetry; it became increasingly political, critical, and exhortative. The "political poems" he and others composed about the Nazi dictatorship over "fifteen years in nights of indignation" "could fill hundreds of volumes," Anders wrote.[20] Tirelessly drawing attention to the fate of European Jewry as Hitler's grip on the continent tightened, Anders mostly relied on the poem as his main consciousness-raising mode of intervention. Through these poems, Anders reached out to his language community, Germanophone, often Jewish and left-wing audiences, via an array of exile publications in Mexico, Chile, Argentina, the United States, and Sweden: *Freies Deutschland, Volksblatt, The German American, Deutsche Blätter*, and *Die neue Rundschau*.

It was with *Aufbau*, the extraordinary publication of the German-Jewish Club of New York City, that Anders established the closest and most enduring link. Under the editorship of the pacifist and Zionist Manfred George, *Aufbau* aided German Jews seeking refuge from Nazism, providing information about jobs, tips about improving their English, and superb news coverage and commentary.[21] In 1939, the same year George took over as its editor, Anders began a connection with the journal that lasted three decades.[22] A few of the poems which first appeared in *Aufbau* or one of the other exile journals Anders later republished in collections of émigré or Holocaust literature.[23] Finally, in 1985, he released many of these poems in a book with the simple title *Tagebücher und Gedichte (Journals and Poems)*.[24]

---

16 As Günther Stern, he published Der Bulle in Das Dreieck: Monatszeitschrift für Wissenschaft, Kunst und Kritik no. 1 (September 1924): 12.

17 See his three poems Der verlorene Sohn, Gebet um Regen, and Hochzeit, in Jo Lherman, ed., Die Lyrik der Generation: Eine Anthologie unveröffentlichter Gedichte sechzig deutscher Autoren, Berlin 1925, 53.

18 See their Rilkes 'Duineser Elegien,' Neue Schweizer Rundschau 23, no. 11 (1930): 855–871.

19 For an example of these early interests in aesthetics and art history, see Anders' essay, Zur Problematik kunstwissenschaftlicher Grundbegriffe: Anlässlich Coellens Buch: 'Methode der Kunstgeschichte,' Archiv für systematische Philosophie und Soziologie XXIX (1926): 213–219.

20 Über Gedichte, in Tagebücher und Gedichte, Munich 1985, 269 (hereafter TG). This piece was written in New York in 1949.

21 See the overview of George's life in the obituary, Dr. Manfred George, 72, Dies; Editor of German Weekly Here; Novelist and Biographer Made Aufbau a Voice of Help to Refugees of Nazism, New York Times, January 1, 1966.

22 As far as I have been able to determine, the first piece by Anders to appear in the newspaper was his poem Aber vorher, Aufbau, August 1, 1939. Shortly after she arrived in the United States, Hannah Arendt also established a connection with Aufbau. For these texts, see Hannah Arendt, Vor Antisemitismus ist man nur noch auf dem Monde sicher: Beiträge für die deutsch-jüdische Emigrantenzeitung "Aufbau" 1941–1945, Munich 2000.

23 For example, Anders' poems Und was hätt'st du getan?, Heimkehrender Mörder spricht zu seiner Hand, Zeitungsnachricht, Die Stunde des Schaufelns, and Späte Benachrichtigung, some of which were originally released separately in exile publications, were published together in the excellent Heinz Seydel, ed., Welch Wort in die Kälte gerufen: Die Judenverfolgung des Dritten Reiches im deutschen Gedicht, Berlin 1968, 322, 335–336, 360, 394–395, 396.

24 For the entirety of the poems, over a hundred of them altogether, see TG, 275–394.

Several of the headings Anders chose for the volume's selection of poems—"Emigration," "War," "Of Death and Killing," "Terror-Images," and a section simply labeled "Jewish," signaled, retrospectively, a major reorientation for his poetry, if not for poetics itself. These poems tri-angulate émigrés who had escaped the SS, those Jews facing violence and death at the hands of the Nazis, and German soldiers and civilians.[25] Studied as a whole, they bind histories of expulsion, resettlement in foreign lands, and homesickness with those of war and geno-cide. Because of this forbidding subject matter, Anders insisted that the "call (Anruf) of my poems—to children, to whom dying, to adults, to whom killing, was their everyday existence (Alltäglichkeit)—excludes any esotericism."[26] Finding the "correct tone" required a "direct-ness" which not only shunned esotericism but avoided a "false popular tone (Volkston)."[27] The search for a precise language adequate to the horrors defining that time compelled him even when he had to write on his "knees rather than at a desk; always for no one or for tomorrow's people rather than for impatient editors; always for the drawers or the valise, never for the bookcase."[28] What was the goal of this linguistic "directness"? Anders' aim, as he related to Heinrich Mann, was to generate "didactic terror" through his poems.[29]

In what follows, I do not offer an assessment of Anders' talents as a poet nor do I consider the liminal character of his literary endeavors, work already undertaken by Bernhard Fetz.[30] Rather, I investigate the sources for and the outcome of his intent to induce terror in audi-ences. What resulted I categorize as a poetics of destruction, a remarkable poetics dedicated to securing an adequate and powerful language to communicate atrocity, in this case prin-cipally the state-directed, systematic, continent-wide extermination program of the Hitler dictatorship. As we shall see, from the start, Anders' poetics of destruction was always self-reflexive about its own inherent limitations.

It must be kept in mind that Anders' poetry-writing during the 1940s overlapped with his involvement with rescue efforts. While Hannah Arendt and her second husband Heinrich Blücher were in Marseille, trying to leave France for the United States, he worked diligently to aid them. In January 1941, after securing affidavits and visas for them, Anders implored the novelist Lion Feuchtwanger to help raise money for the couple.[31] Six weeks later, Anders wrote back to Feuchtwanger informing him that Arendt and her family would be able to make it to the US (they arrived in New York via Lisbon in May 1941). Quoting a letter he had received from Arendt, he notified Feuchtwanger of the "cases" of the Social Democratic Party politicians Rudolf Hilferding and Rudolf Breitscheid, who had been turned over by the Vichy

25 For similar remarks about Anders' thematic organization of the volume's collection of poems, see Holzner, Philippika im Lärm der Sterbenden, 37.
26 Über Gedichte, in TG, 270.
27 Ibid., 271, 270. In this context, see also Anders' Die Dichtstunde, Merkur no. 49 (March 1952): 224–240.
28 See the translation of Anders' 1962 essay Der Emigrant (The Emigré) in this volume, 186.
29 Günther Anders to Heinrich Mann, April 17, 1946, Heinrich Mann Papers, FML-USC. In this letter, Anders uses the term "didactic terror" to refer to the poem, Die Reise zum Meeresgrund (which he enclosed with the letter). I apply this phrase to all of Anders' poems about the Holocaust and contend that a careful examination of the latter will justify this claim.
30 See Bernhard Fetz, Writing Poetry Today—Günther Anders between Literature and Philosophy, in this volume. See also Fetz's earlier work, Attacke von zwei Seiten: Über Dichten und Philosophieren bei Günther Anders, in Die Dichter und das Denken, 264–273. The latter is part of an extremely helpful Dossier Günther Anders Fetz put together for this volume. One of the earliest attempts to assess Anders as a literary figure was Konrad Paul Liessmann, Die Schönheit der Gorgo: Günther Anders und die Literatur, das pult 65 (1982): 17–23.
31 Günther Anders to Lion Feuchtwanger, January 31, 1941, Lion Feuchtwanger Papers, FML-USC.

police to the Gestapo, and passed on the distressing news that the Nazis would soon be able to seize thousands of other German exiles.[32] Anders had had good reason to be distressed, even with the good news concerning Arendt.

Among the unfortunate, who could not and did not get out of German-dominated Europe in time, was Anders' distant cousin Walter Benjamin. After being detained briefly by Spanish border police, Benjamin took his life by swallowing morphine tablets, dying on 26 September, 1940 in the small town of Portbou.[33] Anders learned of Benjamin's suicide from Arendt, who carried with her several of Benjamin's manuscripts, including the famed "On the Concept of History."[34]

Immediately following this shocking news, Anders penned a poem in memory of his cousin. Titled *"Das Vermächtnis* (The Legacy)," the poem appeared in an October 1940 issue of *Aufbau* along with Theodor W. Adorno's essay on Benjamin as a thinker.[35] Anders' poem conveys very little about Benjamin as a person or a thinker. Instead, "The Legacy" proclaims to Benjamin's tormentors that those of "us, those who, accidentally, still outlasted him [Benjamin]" will draw strength from this terrible loss.[36] As the "hall of the dead becomes dreadfully full," Anders writes, "no can predict whether you will/be the next to disappear/ but some will remain/some accidentally still remain/who makes no difference."[37] Mixing grief over Benjamin's death and apprehension about the living with clear defiance, "The Legacy" announces to the Nazis that so long as some still live the anti-fascist struggle will continue. Over twenty years later, Anders numbered Benjamin among the millions interred in "wrong graves, in graves in the wrong place, in graves to which their surviving relatives will never find their way" scattered around the globe during the Second World War.[38]

During this early and disheartening phase of the war, a phase marked by Benjamin's death, serial German triumphs on the battlefield, and ghettoization and ethnic cleansing behind the lines, Anders devoted more time to his poetic labors, producing an extraordinary series of poems on the suffering of European Jewry. He spoke of the resentment faced by those who had escaped Hitler only, in turn, to be compelled to continually seek out more hospitable environments.[39] Elsewhere, Anders tapped the long history of Jews as pariahs. He had already invoked the tale of Ahasver, the Wandering Jew, before he departed from Paris.[40] In a 1939 piece, he refers to a wind from Babylon now blowing through the Łódź Ghetto.[41] Knowing no "terminus (Endstation)," this wind will "still blow tomorrow/tomorrow it blows for your

32 Günther Anders to Lion Feuchtwanger, March 17, 1941, in ibid. After being tortured by the Gestapo, Hilferding died in February 1941. Breitscheid, who was imprisoned in Buchenwald, survived there until August 1944.

33 Bernd Witte, Walter Benjamin: An Intellectual Biography, trans. James Rolleston, Detroit 1991, 205.

34 For how he learned of Benjamin's death from Arendt and, in turn, informed Brecht of the tragedy, see Günther Anders to Erdmut Wizisla, September 23, 1988, quoted in Erdmut Wizisla, Walter Benjamin and Bertolt Brecht—The Story of a Friendship, trans. Christine Shuttleworth, New Haven 2009, 180n.

35 Günther Anders, Das Vermächtnis, Aufbau, October 18, 1940. Adorno's essay in the same issue is called Zu Benjamins Gedächtnis.

36 Ibid.

37 Ibid.

38 The Emigré, 178, n. 4.

39 See one of the last of these poems, the 1942 Die Stimme des Entmutigers flüstert, in TG, especially p. 288.

40 See the 1935 Ahasver besingt die Weltgeschichte, in ibid., 379–380.

41 Schlaflied für ein Emigrantenkind, in ibid., 377. I should note here that if the date for the poem's composition is accurate, Anders must have written it immediately after learning of the establishment of the ghetto in Łódź in December 1939.

son."[42] The nightmare currently lived by Jews in Hitler's Europe, the poem insinuates, belongs to and continues a disgraceful history stretching back to the Babylonian Captivity.

The next year, Anders addressed the case of 300 Jews fleeing Marshal Ion Antonescu's Romania for Palestine in *"Nein, dankbar sie sind nicht* (No, They Are Not Grateful)."[43] The text, introduced with a description of a report from a Belgrade newspaper about the refugees, narrates a horrific situation. In this case, stranded on steamers in the harbor of Tulcea, on the Danube River, they could not embark for their destination. If the refugees tried to leave the ships, they would be shot by the men of the fascist Iron Guard.[44] That same year, Anders wrote another poem, this time utilizing the figure of Eratosthenes from the world of ancient Greece to appeal to people to recognize the enormity of a coming danger. Disconsolate, the speaker laments "the murderers are ten days away?/ And, except for me, is there no one here who screams?"[45] Anders' despair concerning the plight of Jewish refugees caught up in the war and the lack of alarm about their situation is so palpable in this set of works. His despair, it hardly requires adding, was thoroughly warranted, as avenues for escape rapidly vanished by 1941.

For much of 1941–42, Anders composed numerous poems exhorting the German armed forces and civilians to turn against Hitler's monstrous war.[46] After his return to New York in 1943, rumors about Nazi extermination camps reached him that summer. They were confirmed, he recalled, in early 1944.[47] As published excerpts from Anders' journals from 1944 indicate, these awful reports of mass killing hastened a fundamental rethinking of his philosophical conception of the human being already underway.[48]

In response, Anders redirected his attention to the nightmare lived by European Jews, completing a series of stunning poems about their destruction. One can mark a clear thematic shift in these works from concern over persecution and expulsion to horror and shock over the growing evidence of Hitler's new policy of total extermination. While, much later, he used "Auschwitz" as a general term for the genocide, Anders' poems from 1943–49 adhered to a more differentiated approach to the Nazis' turn to extermination. These works not only attended to the industrialized murder process so often associated in Anders' later philosophy (and that of many other intellectuals) with Auschwitz but also explored less technocratic meth-

---

42 Ibid.

43 See Nein, dankbar sie sind nicht, in ibid., 378–379. The poem was originally published under the title Eigentlich, Aufbau, November 1, 1940.

44 Ibid. I have been unable to determine exactly which incident Anders reports here. Perhaps he referred to the efforts to bring over 3000 Jews from Vienna to Palestine via Tulcea in October and November 1940. Seized by the British and placed on a French ship, the *Patria*, bound for Mauritius, 267 of them were killed when the Haganah detonated a bomb to disable the vessel, sinking it in the process. Anders might also have been describing the Kladovo episode of late 1939-early 1940 when 1200 Jews, mostly members of Zionist youth organizations, tried to make their way through Yugoslavia and Romania, were halted on the Yugoslav side of the Danube, and prohibited by Romanian border authorities from going any farther. Living on unheated barges on the Danube through the winter, many of the Kladovo group were later swept up during the German invasion of Yugoslavia in April 1941 and subsequently murdered. For more on these incidents, see Saul Friedländer, The Years of Extermination: Nazi Germany and the Jews, 1939–1945, New York 2007, 88–90.

45 See Was Wissen ist, in TG, 312.

46 For some of these poems, see the Krieg section of TG, 321–332. Anders' very interesting poems on the war deserve a separate study.

47 See his Nach 'Holocaust' 1979, in Besuch im Hades, Munich 1979, 198 (hereafter BiH). It is worth noting that Anders uses the term *"Vernichtungslagern"* in these statements.

48 See the selections Anders published from his journals, Rückblendung 1944–1949, in ibid., 37–46.

ods of murder. Experimenting with different rhyme schemes and occasionally with free verse, Anders focused in these works on depicting the varied if always heartbreaking experiences of victims. Just as he did in "No, They Are Not Grateful," he often integrated newspaper reports into the text in order to counter inevitable disbelief about the subject matter he covered.

What is particularly chilling about so many of these poems is how they revolve around children. Among them, Anders created a work to soothe an emigrant child at bedtime.[49] Several years later, he revisited the theme of consolation with a poem about a small, naïve child and his mother aboard a deportation train to one of the Nazi camps. In this case, though, after he brings up pleasant memories of past family trips, the boy, believing he is on another vacation, tells his mother that everything is all right. These comforting words are uttered as they arrive at their terrible destination.[50] "*Europäisches Kinderlied* (Song of Europe's Children)," from 1945, depicts the dreadful situation of refugee children coping with hunger and the absence of shelter. These urchins "have nothing on Earth/no clothes, no bed and no food."[51] Reduced to scavenging, they have no better prospects ahead.

> The morning hour comes cold,
> then we sniff around like dogs
> in the garbage and debris and blood.
> And what filth we find,
> potatoes or crusts,
> we devour (*fressen*) before the neighbor does.[52]

"What only should become of us?" the poem asks.[53] "*Zeitungsnachricht* (Newspaper Message)," also written in the first person, relays the pleas of a five-year-old liberated from Buchenwald, one of the few Nazi camps Anders explicitly names in these poems.[54] The child begs to be permitted to stay in Buchenwald, its place of birth and the only world it knows.

"*Verlaufenes Kind* (Child Gone Astray)," from 1945, Anders prefaces with a newspaper story about the discovery of small skeletons, the remains of children marched through the darkness, then shot.[55] There, Death personified consoles a child in its last moments. "Give up, my child," "stay here, my child," he implores.[56] Death's voice hovers over the dying victim and promises lasting peace.

> Since secretly beast and stone
> and root have sworn to be hospitable
> for you there.
> And even the earth invites you
> with gates left open.[57]

---

49 See the 1939 Schlaflied für ein Emigrantenkind, in TG, 377–378.
50 Peer Gynt im Deportationszug, in ibid., 381–382. This poem was written in 1947.
51 Europäisches Kinderlied, in ibid., 356.
52 Ibid.
53 Ibid.
54 Zeitungsnachricht, in ibid., 362.
55 Verlaufenes Kind, in ibid., 363.
56 Ibid.
57 Ibid.

As the poem's lines comfort, as much as possible, the child facing its end, they sear the reader. Betraying some knowledge of the Nazi death marches of the war's last months, Anders' "Child Gone Astray," in its envisioning of the most helpless as they perished, is one of his bravest works. All of these poems featuring children expressed Anders' deep anxiety about the most vulnerable of those affected by the war.[58] What kind of human beings would deliberately and systematically target children? Who would build a new society after the Third Reich's collapse, if not the young?

Also dating from the war's final year, "*Die Stunde des Schaufelns* (The Hour of Shoveling)" pauses over the act of digging, digging one's own grave in "snow-covered forests."[59] Here, speaking to the dead, the poet strains to conceive the steps which led to this final, inhuman action before violent death. The ability to recall the person's very visage becomes fraught with difficulty. It "seems untrue/what is too hard/to preserve (bewahren)," the poem bemoans.[60] On the one hand, this text can be read as a plea to also remember the victims of the face-to-face killing perpetrated by the Einsatzgruppen in the forests across Eastern Europe. At the same time, the poem meditates on how such cold-blooded mass killing tests the capacity, tests the willingness for recollection. The poem's most poignant line is "We remember (*gedenken*) much too little of the hour of your shoveling."[61]

As the conflict in Europe finally concluded with the Third Reich's collapse and more detailed information about the "Final Solution" circulated, Anders increasingly focused his poetry-writing around the Nazi death camps. In 1945, he composed an obituary for Alma Rosé (1906–1944), the daughter of the violinist Arnold Rosé, niece of Gustav Mahler, and an accomplished violinist in her own right.[62] Rosé was deported in 1943 to Auschwitz-Birkenau, where the SS permitted her to lead a women's orchestra. Her orchestra performed music as inmates began and ended their work details. Perhaps, they also played while "selections" were carried out, though that is uncertain. Anders' obituary, while leaving the camp unnamed, told a story of how Rosé, when ordered by the commandant (also unnamed) to perform music during "executions (*Hinrichtungen*)," smashed her violin and then hanged herself. With the details of her death uncertain, Anders chose to portray Rosé's suicide as a final act of heroic defiance.[63] Even if his account was inaccurate, the text evoked a determination to ensure that Rosé and the murdered Jews be remembered. Anders rightly feared that "already tomorrow no person will any longer believe us."[64]

Anders' private papers from this time have yielded more poems about the Shoah. One of these unpublished pieces, "*Die Gaskammern von Theresienstadt* (The Gas Chambers of Theresienstadt)," he planned for inclusion in a "German school reader (deutsche Schullesebuch)."[65] Before the unfinished poem breaks off, it describes a roll call in the camp when the SS forced

---

58 The situation of Jewish children and adolescents is extensively documented in Patricia Heberer, Children During the Holocaust, Lanham 2011.

59 See Die Stunde des Schaufelns, in TG, 383, 384.

60 These lines are repeated in the opening and closing of the poem. See ibid., 383, 384.

61 Ibid., 383, 384.

62 Nachruf, Deutsche Nachrichten 3, no. 21 (1945): 1.

63 The details of Rosé's time in Auschwitz-Birkenau and of her death were debated for decades. It seems that she died from food poisoning after performing at a SS party in April 1944. It is still uncertain whether she poisoned herself. See Richard Newman and Karen Kirtley, Alma Rosé: Vienna to Auschwitz, London 2000.

64 Nachruf, 1.

65 Die Gaskammern von Theresienstadt, ÖLA-ÖNB, NGA 237/04.

Jewish inmates to stand in the snow until a satisfactory count was completed. Another of these works from his *Nachlass*, "*Das Haus der Penelope* (The House of Penelope)," dated, according to Anders' own notes, to September 1945, tells of Jews ordered to build a new facility in Theresienstadt: a gas chamber. As the Red Army relentlessly closes in, the inmates agree to sabotage the construction process and many of them are punished for it by being sent to Auschwitz.[66] This poem, existing only in draft form, is quite revealing in that it shows what Anders believed—in this case wrongly (Theresienstadt was not equipped with gassing facilities)—about the murder process only a few months after the war's end.

Anders' preoccupation with the Shoah did not subside with the Nazi regime's collapse in May 1945. On the contrary, we know, from his correspondence, that he monitored reports in Aufbau about efforts to reunite survivors with loved ones and friends into 1947.[67] Fifteen months later, in a letter to his young nephew, David Michaelis, Anders celebrated the founding of the state of Israel.[68] Following 2000 years of statelessness and with Nazi Germany's total war against European Jewry only recently stopped, Jews once again had a state of their own, a state that, he warned his nephew, must succumb neither to thoughtless condemnation of Jews from earlier historical eras nor to anti-Arab ethnonationalism.[69] Some of Anders' most significant poetic reflection on the genocide dates from the context of these early postwar years.

Immediately after the war, Anders did translation work for *Aufbau*, rendering from Yiddish a poem written by a Riwe Kwiatowski. Kwiatowski, a Polish Jew and inmate, at various times, in Auschwitz, Stutthoff, and the latter's subcamp Kokoszki, had been liberated by the Red Army along with fifty-three other girls. Her hands and feet amputated due to terrible frostbite, she dictated a poem, a "prayer" to God to strip her "tormented soul" away from her as well as the very designation "human being (*Mensch*)" and make her into an ox or a nag. She could no longer bear to see the barbed wire and guard tower or hear the whimpering by the inmates at the ghetto wall.[70] Thanks to Anders' translation, the readership of *Aufbau* had access to this prayer of a survivor who had experienced so much violence that she could desire literal dehumanization.

Among Anders' own poems from this time, one of the most unforgettable is the 1948 "*Und Was hätt'st du getan?* (And What Would You Have Done?)," which envisioned the impossible circumstances Jews endured in the camps. He opened the poem with a quotation from a newspaper report that exposed how the Nazis forced camp inmates (he did not mention which camp) to clean out the ovens and dispose of the ashes of friends and relatives before they themselves were killed. As rewards, "extra soup" and "doubled rations" were granted to these inmates.[71] While not calling them by name, Anders clearly meant the *Sonderkommando* (Special Commando) units, comprised mostly of Jews and deployed by the SS to remove corpses from the gas chambers, extract gold teeth and any valuables from the dead, and take

---

66 Das Haus der Penelope, in ibid.

67 This information can be found in Günther Anders to Max Rychner, February 8, 1947, ÖLA-ÖNB, NGA 237/04.

68 See Anders' Mein lieber David: Brief an meinem mir noch unbekannten Neffen in Jerusalem, von ihm zu lesen in fünfzehn Jahren: Geschrieben am historischen Tage der Proklamation des Jüdischen Staates, Aufbau, May 28, 1948.

69 Ibid.

70 Riwe Kwiatowski, Gebet einer Ghettojüdin, trans. Günther Anders, Aufbau, February 22, 1946. The poem had originally appeared in the Łódź Yiddish newspaper, Das Naje Lebn. All the biographical information about Kwiatowski is taken from the unsigned introduction to the poem.

71 Und was hätt'st du getan?, in TG, 331–332.

care of the ashes once the crematoria had done their work. Gleaning from the report insight into the enormous moral ambiguity later characterized by Primo Levi as the "gray zone," Anders strained to imagine a situation where one might survive and, for a brief period, fare better than the other prisoners as long as the capability for such gruesome labor still held.[72] A hell of this sort, the poem continued, had been spared the author and his readership: "Not for you, not for me.—how untested we remained!"[73] With its bluntly worded title, the poem spurned hasty moral judgments or assumptions on the part of those who had not been there.

In 1949, Anders submitted to *Aufbau* another gripping poem. Directed "*Dem Mörder meines Freundes L.* (To the Murderer of My Friend L.)," the text warned the murderer that though "we are unknown to one another," "you will never be rid of me."[74] A "bond runs from my grief to the blow of your rifle-butt (*Kolbenstoss*)" that is unbreakable.[75] Even if the identity of L. is not clear, much less that of the killer, the hunger for retribution for his murdered friend is unmistakable. Similarly, Anders depicted elsewhere a scenario of a "murderer" who, returning home, could only expect to be greeted with alarm, distrust, and, eventually, vengeance. Here, too, the insistence on justice, if a much delayed justice, is absolutely central. The narrator states,

Nothing frightens me as
the image of the fist which is greater than you.
I stand naked in the barbarism of truth (*Barbarei der Wahrheit*),
without illusion—without a chance. And nothing remains but
to wait.[76]

The poem sketches a situation, all too familiar to historians, where perpetrators (their criminal acts are never delineated) resume their lives after the war dwelling among those who legitimately fear and seek revenge against them.

As he continued to write poetry about the experiences of being hunted and killed and of unpunished injustice, Anders sought adequate metaphors to grasp the Holocaust in its entirety. This is particularly evident in the 1946 "*Die Reise zum Meeresgrund* (The Journey to the Seafloor)," an imposing work, that, unfortunately, Anders never republished.[77] Lengthier than most of his other poems and fashioned as a "prologue to the history of the Second World War," "The Journey to the Seafloor" prepares its reader for a metaphorical journey below the waves. "No stream knows its depths/no sea its own weight," the opening lines read.[78] Only humans possess the talents of conceptualization and measurement. In a surprising and unsettling move, the poem speaks of how the scale of the crimes committed by "*our fathers*" neces-

---

72   For his indispensable notion of the "gray zone," see Primo Levi, The Drowned and the Saved, trans. Raymond Rosenthal, New York 1988, Ch. 2.
73   Ibid., 332.
74   Dem Mörder meines Freundes L., Aufbau, October 7, 1949. It is also available in *TG*, 329–330, in the section titled Krieg and 1947 is given as the poem's date of composition. The quotation is taken from the latter, 329.
75   Ibid.
76   Heimkehrender Mörder spricht zu seiner Hand, in Welch Wort in die Kälte gerufen, 335. Heinz Seydel, the editor of this volume, includes this work in a selection of poems called Vernichtungslager.
77   Die Reise zum Meeresgrund: Vorspruch zur Geschichte des 2. Weltkrieges, The German American, April 15, 1946.
78   Ibid.

sitated new concepts and measurements.[79] To meet this challenge, one must, like a diver, endure a traumatizing descent into the death and carnage wrought by the war and already submerged and out of sight. The poem warns that, on the way down, the diver will glimpse "many evil things," gas chambers and ovens—and the dead who once filled them.[80] Among the murdered will be those known to the diver. They will "seize you by the ankles" and "hold you like an anchor," each one displaying the "numbers burned into their flesh" and begging to recount their demise.[81] Intending, as he related to Heinrich Mann, to terrorize the reader with it, Anders' "The Journey to the Seafloor" asserts that any legitimate history of the war would have to confront the extermination of the Jews in order to preclude public awareness of the genocide from dissipating in the war's aftermath. In this case, history-writing would, the poem says, courageously transmit the screams and blows witnessed in the depths.

"Ashes," which he placed in a section of Journals and Poems titled "Schreckbilder (Terror-Images)," offered a very different metaphor for the post-Holocaust world as a whole, a metaphor directly derived from the killing process itself. Composed in 1947, "Ashes," too, featured the scream already encountered in poems such as "What Knowing Is." In this case, a scream reached the ears of the poet yet he did not see any mouth. Nevertheless, this disembodied howl foretold a world totally blackened with soot: "Only ashes should be left so I heard the voice scream."[82] All that the narrator's generation's fathers had labored to preserve and all the dreams the poet still nurtured had been incinerated. "If I did not see its body," the poem goes on about the source of the shrieking, "it remained there as ashen rain and covered me entirely."[83] An eerie world, one of universal desolation, emerges by the poem's conclusion. Everything is despoiled by its contact with the burned remnants of the murdered. Given the depth, duration, and intensity of his immersion in these reflections on mass annihilation, it is incredible that Anders could produce the lovely *Mariechen* (*Little Mary*) or a book about love in this period.[84]

As trenchant as they are, Anders' desperate efforts to convey something about the monstrousness of the Nazi genocide are burdened with an underlying apprehension, an apprehension about the capacity of language to say anything just and substantive about the physical extermination of a people. Long familiar to Holocaust scholars, the issue of "language and silence" was deliberately thematized in Anders' poetry from the 1940s.[85] In 1940, he bemoaned "how poor we are, we poets of today" compared to the "gravity (*Schwerkraft*)" possessed by "the ancestors."[86] Four years later, Anders put to paper a "*Sprachelegie* (Elegy of Language)," where he tells of how "the good land of language lies devastated."[87] After surveying the devastation, the poem looks forward to a rebirth of language. The 1943 "*Unser Teil* (Our Part)"

---

79 Ibid. Italics added.
80 Ibid.
81 Ibid.
82 Asche, in TG, 389.
83 Ibid., 390.
84 Mariechen: Eine Gutenachtgeschichte für Liebende, Philosophen und Angehörige anderer Berufsgruppen, Munich 1987. On p. 83, Anders points out that he wrote the manuscript in 1946. Lieben gestern: Notizen zur Geschichte des Fühlens, Munich 1986. Written in New York in 1947–49, Anders originally intended to title the book Lieben heute.
85 I refer here to George Steiner's classic Language and Silence: Essays on Language, Literature, and the Inhuman New York 1967. In a very large literature on the topic, see two crucial works: Saul Friedländer, Reflections of Nazism: An Essay on Kitsch and Death, trans. Thomas Weyr, New York 1984; Horowitz, Voicing the Void, Ch. 2.
86 Über das Ende des Dichtens, in TG, 376.
87 Die Sprachelegie, in ibid., 393.

addressed much more explicitly the dilemmas to communication posed by the genocide, just as relatively reliable information about it became available. "And if you could speak a sentence (*Spruch*) for every immolated and slain person (*jeden Verbrannten und Erschlagenen*)—how far would your voice carry?"[88] When "even the most faithful word quickly dissipates," what was an adequate, ethical response on behalf of "the forgotten, the never mentioned, the never reported," the poem asks.[89] At roughly the same time, in "*Die Meldung* (The Report)," penned in 1944 or 1945, Anders offered more philosophical elaboration on obstacles to belief, comprehension, and mourning identified so briefly in the obituary for Alma Rosé. Two astonishing parts of the text elucidate these obstacles.

> Since three are father, mother and child.
> Every heart can adjudicate (*ermessen*) three dead.
> Yet we millions are already today forgotten,
> because three million are much too many.
>
> So long as one does not yet believe us about the ovens,
> and not the mills that have broken us to pieces,
> For us ashes and bones
> being dead remains forbidden (*nicht erlaubt*).[90]

Here, Anders voices the dead endangered by an oblivion beyond death. According to this poem's line of argument, forgetting or suppressing the past might not only result, in the case of the Holocaust, from conscious wishes to deny it but also from intrinsic socio-psychological inabilities to come to terms with it.

In a related piece, Anders gave voice to those killed by the Nazis as well as to survivors. The "murdered," despairing if any "chronicler" would record the "last parts of our existence," question whether, in a dramatic reversal of Hegel's claim that the "whole is the true," "the whole instead remains the mute (*Stumme*)?"[91] As forthright and apprehensive as these writings are about the limits of language, they do not bespeak, however, a rejection of the poetic mode of expression. Rather, they seem to promote a self-reflexivity about the fragile capacities of poetry when faced with the most extreme phenomena like the Shoah. On this point, the thrust of Anders' poems about the Judeocide coincides with the initial formulation of his "theory of the 'nonsynchronization of the human being with itself' ('*Ungleichgeschaltetheit des Menschen mit sich selbst*')," a theory he believed could account for the shortcomings, not only of language but of all human faculties, exposed by the ceaseless development of modern technology.[92]

---

88 Unser Teil, in ibid., 326.

89 Ibid., 327.

90 These non-consecutive parts of Die Meldung are in ibid., 385.

91 See Die Summe of Erlittenen, in ibid., 358. On p. 359, the survivors answer this question resolutely in the affirmative.

92 Rückblendung, in BiH, 47. For an early formulation of this concept of "nonsychronization," see Anders' neglected Der Mensch ist kleiner als er selbst, Aufbau, August 2, 1940. These insights about the limits of human capacities should be brought into a productive dialogue with the work of Carolyn Dean, especially her The Fragility of Empathy after the Holocaust, Ithaca, 2004.

* * * *

After careful study of these remarkable poems, it is difficult to exaggerate the impact of the Shoah on Anders. The extermination of European Jewry left deep, irremovable scars on his psyche. Even from the relative obscurity he endured in the United States for most of the 1940s, the composition of these "political poems" likely helped him respond to constant sentiments of isolation and powerlessness. With these pieces, Anders, one of the "shame-filled community of the accidentally not gassed (schamvolle Gemeinde der zufällig nicht Vergasten)," contributed vitally, in retrospect, to the German émigrés' "culture of resistance" by throwing light on the Third Reich's darkest, unprecedented crimes.[93] Although still not that well known, his very important collection of poems should not be overlooked by scholars.

Anders' poetry about the Holocaust can be understood, to borrow Sara Horowitz's phrase, as a "radical imagining that confronts the mass death that has occurred."[94] This "radical imagining," it must be stressed, encompassed but also extended beyond the mechanized annihilation system of Auschwitz-Birkenau. More nuanced in many respects than his post-1950 thought about the Holocaust, the poems analyzed in this essay address virtually every aspect of the genocide: ghettos, deportation, mass shooting, and the extermination camps. "Auschwitz" does not yet claim primacy in his theoretical imagination.[95] These works preserved the memory of what happened against expected denials and unbelief yet also, self-critically, scrutinized the potential of language to respond to the enormity of such barbarism.

Through the late 1940s, then, Anders still construed the poem as a viable critical aesthetic form to depict the extermination of the Jews. Poems could communicate to and thus enlighten others about this epoch-defining terror. After 1950, after he and Elisabeth Freundlich resettled in post-Nazi Vienna, Anders gradually abandoned the writing of poetry and adopted the critical essay, the "philosophical journal," and the "open letter" as forms of didactic, terror-raising exposition. Faced with the specter of the possible repetition of Auschwitz and Hiroshima, "my muse," he contended, "had died, if not right away, of fright (*an Schrecken*)."[96] According to the later Anders, art, as a whole, including poetry, not only failed to grasp these extreme events but actually hindered the emergence of a critical consciousness, hence his support for Adorno's much disputed statements about writing poetry "after Auschwitz."

Nevertheless, Anders did not forsake the "political poem" altogether. The poems from the 1940s were not discarded. His willingness to republish so many of these works in *Journals and Poems* will benefit any who, like Anders, "unintimidated report/the journey to the seafloor."[97]

---

93 The Émigré, p. 183, n. 8.

94 The phrase comes from Sarah Horowitz's excellent Voicing the Void, 14, where she addresses the short stories of Ida Fink.

95 One can perhaps see a turn in Anders' thinking in his 1949 Dichten heute. There he announced that the "motives for terror" in his new thinking would be the "self-destruction of humanity, the self-made apocalypse, the gas-ovens." See Dichten heute: Aus Tagebüchern, Die Wandlung no. 1 (January 1949): 50. It is not only the attention to the Bomb in this statement which deserves scrutiny but also the way that the "gas-ovens" stand in for the Holocaust as a whole in a way that they had not with the poems.

96 See Anders' 1985 interview with Fritz Raddatz, Brecht konnte mich nicht riechen, in GAa, 111.

97 The quotation is from the final lines of Die Reise zum Meeresgrund.

Jean-Pierre Dupuy*

An *Andersian* Approach to Nuclear Deterrence

As many doomsayers, Günther Anders never saw in his lifetime what he was prophesying: a nuclear war. He didn't even see a conventional (direct) confrontation between two nuclear powers. Does that mean that he was wrong and that nuclear deterrence was working efficiently? Throughout this period it was as though the bomb had protected us from the bomb—an astonishing paradox that some of the most brilliant minds sought to explain with only very limited success. The very existence of nuclear weapons, it would appear, had prevented the world from disappearing in a nuclear holocaust.

As far as I know, Anders never wrote specifically about the mad "logic" of nuclear deterrence and its metaphysical implications. He thought that was the kind of philosophy that was only of interest to philosophers. However, he wrote extensively about nuclear weapons in general.[1] I believe it is possible to extend his analyses to the case of nuclear deterrence in a way that confirms his most essential intuitions. *Horresco referens*, I will strive to do that resorting to concepts borrowed from analytic philosophy and metaphysics, a method he probably would have deplored. I hope I will be forgiven if I show that in that way I can consolidate his highly pessimistic views on the world.

1. Premise: Anders on Nuclear Weapons

On 6 August 1945 an atomic bomb reduced the Japanese city of Hiroshima to radioactive ashes. Three days later, Nagasaki was struck in its turn. In the meantime, on 8 August, the International Military Tribunal at Nuremberg provided itself with the authority to judge three types of crime: crimes against peace, war crimes, and crimes against humanity. In the space of three days, then, the victors of the Second World War inaugurated an era in which unthinkably powerful arms of mass destruction made it inevitable that wars would come to be judged criminal by the very norms that these victors were laying down at the same moment. This "monstrous irony" was forever to mark the thought of the most neglected German philosopher of the twentieth century, Günther Anders.

Anders was born Günther Stern, on 12 July 1902, to German Jewish parents in Breslau (now the Polish city of Wrocław). His father was the famous child psychologist Wilhelm Stern, remembered for his concept of intelligence quotient (or IQ). Günther worked in the 1930s as an art critic in Berlin. His editor, Bertolt Brecht, suggested that he call himself something *dif-*

---

* Ecole Polytechnique, Paris, and Stanford University. jpdupuy@stanford.edu

1 The book of his I prefer in this domain is Hiroshima ist überall, Munich, Beck 1982. I have edited and published the French translation under the title: Hiroshima est partout, Paris, Seuil 2005.

ferent, and from then on he wrote under the name Anders ("Different" in German). This was not the only thing that distinguished him from others. There was also his manner of doing philosophy, which he had studied at Freiburg with Husserl and Heidegger. Anders once said that to write moral philosophy in a jargon-laden style accessible only to other philosophers is as absurd and as contemptible as a baker's making bread meant only to be eaten by other bakers. He saw himself as practicing "occasional philosophy," a kind of philosophy that "arises from concrete experiences and on concrete occasions." Foremost among those "concrete occasions" was the conjunction of Auschwitz and Hiroshima—the moment when the destruction of humanity on an industrial scale entered the realm of possibility for the first time.

Anders seems not to have been very well liked, at least not by his first wife, Hannah Arendt. She had been introduced to him by their classmate at Freiburg, Hans Jonas—each of them a former student of Heidegger, as he was; each of them Jewish, as he was; each of them destined to become a more famous philosopher, and a far more influential one than he would ever be. The memory of Günther Anders matters because he is one of the very few thinkers who had the courage and the lucidity to link Hiroshima with Auschwitz without depriving Auschwitz of the sad privilege it enjoys as the incarnation of bottomless moral horror. He was able to do this because he understood (as Arendt herself did, though probably somewhat later) that even if moral evil, beyond a certain threshold, becomes too much for human beings to bear, they nonetheless remain responsible for it, and that no ethics, no standard of rationality, no norm that human beings can establish for themselves has the least relevance in evaluating its consequences.

It takes courage and lucidity to link Auschwitz and Hiroshima, because still today in the minds of many people—including, it would appear, a very large majority of Americans—Hiroshima is the classic example of a necessary evil. Having invested itself with the power to determine—if not the best of all possible worlds, then at least the least bad among them—America placed the bombing of civilians and their murder in the hundreds of thousands on one of the scales of justice, and on the other, an invasion of the Japanese archipelago that, it was said, would have cost the lives of a half-million American soldiers. Moral necessity, it was argued, required that America choose to put an end to the war as quickly as possible, even if this meant shattering once and for all everything that until then had constituted the most elementary rules of just war. Moral philosophers call this a consequentialist argument: when the issue is one of surpassingly great importance, deontological norms—so called because they express a duty to respect absolute imperatives, no matter what the cost or effects of doing this may be—must yield to the calculus of consequences. But what ethical and rational calculation could justify sending millions of Jewish children from every part of Europe to be gassed? There lies the difference, the chasm, the moral abyss that separates Auschwitz from Hiroshima.

In the decades since, however, persons of great integrity and intellect have insisted on the intrinsic immorality of atomic weapons, and the ignominy of bombing Hiroshima and Nagasaki, in particular. In 1956, the Oxford philosopher and Catholic thinker Elizabeth Anscombe made an enlightening comparison that threw into stark relief the horrors to which consequentialist reasoning leads when it is taken to its logical conclusion. Let us suppose, she said, that the Allies had thought at the beginning of 1945 that in order to break the Germans' will to resist and to compel them to surrender rapidly and unconditionally, thus sparing the lives of a great many Allied soldiers, it was necessary to massacre hundreds of thousands of civilians, women and children included, in two cities in the Ruhr. Two questions arise. First, what difference would there have been, morally speaking, between this and what the Nazis did in Czechoslovakia and Poland? Second, what difference would there have been, morally speaking, between this and the atomic bombing of Hiroshima and Nagasaki?[2]

In the face of horror, moral philosophy is forced to resort to analogies of this sort for it has nothing other than logical consistency on which to base the validity of its arguments. In the event, this minimal requirement of consistency did not suffice to rule out the nuclear option nor to condemn it afterwards. Why? One reply is that because the Americans won the war against Japan, their victory seemed in retrospect to justify the course of action they followed. This argument must not be mistaken for cynicism. It involves what philosophers call the problem of moral luck. The moral judgment that is passed on a decision made under conditions of radical uncertainty depends on what occurs *after* the relevant action has been taken—something that may have been completely unforeseeable, even as a probabilistic matter.

Robert McNamara memorably describes this predicament in the extraordinary set of interviews conducted by the documentarian Errol Morris and released as a film under a most Clausewitzian title, *The Fog of War* (2003). Before serving as Secretary of Defense under Presidents Kennedy and Johnson, McNamara had been an advisor during the war in the Pacific to General Curtis LeMay, who was responsible for the firebombing of sixty-seven cities of Imperial Japan, a campaign that culminated in the dropping of the two atomic bombs. On the night of 9–10 March 1945 alone, one hundred thousand civilians perished, burning to death in Tokyo. McNamara approvingly reports LeMay's stunningly lucid verdict: "If we'd lost the war, we'd all have been prosecuted as war criminals."

Another possible reply is that consequentialist morality served in this instance only as a convenient pretext. A "revisionist" school of American historians led by Gar Alperovitz has pleaded this case with great conviction, arguing that in July 1945 Japan was on the point of capitulation.[3] Two conditions would have had to be satisfied in order to obtain immediate surrender: first, that President Truman agree to an immediate declaration of war on Japan by the Soviet Union; second, that the Japanese surrender be accompanied by an American promise that the emperor would be allowed to continue to sit on his throne. Truman refused both conditions at the conference at Potsdam, a few days after 16 July 1945. On that day, the President had received "good news." The bomb was ready, as the successful test at Alamogordo had brilliantly demonstrated.

Alperovitz concludes that Truman sought to steal a march on the Soviets before they were prepared to intervene militarily in the Japanese archipelago. The Americans played the nuclear card, in other words, not to force Japan to surrender, but to impress the Russians. In that case the Cold War had been launched on the strength of an ethical abomination, and the Japanese reduced to the level of guinea pigs, for the bomb was not necessary to obtain the surrender. Other historians reckon that whether or not necessary, it was not a sufficient method of obtaining a surrender.

The historian Barton J. Bernstein has proposed a "new synthesis" that departs from both the official and the revisionist accounts.[4] The day after Nagasaki, the War Minister, General Korechika Anami, and the Vice Chief of the Naval General Staff, Admiral Takijiro Ōnishi,

---

2 G. E. M. Anscombe, Mr. Truman's Degree , in Collected Philosophical Papers, vol. 3, Ethics, Religion and Politics, Minneapolis 1981.

3 Gar Alperovitz, The Decision to Use the Atomic Bomb and the Architecture of an American Myth, Vintage 1996.

4 Barton J. Bernstein, Understanding the Atomic Bomb and the Japanese Surrender : Missed Opportunities, Little-Known Near Disasters, and Modern Memory, *Diplomatic History*, 19, 2, March 1995, 227–273.

urged the emperor to authorize a "special attack *[kamikaze]* effort," even though this would mean putting as many as twenty million Japanese lives at risk, by their own estimate, in the cause of ultimate victory. In that case, two bombs would not suffice. So convinced were the Americans of the need to detonate a third device, Bernstein says, that the announcement of surrender on 14 August—apparently the result of chance and of reversals of alliance at the highest level of the Japanese government, still poorly understood by historians—came as an utter surprise. But Bernstein takes the argument a step further. Of the six options available to the Americans to force the Japanese to surrender without an invasion of the archipelago, five had been rather cursorily analyzed, singly and in combination, and then rejected by Truman and his advisors: continuation of the conventional bombing campaign supplemented by a naval blockade; unofficial negotiations with the enemy; modification of the terms of surrender including a guarantee that the emperor system would be preserved; awaiting Russian entry into the war; and a non-combat demonstration of the atomic bomb. As for the sixth option, the military use of the bomb, it was never discussed—not even for a moment: it was simply taken for granted. The bombing of Hiroshima and Nagasaki followed from the bomb's very existence. From the ethical point of view, Bernstein's findings are still more terrible than those of Alperovitz: dropping the atomic bomb, perhaps the gravest decision ever taken in modern history, was not something that had actually been decided.

These revisionist interpretations do not exhaust the questions that need to be asked. There are at least two more. First, how are we to make sense of the bombing of Hiroshima, and more troubling still, of Nagasaki, which is to say the monstrously absurd determination to persist in infamy? Second, how could the consequentialist veneer of the official justification for these acts—that they were extremely regrettable, but a moral necessity just the same—have been accepted as a lawful pretext, when it should have been seen instead as the most execrable and appalling excuse imaginable?

Not only does the work of Günther Anders furnish an answer to these questions, it does so by relocating them in another context. Anders, a German Jew who had emigrated to France and then to America, returning to Europe in 1950—everywhere an exile, the wandering Jew—recognized that on 6 August 1945 human history had entered into a new phase, its last. Or rather that the sixth day of August was only a *rehearsal* for the ninth—what he called the "Nagasaki syndrome." The dropping of the first atomic bomb over civilian populations introduced the impossible into reality and opened the door to more atrocities in the same way that an earthquake is followed by a series of replicas. History became obsolete that day, as Anders put it. Now that humanity was capable of destroying itself, nothing would ever cause it to lose this "negative all-powerfulness," not even a general disarmament, not even a total denuclearization of the world's arsenals. *Now that apocalypse has been inscribed in our future as fate, the best we can do is to indefinitely postpone the final moment.* We are living under a suspended sentence, as it were, a stay of execution. In August 1945, Anders says, humanity entered into the era of the "reprieve" *(die Frist)* and the "second death" of all that had existed: since the meaning of the past depends on future actions, the obsolescence of the future, its programmed end, signifies not that the past no longer has any meaning, but that it never had one.[5]

---

5   Günther Anders, Die Atomare Drohung: Radikale Überlegungen zum atomaren Zeitalter, 6th ed., Munich 1993. For a French philosopher, these assertions immediately conjure up a number of philosophemes that she is prompt to associate with the name of Jean-Paul Sartre. We have good reasons today to believe that the influence went in the other direction.

To ascertain the rationality and the morality of the destruction of Hiroshima and Nagasaki amounts to treating nuclear weapons as a means in the service of an end. A means loses itself in its end as a river loses itself in the sea, and ends up being completely absorbed by it. But the bomb exceeds all the ends that can be given to it, or found for it. The question whether the end justifies the means suddenly became obsolete, like everything else. Why was the bomb used? Because it *existed*. The simple fact of its existence is a threat, or rather a promise that it will be used. Why has the moral horror of its use not been perceived? What accounts for this "blindness in the face of apocalypse"? Because beyond certain thresholds, our power of doing infinitely exceeds our capacity for feeling and imagining. It is this irreducible gap that Anders called the "Promethean discrepancy." Thus Hannah Arendt, for example, was to diagnose Eichmann's psychological disability as a "lack of imagination." Anders showed that this is not the weakness of one person in particular; it is the weakness of every person when his capacity for invention (and for destruction) becomes disproportionately enlarged in relation to the human condition.

"Between our capacity for making and our capacity for imagining," Anders says, "a gap is opened up that grows larger by the day." The "too great" leaves us cold, he adds. "No human being is capable of imagining something of such horrifying magnitude: the elimination of millions of people."

2. Paradoxes of Nuclear Deterrence

A pacifist would say: surely the best way for humanity to avoid a nuclear war is not to have any nuclear weapons. This argument, which borders on the tautological, was irrefutable before the scientists of the Manhattan Project developed the atomic bomb. Alas, it is no longer valid today. Such weapons exist, and even supposing that they were to cease to exist as a result of universal disarmament, they could be recreated in a few months. Errol Morris, in *The Fog of War*, asks McNamara what he thinks protected humanity from extinction during the Cold War when the United States and the Soviet Union permanently threatened each other with mutual annihilation. Deterrence? Not at all, McNamara replies: "We lucked out." Twenty-five or thirty times during this period, he notes, mankind came within an inch of apocalypse.

For more than four decades during the Cold War, the discussion of "mutual assured destruction" (MAD) assigned a major role to the notion of *deterrent intention* on both the strategic and the moral level. And yet, the language of intention can be shown to constitute the principal obstacle to understanding the logic of deterrence.

In June 2000, meeting with Vladimir Putin in Moscow, Bill Clinton made an amazing statement that was echoed almost seven years later by Secretary of State Condoleezza Rice, speaking once again to the Russians. The antiballistic shield that we are going to build in Europe, they explained in substance, is only meant to defend us against attacks from rogue states and terrorist groups. *Therefore be assured:* even if we were to take the initiative of attacking you in a first nuclear strike, you could easily get through the shield and annihilate our country, the United States of America.

Plainly, the new world order created by the collapse of Soviet power in no way made the logic of deterrence any less insane. This logic requires that each nation exposes its own population to certain destruction by the other's reprisals. Security becomes the daughter of terror.

For if either nation were to take steps to protect itself, the other might believe that its adversary considers itself to be invulnerable, and so, in order to prevent a first strike, hastens to launch this strike itself. It is not for nothing that the doctrine of mutually assured destruction came to be known by its acronym, MAD. In a nuclear regime, nations are at once vulnerable and invulnerable: vulnerable because they can die from attack by another nation; invulnerable because they will not die before having killed their attacker—something they will always be capable of doing, no matter how powerful the strike that will have brought them to their knees.

There is another doctrine, known as NUTS (Nuclear Utilization Target Selection), that calls for a nation to use nuclear weapons in a surgical fashion to eliminate the nuclear capabilities of an adversary while protecting itself by means of an antimissile shield. It will be obvious that MAD and NUTS are perfectly contradictory, for what makes a type of weapon or vector valuable in one case robs it of much utility in the other. Consider submarine-launched missiles, which have imprecise trajectories and whose mobile hosts are difficult to locate. Whereas nuclear-equipped submarines hold little or no theoretical interest from the perspective of NUTS, they are very useful—indeed, almost ideal—from the perspective of MAD since they have a good chance of surviving a first strike and the very imprecision of their guidance systems makes them effective instruments of terror. The problem is that the Americans say that they would like to go on playing MAD with the Russians and perhaps the Chinese, while practicing NUTS with the North Koreans, the Iranians, and, until a few years ago, the Iraqis. This obliged them to show that the missile defense system they had been hoping to build in Poland and the Czech Republic would be penetrable by a Russian strike while at the same time capable of stopping missiles launched by a "rogue state."

That the lunacy of MAD, whether or not it was coupled with the craziness of NUTS, should have been considered the height of wisdom, and that it should have been credited with having kept world peace during a period whose return some people wish for today, passes all understanding. Few persons were at all troubled by this state of affairs, however, apart from American bishops—and President Reagan. Once again we cannot avoid asking the obvious question: why?

For many years the usual reply was that what is at issue here is an intention, not the carrying out of an intention. Moreover, it is an intention of an exceedingly special kind: its being formed has the consequence that the conditions that would lead to its being acted on are not realized. Hypothetically, since one's enemy is dissuaded from attacking first, one does not have to preempt his attack by attacking first, which means that no one makes a move. One forms a deterrent intention, in other words, *in order* not to put it into effect. Specialists speak of such intentions as being inherently "self-stultifying,"[6] but this plainly does no more than give a name to an enigma. It does nothing to resolve it.

No one who inquires into the strategic and moral status of deterrent intention can fail to be overwhelmed by paradox. Because deterrent intention cannot be efficient without the meta-intention to act on it if the circumstances require, what seems to shield deterrent intention from ethical rebuke is the very thing that renders it strategically useless. Deterrent intention, like primitive divinities, appears to unite absolute goodness—since it is a result of this intention that nuclear war has not taken place—with absolute evil, since the act of which it is the intention is an unutterable abomination.

---

6   Gregory Kavka, Moral Paradoxes of Nuclear Deterrence, Cambridge, Cambridge University Press 1993.

Throughout the Cold War, two arguments were made that seemed to show that nuclear deterrence in the form of MAD could not be effective.[7] The first argument has to do with the non-credible character of the deterrent threat under such circumstances: if the party threatening a lethal and suicidal response to aggression that endangers its "vital interests" is assumed to be at least minimally rational, then calling its bluff—say, by means of a first strike that destroys a part of its territory—ensures that it will not carry out its threat. The very purpose of this regime, after all, is to issue a guarantee of mutual destruction in the event that either party upsets the balance of terror. In the aftermath of a first strike, what chief of state having only a devastated nation to defend would run the risk of putting an end to the human race by launching a vengeful retaliatory strike? In a world of sovereign states endowed with this minimal degree of rationality, the nuclear threat has no credibility whatsoever. Jonathan Schell summarizes this argument beautifully:

> Since in nuclear-deterrence theory the whole purpose of having a retaliatory capacity is to deter a first strike, one must ask what reason would remain to launch the retaliation once the first strike had actually arrived. It seems that the logic of the deterrence strategy is dissolved by the very event—the first strike—that it is meant to prevent. Once the action begins, the whole doctrine is *self-canceling*. It would seem that the doctrine is based on a monumental logical mistake: one cannot credibly deter a first strike with a second strike whose raison d'être dissolves the moment the first strike arrives.[8]

Another quite different argument was put forward that likewise pointed to the incoherence of the prevailing strategic doctrine. To be effective, nuclear deterrence must be absolutely effective. Not even a single failure can be allowed, since the first bomb to be dropped would already be one too many. But if nuclear deterrence is absolutely effective, it cannot be effective. As a practical matter, deterrence works only if it is not 100% effective. One thinks, for example, of the criminal justice system: violations of the law must occur and be punished if citizens are to be convinced that crime does not pay. However, in the case of nuclear deterrence, the first transgression is fatal.

The most telling sign that nuclear deterrence did not work is that it did nothing to prevent an unrestrained and potentially catastrophic arms build-up. If indeed it did work, nuclear deterrence ought to have been the great equalizer. As in Hobbes' state of nature, the weakest nation—measured by the number of nuclear warheads it possesses—is on exactly the same level as the strongest since it can always inflict "unacceptable" losses, for example by deliberately targeting the enemy's cities. France enunciated a doctrine ("deterrence of the strong by the weak") to this effect. Deterrence is therefore a game that can be played—indeed, that must be able to be played—with very few armaments on each side.

Belatedly, it came to be understood that in order for deterrence to have a chance of succeeding, it was absolutely necessary to abandon the notion of deterrent *intention*. The idea that human beings, by their conscience and their will, could control the outcome of a game as

---

7   See the excellent synthesis of the debate by Steven P. Lee, Morality, Prudence, and Nuclear Weapons, Cambridge, Cambridge University Press 1996.
8   Jonathan Schell, The Fate of the Earth, New York, Avon Books 1982, 227.

terrifying as deterrence was manifestly an idle and abhorrent fantasy. In principle, the mere *existence* of two deadly arsenals pointed at each other, without the least threat of their use being made or even implied, is enough to keep the warheads locked away in their silos.

This solution came with a name: *existential* deterrence. Is the intention or the threat to retaliate and launch a counter-attack that will lead to the Apocalypse the problem? Let us get rid of the intention. As two major philosophers put it: "The existence of a nuclear retaliatory capability suffices for deterrence, regardless of a nation's will, intentions, or pronouncements about nuclear weapons use" [Gregory Kavka]; or: "It is our military capacities that matter, not our intentions or incentives or declarations" [David K. Lewis]. If deterrence is existential, it is because the existence of the weapons alone deters. Deterrence is inherent in the weapons because "the danger of unlimited escalation is inescapable." As Bernard Brodie put it in 1973:

> It is a curious paradox of our time that one of the foremost factors making deterrence really work and work well is the lurking fear that in some massive confrontation crisis it may fail. Under these circumstances *one does not tempt fate.*[9]

The kind of rationality at work here is not a calculating rationality, but rather the kind of rationality in which the agent contemplates the abyss and simply decides never to get too close to the edge. As David Lewis puts it: *"You don't tangle with tigers—it's that simple."* The probability of error is what makes deterrence effective. But error, failure or mistake, here, is not strategic. It has nothing to do with the notion that a nation, by irrationally running unacceptable risks, can limit a war and achieve advantage by inducing restraint in the opponent. Thomas Schelling popularized this idea—known as the "rationality of irrationality" theory—in his landmark *Strategy of Conflict*, published in 1960. Here, by contrast, the key notion is *"Fate."* The error is *inscribed* in the future. In other terms, the game is no longer played between two adversaries. It takes on an altogether different form. Neither is in a position to deter the other in a credible way. *However, both want and need to be deterred.* The way out of this impasse is brilliant. It is a matter of creating jointly a fictitious entity that will deter both at the same time. The game is now played between one actor, humankind, whose survival is at stake, and its double, namely its own violence exteriorized in the form of fate. The fictitious "tiger" we'd better not tangle with is nothing other than the violence that is in us but that we project outside of us: it is as if we were threatened by an exceedingly dangerous entity, external to us, whose intentions toward us are not evil, but whose power of destruction is infinitely superior to all the earthquakes or tsunamis that Nature has in store for us. Günther Anders and Hannah Arendt were right: we are living under a new regime of evil—*an evil without harmful intent.*

Heidegger famously said, *"Nur noch ein Gott kann uns retten"* ["Only a God can still save us."]. In the nuclear age, this (false) God is the self-externalization of human violence into a nuclear holocaust inscribed in the future as destiny. This is what the fictitious tiger stands for.

In this light, to say that deterrence works means that so long as one does not recklessly tempt the fateful tiger, there is a chance that it will forget us—for a time, perhaps a long, indeed a very long time—but not forever. From now on, as Günther Anders had already understood and announced from a philosophical perspective at the antipodes of rational choice theory, we are living on borrowed time (*die Frist*).

---

9   Bernard Brodie, War and Politics, New York, Macmillan 1973.

We must then conclude that Anders was right: Hiroshima (or, rather, Nagasaki) is not only everywhere, from now on it is with us at any point in time, since treating the future as fate, as some of the best strategists put it, amounts to collapsing time and making the (catastrophic) future present.

In his *Memoirs*, Robert McNamara asserts that several dozen times during the Cold War humanity came ever so close to disappearing in a radioactive cloud. Was this a failure of deterrence? Quite the opposite: it is precisely these unscheduled expeditions to the edge of the black hole that gave the threat of nuclear annihilation its dissuasive force. "We lucked out," McNamara says. Quite true—but in a very profound sense it was this repeated flirting with apocalypse that saved humanity. Those "near-misses" were the condition of possibility of the efficiency of nuclear deterrence. Accidents are needed to precipitate an apocalyptic destiny. Yet unlike fate, an accident is not inevitable: it *can* not occur.

The key to the paradox of existential deterrence is found in this dialectic of fate and accident: nuclear apocalypse must be construed as something that is *at once necessary and improbable*. Yet, is there anything really new about this idea? Its kinship with tragedy, classical or modern, is readily seen. Consider Oedipus, who kills his father at the fatal crossroads, or Camus's "stranger," Meursault, who kills the Arab under the blazing sun in Algiers—these events appear to the Mediterranean mind both as accidents and as acts of fate, in which *chance and destiny are merged and become one*.

Accident, which points to chance, is the opposite of fate, which points to necessity; but without this opposite, fate cannot be realized. A follower of Derrida would say that accident is the *supplement* of fate, in the sense that it is both its contrary and the condition of its occurring.

In the nuclear era, all that is left to us is a game of immense hazard and jeopardy that amounts to constantly playing with fire: we cannot risk coming too close, lest we perish in a nuclear holocaust; nor can we risk standing too far away, lest we forget the danger of nuclear weapons. In principle, the dialectic of fate and chance permits us to keep just the *right distance* from the black hole of catastrophe: since apocalypse is our fate, we are bound to remain tied to it; but since an accident has to take place in order for our destiny to be fulfilled, we are kept separate from it.

3. The Good News in Reverse: The End of Hatred and Resentment

Likely it is owing to the influence of Christianity that evil has come to be most commonly associated with the intentions of those who commit it. And yet the evil of nuclear deterrence in its existential form is an evil disconnected from any human intention, just as the sacrament of the bomb is a sacrament without a god. In this context worse news than the imminent end of hatred and resentment cannot be imagined.

In 1958, Günther Anders went to Hiroshima and Nagasaki to take part in the Fourth World Conference against Atomic and Hydrogen bombs. After many exchanges with survivors of the catastrophe, he noted in his diary: "Their steadfast resolve not to speak of those who were to blame, not to say that the event had been caused by human beings; *not to harbor the least resentment, even though they were the victims of the greatest of crimes*—this really is too much for me, it passes all understanding." And he adds: "They constantly speak of the catastrophe as if it were an earthquake or a tidal wave. They use the Japanese word, *tsunami*."

Anders on his way to Hiroshima,
on his trip to the „Fourth World Conference
against A and H Bombs and for Disarmament"
in Tokyo/Japan, 1958.
Photo: Anders Papers, Literature Archives,
Austrian National Library

The evil that inhabits the "nuclear peace" is not the product of any malign intention. It is the inspiration for passages of terrifying insight in Anders' book, *Hiroshima ist überall*, words that send a chill down the spine: "The fantastic character of the situation quite simply takes one's breath away. At the very moment when the world becomes apocalyptic, and this owing to our own fault, it presents the image … of a paradise inhabited by murderers without malice and victims without hatred. Nowhere is there any trace of malice, there is only rubble." And Anders prophesies: "No war in history will have been more devoid of hatred than the war by tele-murder that is to come. … [T]his absence of hatred will be the most inhuman absence of hatred that has ever existed; absence of hatred and absence of scruples will henceforth be one and the same."[10]

Violence without hatred is so inhuman that it amounts to a transcendence of sorts—perhaps the only transcendence yet left to us.

---

10 Günther Anders, Hiroshima ist überall, "Tagebuch aus Hiroshima und Nagasaki," Munich, C.H.Beck 1995.

Elisabeth Röhrlich

"To Make the End Time Endless:" The Early Years of Günther Anders' Fight against Nuclear Weapons

The dropping of the atom bombs on Hiroshima and Nagasaki had a crucial impact on Günther Anders' work as a philosopher. For Anders, with the day of the Hiroshima bombing a new age began in which man had "the power to transform any given place on our planet, and even our planet itself, into a Hiroshima." This thought remained central throughout his later writings, yet the impact of Hiroshima was more than academic. Anders called on his readers to "fight against this man made apocalypse" and to do everything in their power "to make The End Time endless."[1] Anders himself became a leading figure in the early peace movement of the 1950s and 1960s.

Against this background it is not surprising that recent scholarship on the history of the transnational disarmament movement has rediscovered Günther Anders as a key philosopher of the nuclear age. Holger Nehring uses Anders' "Thesis of the Nuclear Age" as the starting point for his comparative history of the British and West German protest movements.[2] A recently published edited volume on the social and intellectual history of the Cold War introduces Anders as one of the main thinkers of atomic apocalypse.[3] However, what is still missing is a deeper examination of Anders' actual involvement in the peace movement, his anti-nuclear activities (rather than just his anti-nuclear thinking), and the national and transnational networks that were part of these activities. This chapter aims to address this striking gap in research and focuses on Anders' fight against nuclear weapons during the 1950s and 1960s when the first wave of a mass nuclear disarmament movement emerged. Anders was one of the leading figures of the peace movement in Austria. His writings on the nuclear question laid the foundation for these activities. Apart from that, Anders' fight against nuclear weapons also involved much more tangible activities such as the participation in anti-nuclear weapons conferences and the establishment of an Austrian disarmament committee.[4]

---

1   Günther Anders, Theses for the Nuclear Age, in: The Massachusetts Review, Vol. 3, No. 3 (Spring 1962): 493–505 (here: 493–494). See p. 187 in this volume.

2   Holger Nehring, Politics of Security: British and West German Protest Movements and the Early Cold War, Oxford 2013, 1.

3   Christian Dries, "Zeitbomben mit unfestgelegtem Explosionstermin": Günther Anders und der Kalte (Atom) Krieg, in: Patrick Bernhard/Holger Nehring, eds., Den Kalten Krieg denken: Beiträge zur sozialen Ideenge-schichte (Frieden und Krieg: Beiträge zur historischen Friedensforschung; 19), Essen 2013, 63–87; also see: Philipp Gassert, Popularität der Apokalypse: Zur Nuklearangst seit 1945, in: Aus Politik und Zeitgeschichte (14 November 2011): 48–54.

4   The Günther Anders Papers at the "Österreichisches Literaturarchiv" (Vienna) are the most important historical source for Günther Anders' involvement in the early peace movement (hereinafter referred to as Anders Papers).

The first advocates of nuclear disarmament were scientists, many of whom had contributed to the Manhattan Project. After the development of the American and Soviet hydrogen bombs and a series of nuclear tests by the United States, the disarmament movement gained new momentum in the early 1950s. In July 1955, the so-called "Russell-Einstein-Manifesto" warned of the destructive power of nuclear weapons. The Manifesto became the founding document of the Pugwash Conferences on Science and World Affairs.[5] In late 1957, British peace activists established the Campaign for Nuclear Disarmament (CND) that shortly developed into a mass movement and prompted the formation of similar organizations in other European countries. Only after the turning points of the 1962 Cuban Missile Crisis and the signing of the Limited Test Ban Treaty in 1963 did the influence of the transnational disarmament movement slow down. The NATO Double-Track Decision of 1979 again gave rise to a new transnational mass disarmament movement.[6]

This chapter is based on archival research in the papers of Günther Anders and two other Austrian peace activists, Robert Jungk and Hans Thirring. These archives have been strikingly neglected in the before mentioned works on Anders. The chapter aims to contribute to the growing scholarship on Anders by examining the as yet under-researched social and political context of his work. Without wanting to perpetuate what Jason Dawsey has aptly called "the classic (and flawed) bifurcation of activists and theorists,"[7] the chapter puts the emphasis on Günther Anders' role in the peace movement rather than on his philosophical work. Even though the peace movement transcended national boundaries, the individual organizations were highly influenced by local and national developments. Holger Nehring has therefore described the transnational peace activists as "national internationalists." He argues that the members of national disarmament initiatives addressed international problems but nevertheless "continued to observe the world from their individual perspectives: national, regional and local forms thus remained important."[8]

This chapter is divided into four parts. The first part looks at Austria, Anders' home after his years of exile, and addresses how the nuclear question affected the neutral country at the borders of the Iron Curtain. The second part examines the emergence of an Austrian peace movement and Anders' role in it. In the subsequent third part, the chapter focuses on Anders' relationship to Japan and his encounters with the victims of the atomic bombings.

---

5   The Russell-Einstein-Manifesto, 9 July 1955, in: Andrew G. Bone, ed., The Collected Papers of Bertrand Russell (Vol. 28, Man's Peril, 1954–1955), London 2003, 247–272.
6   For an excellent history of the disarmament movement see: Lawrence S. Wittner, One World or None: A History of the World Nuclear Disarmament Movement Through 1953 (The Struggle Against the Bomb, Vol. 1), Stanford 1993; Lawrence Wittner, Resisting the Bomb: A History of the World Nuclear Disarmament Movement, 1954–1970 (The Struggle Against the Bomb, Vol. 2), Stanford 1997; and Lawrence Wittner, Toward Nuclear Abolition: A History of the World Nuclear Disarmament Movement, 1971 to the Present (The Struggle Against the Bomb, Vol. 3), Stanford 2003. Also see the shorter version of the book: Lawrence Wittner, Confronting the Bomb: A Short History of the World Nuclear Disarmament Movement, Stanford 2009.
7   Jason Dawsey, After Hiroshima: Günther Anders and the History of Anti-Nuclear Critique, in: Matthew Grant/ Benjamin Ziemann, eds., Unthinking the Imaginary War: Intellectual Reflections of the Nuclear Age, Stanford (in preparation). I thank Jason Dawsey for giving me the manuscript of the article.
8   Holger Nehring, National Internationalists: British and West German Protests against Nuclear Weapons, the Politics of Transnational Communications and the Social History of the Cold War, 1957–1964, in: Contemporary European History (Vol. 14, No. 4, Theme Issue: Transnational Communities in European History, 1920–1970), November 2005: 559–582.

The fourth part turns back to the Vienna context and examines the anti-communist suspicions that Anders and his fellow peace activists often had to face.

Austria and Nuclear Energy Optimism in the 1950s[9]

Austria was the home of Günther Anders' second wife, Elisabeth Freundlich. In 1950, after years of exile in the United States, the couple moved back to Freundlich's native city of Vienna. They divorced in 1955, but Anders remained in Vienna and lived there until his death in late 1992.[10] For a philosopher of the nuclear age and disarmament activist like Anders, Austria provided a particular backdrop. The Cold War shaped the postwar history of Austria, which was close to the Iron Curtain, in decisive ways. As a result of the Austrian policy of neutrality, Vienna became a hub for international diplomacy. Nuclear issues were an important part of the country's new profile as the establishment of the International Atomic Energy Agency (IAEA) in 1957 clearly shows.

In 1955, after ten years of four-power military occupation, Austria regained its national sovereignty with the Austrian State Treaty. In the same year the country declared that it would remain neutral.[11] The small size of the state, the policy of neutrality, and the reluctant attitude toward returning refugees had a noticeable impact on the Austrian cultural and intellectual scene.[12] This was also felt by Anders. In 1956, the German journalist Robert Jungk was pondering whether he should move to Vienna. Anders warned his German colleague about Austria's isolation. He described the country as an intellectual wasteland and held the opinion that Austria's "neutralization" (*Neutralisierung*) would only disguise the lack of liberality (*Liberalität*). As a matter of fact, Anders explicitly excluded himself from this characterization of Vienna's intellectual scene.[13]

In the wake of the State Treaty, the young and neutral Second Republic of Austria struggled with the task to find a new role in international affairs. Nuclear matters played a pivotal role in these endeavors as the establishment of the IAEA in Vienna underlined. The Agency's creation traced back to US President Eisenhower's "Atoms for Peace" speech before the United Nations General Assembly in December 1953. Following Stalin's death and the development of the Soviet hydrogen bomb, the speech was an initiative to open a "new channel for peaceful discussion" between the two Cold War rivals and to facilitate international cooperation in the field of nuclear energy. Eisenhower contrasted the threat of nuclear weapons with the benefits of civilian applications of nuclear science and technology in agriculture, medicine, and power generation. Due to this promise of global progress and welfare, "Atoms for Peace"

---

9   This part of the chapter is based on archival research that was made possible through a generous research grant of the Oesterreichische Nationalbank (Anniversary Fund, project number: 14405) and a travel grant by the Bostiber Institut for Austrian American Studies.

10 Jason Dawsey, Where Hitler's Name is Never Spoken: Günther Anders in 1950s Vienna, in: Contemporary Austrian Studies, Vol. 21 (2012): 212–439.

11 For the Austrian State Treaty and the postwar history of Austrian foreign relations see: Arnold Suppan et. al., eds., Der österreichische Staatsvertrag 1955: Internationale Strategie, rechtliche Relevanz, nationale Identität. The Austrian State Treaty 1955: International Strategy, Legal Relevance, National Identity, Vienna 2005; Günter Bischof, Austria in the First Cold War, 1945–1955: The Leverage of the Weak, Basingstoke 1999.

12 For this phenomenon see: Oliver Rathkolb, Die paradoxe Republik: Österreich 1945 bis 2005, Wien 2005.

13 Günther Anders to Robert Jungk, 14 December 1956, Box: Anders-Jungk correspondence, Anders Papers.

was received enthusiastically by many delegations and became a propaganda success for the United States.[14] The Austrian Ambassador to the United Nations, Heinrich Haymerle, reported to Vienna that Eisenhower's speech was one of the most impressive ever held before the UN General Assembly.[15]

While the peace movement of the 1950s centered its attention on the threat of nuclear weapons, atomic hopes were an equally important part of the spirit of the decade. Walt Disney's "Our Friend the Atom" that shaped a whole generation of nuclear energy optimists is probably the most famous and widespread example of atomic euphoria in the mid-1950s.[16] The prevailing nuclear optimism found another expression in the International Conference on the Peaceful Uses of Atomic Energy, which was held at the UN Office in Geneva in 1955. The conference brought together scientists and engineers from all over the world and helped to reestablish the exchange of nuclear physicists from East and West after the scientific isolation of the war decade. This UN event became the largest scientific conference the world had seen until that date—a fact that clearly showed that nuclear physics was about to become the dominating science of the time.[17]

The blessings of the "benign atom" also appealed to the Austrian government. When the negotiators of the IAEA Statute considered where to establish the headquarters of the new international organization, the Foreign Ministry actively lobbied for an Austrian location. The Soviet Union had officially entered the multilateral negotiations to set up the IAEA in 1955 and proposed to erect the organization's headquarters in the capital of a neutral country. The Soviet Union suggested Vienna, Stockholm, and Geneva.[18] India, and particularly the famous 'father' of the Indian nuclear program Homi Bhabha (who adored European culture) was another early supporter of an Austrian location.[19] The Austrian foreign ministry responded enthusiastically to this proposal. Establishing an important international organization like the IAEA in Austria could be a means to regain international prestige and "to reenter the blood circulation of the world."[20] Karl Gruber, at that time Austrian Ambassador to the United States, was the liveliest cheerleader for establishing the IAEA in Vienna. The US government, however, remained skeptical toward the Soviet proposal. The United States Atomic Energy Commission (AEC) insisted on an American location, and the State Department initially favored Geneva over Vienna.

---

14 For the history of "Atoms for Peace" and the full text of the speech see: Ira Cherus, Eisenhower's Atoms for Peace, College Station 2002. For "Atoms for Peace" and American Cold War propaganda see: Kenneth Osgood, Total Cold War: Eisenhower's Secret Propaganda Battle at Home and Abroad, Lawrence 2008. On Eisenhower's speech and the creation of the IAEA see: Elisabeth Röhrlich, Eisenhower's Atoms for Peace: The Speech that Inspired the Creation of the IAEA, IAEA Bulletin (December 2013): 3–4.

15 Heinrich Haymerle to Leopold Figl, New York, 9.12.1957, in: Austrian State Archives, Archiv der Republik, BMfaA II-Pol, Box 252, 193 UN, UNO 2–3, GZ 316 301 Pol 53.

16 Walt Disney Productions/Heinz Haber, Our Friend the Atom, 1956.

17 On the Geneva Conference see: John Krige, Atoms for Peace, Scientific Internationalism, and Scientific Intelligence, in: Osiris 1/2006: 161–181.

18 Gerard C. Smith to Lewis Strauss, 15 May 1956, General Records of the Department of State. Office of the Secretary. Office of the Special Assistant for the Secretary of State for Atomic Energy and Outer Space, File: 10.15 IAEA Headquarters Location 1955–1959, II, Box 139, RG 59, National Archives, College Park (hereinafter referred to as NARA II).

19 Bertrand Goldschmidt, The Origins of the International Atomic Energy Agency, in: David Fischer, ed., International Atomic Energy Agency: Personal Reflections, Vienna 1997, 1–14 (here: 9).

20 Amtssitz der IAEO in Wien: Überblick über die Bemühungen des BKA, AA, 24 January 1958, 536378-VR/58, Völkerrechtsbüro, Archives of the Austrian Foreign Ministry, Vienna.

But soon the Department realized that supporting the Austrian application offered political benefits; even though Austria's neutrality was young and untested, the country was seen as an integral part of the ideological West. For the State Department, it was therefore key to avoid the impression that Austria was "dropped politically by the West."[21] The State Department finally outvoted the AEC. In October 1957, the first General Conference of the IAEA took place in Vienna. The conference delegates were shocked by news of the launch of the Soviet artificial satellite Sputnik—an incident that intensified the Cold War again. Yet, the Austrian press celebrated the Agency's creation as a major success of the government's foreign policy. Austrian newspapers printed headlines like "People are looking at us around the world."[22] In the words of the leading journalist Hugo Portisch, Vienna had become the "world's center of the atom."[23]

With the establishment of the IAEA Austria tied in with earlier traditions, most notably the holding of the famous Congress of Vienna in 1815. Against the background of the Cold War, international events like the opening of the IAEA were a tool to underscore the country's neutrality. Scientific cooperation in the nuclear field was in line with a strategy that historian of science, Bruno Strasser, has called the "coproduction of neutral science and neutral state."[24] When in September 1955 the American Ambassador to Austria Llewellyn E. Thompson inaugurated the "Atoms for Peace Library" in Vienna, the Austrian Foreign Minister Leopold Figl declared: "Our country has never forgotten that you gave us food when our people were starving. And we feel blessed that you will now help our country to enter the nuclear age."[25]

Anders thus developed his nuclear critique in a country that was at the heart of the new evolving international nuclear order. His writings and activities in these early years, however, were little influenced by these developments. It was rather the threat of the bomb than the potential dangers of the civilian nuclear applications as promoted by the IAEA that were at the core of Anders' work.

The Formation of a Nuclear Disarmament Movement in Austria

Compared to the large anti-nuclear movements in West Germany, the United Kingdom, and neighboring Switzerland, the Austrian peace movement developed at a much slower pace. Lawrence Wittner, the historian of the world nuclear disarmament movement, has argued that this was probably due to the fact that nuclear weapons were perceived as a less imminent

21 Austrian Interest in Selection of Vienna as Permanent Site for IAEA, 24 May 1956, General Records of the Department of State. Office of the Secretary. Office of the Special Assistant for the Secretary of State for Atomic Energy and Outer Space, File: 10.15 IAEA Headquarters Location 1955–1959, II, RG 59, Box 139, NARA II; Report from U.S. Embassy in Austria (n.d., n.a.), General Records of the Department of State. Office of the Secretary. Office of the Special Assistant for the Secretary of State for Atomic Energy and Outer Space, File: 10.15 IAEA Headquarters Location 1955–1959, I, RG 59, Box 139, NARA II.

22 Die Menschen überall in der Welt sehen auf uns, in: Kurier, 1 October 1957 (quoted from: Press Clippings IAEA, Wienbibliothek) (translated from German, E.R.).

23 Hugo Portisch, In den Mauern unserer Stadt, in: Kurier, 1 October 1957 (quoted from: Press Clippings IAEA, Wienbibliothek) (translated from German, E.R.).

24 Bruno J. Strasser, The Coproduction of Neutral Science and Neutral State in Cold War Europe: Switzerland and International Scientific Cooperation, 1951–1969, in: Osiris 1/2009, 165–187.

25 Brigitte Kromp, Die Zentralbibliothek für Physik als Depotbibliothek und regionales Zentrum, unpublished manuscript (Vienna n.d.), 27–28 (translated from German, E.R.).

danger for neutral Austria than for other European countries.[26] For Anders it was, however, important that the movement would expand in countries where the nuclear question was not linked to national defense debates.[27] Anders' most important fellow disarmament activist in Austria was Robert Jungk. Their friendship began in late 1956 when Jungk, who at that time was about to move to Vienna, sent a letter to Anders in order to express his appreciation for Anders' work. The two men had never met in person before. Jungk wrote to Anders: "Today, there is so much that makes us blind, but your book can make us see." And he continued: "As far as I can remember, this is the first 'fan letter' I have ever written."[28] This correspondence laid the foundation for a close (if often complicated) friendship between the two authors.

The anti-nuclear protest movements of the time were composed of a variety of different local, national, and transnational groups, some of which addressed a wider public while others were more defined by specific professions such as physicians or physicists. In 1963, Günther Anders and Robert Jungk founded the Austrian Easter March Committee (Österreichisches Komitee für den Ostermarsch) after the model of the CND's annual Easter Marches in London. The Viennese Easter March of 1963 started with about 600 people in the small town of Mödling near Vienna and ended with over sixteen hundred participants in the center of the city. In the following years, Robert Jungk led the Committee that was then renamed into Action for Peace and Disarmament (Aktion für Frieden und Abrüstung).[29]

A few years earlier, Anders had tried to establish an Austrian section of the Committee against Nuclear Armament (Komitee gegen Atomrüstung). The Committee had been initiated by the writer Hans Werner Richter in West Germany in 1958. Richter was also the founder of a very influential group of German writers, the Group 47 (Gruppe 47).[30] Vis-à-vis representatives of the West German Committee Anders emphasized that he was not happy about the development of the movement in Austria. According to Anders, "no one of interest" had taken part in the first meeting of the Austrian Committee and not a single physicist or physician had shown up.[31]

Anders' transnational networks with European and American disarmament groups and organizations were often more effective than the collaboration with his fellow Austrians. When the first disarmament movement reached its peak of influence in the late 1950s and early 1960s, Anders was in touch with many of the movements' leading figures, among them prominent members of Pugwash such as Bertrand Russell as well as Linus and Ava Helen Pauling. Besides maintaining this written correspondence, Anders traveled a lot and participated in other countries' disarmament initiatives, for instance in a European congress organized by the British CND in January 1959. In the same month, he spoke to the participants of the Students Congress against Nuclear Armament in West Berlin.[32] He was, however, only interested in events that would allow him to play a leading role. When Anders was invited to take part in the London

---

26 Wittner, Struggle against the Bomb 2, 227.
27 Günther Anders to Hajo Schedlich, 4 May 1959, Anders-Jungk correspondence, Anders Papers (translated from German, E.R.).
28 Robert Jungk to Günther Anders, 8 December 1956, Anders-Jungk correspondence, Anders Papers (translated from German, E.R.).
29 Wittner, Struggle against the Bomb 2, 228.
30 Heinz Ludwig Arnold, Die Gruppe 47, Reinbek bei Hamburg 2004.
31 Günther Anders to the "Komitee gegen Atomrüstung," 20 March 1959, Konvolut "Comite gegen Atomrüstung" (sic), Anders Papers (translated from German, E.R.).
32 For an overview of Anders's anti-nuclear activities in the late 1950s and early 1960s see the Anders Papers, Vienna.

Easter March of 1961 but was not asked to give a speech to the participants, he declined the invitation. Referring to his medical condition he said he would not fly to London "only to do some arthritic marching."[33]

The peace movement of the 1950s was marked by an expansion of its participants and members, in contrast to the beginnings of anti-nuclear weapons activism that was dominated by nuclear physicists. Günther Anders was a representative of the humanities. He thus did not become a member of Pugwash, which was dominated by scientists.[34] As mentioned earlier, he was, however, in touch with several important members of the non-governmental organization that aimed to work toward nuclear disarmament and that, thanks to its Western, Soviet, and Indian members, bridged the East-West divide. The Austrian representative to Pugwash was the physicist and social democrat Hans Thirring. In December 1963, Thirring published the brochure "Mehr Sicherheit ohne Waffen" (the so-called Thirring Plan).[35] It presented a (widely discussed yet politically unsuccessful) proposal for the complete disarmament of neutral Austria and the establishment of demilitarized zones in neighboring countries under the supervision of a UN committee. A few years earlier, in 1958, Thirring had organized the third Pugwash Conference on Science and World Affairs, which took place in Austria (Kitzbühel and Vienna) in September of that year. It was the biggest conference in the history of Pugwash and supported by prominent Austrian social democrats such as Federal President Adolf Schärf and State Secretary Bruno Kreisky.[36]

Even though Anders was not a member of Pugwash, he supported the organization's work. The major outcome of the Austrian Pugwash Conference of 1958 was the release of the "Vienna Declaration," which dealt with topics such as the need to end the arms race, the promotion of nuclear disarmament, and international scientific cooperation. The declaration also highlighted the social responsibility of scientists.[37] Anders distributed the "Vienna Declaration" among participants of disarmament conferences other than Pugwash. In a letter to Hans Werner Richter he explained why he supported the Pugwashites. In Anders' view, all the different sections of the international peace movement and its respective national branches shared one goal. He explained: "Somehow it is always the same large congress, even though it takes place sometimes here and sometimes there. It is always the same old solidarity [...] and everywhere you can find the same desperate hope that we can still save what cannot be saved."[38] Anders aimed to include Thirring in his other activities and, for instance, invited him to become a member of the steering committee of the Berlin Student Congress.[39]

The different groups of the peace movement had something else in common: their belief in the peaceful applications of nuclear energy. While the disarmament activists fought against the military uses of nuclear energy, they aimed to accelerate its peaceful applications in science and medicine, agriculture, as well as power generation. Most of Anders' fellow

---

33 Günther Anders to Robert Jungk, 12 April 1961, Anders-Jungk correspondence, Anders Papers.

34 For the history of Pugwash see: Matthew Evangelista, Unarmed Forces: The Transnational Movement to End the Cold War, Ithaca 1999.

35 Brigitte Zimmel/Gabriele Kerber, eds., Hans Thirring: Ein Leben für Physik und Frieden, Wien 1992, 101–108.

36 Joseph Rotblat, Science and World Affairs: History of the Pugwash Conferences (London 1962); Eugene Rabinowitch, The Third Pugwash Conference, in: The Bulletin of the Atomic Scientists, November 1958: 338–340.

37 Vienna Declaration, in: The Bulletin of the Atomic Scientists, November 1958: 341–344.

38 Günther Anders to Hans Werner Richter, Wien, 22 September 1958, Anders Papers.

39 Letter from Student Congress to Hans Thirring, B35 1133, Hans Thirring Papers, Österreichische Zentralbibliothek für Physik, Vienna.

peace activists clearly distinguished the peaceful from the military uses of nuclear energy. This separation had shaped the debates on nuclear matters since the immediate postwar years. Some of the most prominent anti-nuclear weapons declarations of the time were built on praise for the peaceful uses of the benign atom, among them the "Vienna Declaration" of the Pugwashites and the appeal of eighteen distinguished nuclear scientists from Germany. This famous declaration of the "Göttinger 18," published in 1957, ended with a plea for atomic power optimism: "We emphasize that it is of the utmost importance to promote the peaceful applications of nuclear energy with all means, and that we will continue to work for this aim."[40]

To some extent, Anders shared this mainstream thinking. In the 1950s and 1960s, Hiroshima was the central metaphor in his writings on the nuclear age. The nuclear power plant accident in Windscale in the United Kingdom (today Sellafield), on the other hand, did not receive particular attention in Anders' work. Only after the 1986 Chernobyl power plant disaster did Anders begin to write extensively about their potential hazards. "Hiroshima is everywhere" was then supplemented by "Chernobyl is everywhere." Anders approved of this new version of his slogan, which had been phrased by his followers.[41] After the Chernobyl disaster, Anders developed a very radical attitude toward nuclear power generation. According to Anders, the erection and operation of nuclear power plants was "murder and genocide."[42] Next to the dropping of the atom bombs on Hiroshima and Nagasaki, the holocaust was the other central historic rupture that shaped Anders' work. As this quote illustrates, Anders' nuclear critique often united both in one argument.

In the 1950s, Anders' writings focused on the bomb and did not pay much attention to the peaceful uses of nuclear energy. Nevertheless, Anders questioned the prevailing opinion that there was a clear-cut difference between the military and the civilian uses of nuclear energy. In the "Journal from Hiroshima," published in 1959, Anders argued that those who can build peaceful reactors were also able to use the destructive forces of nuclear energy.[43] In another passage of the book, Anders criticized the atomic energy optimism of most of his contemporaries, and the belief in modernity and progress that was part of it. He described how irritated he had been to see an exhibition on the "peaceful uses of atomic energy" at the Hiroshima Museum. For him this was a "shot in the heart"; it left a very cynical impression on him.[44] Unlike the majority of the disarmament activists of his time, Anders did not share the optimistic belief in unlimited progress. Anders' magnum opus, "The Obsolescence of Human Beings" ("*Die Antiquiertheit des Menschen*") is another early and elaborate manifestation of this opinion.[45]

---

40 For the full text see the online platform of the German Historical Museum: http://www.hdg.de/lemo/html/dokumente/JahreDesAufbausInOstUndWest_erklaerungGoettingerErklaerung/index.html (translated from German, E.R.)

41 10 Thesen zu Tschernobyl, Anders Papers.

42 Volker Hage, Günther Anders: Philosoph der Liebe, in: Die Zeit, 7 November 1986 (translated from German, E.R.).

43 Günther Anders, Hiroshima ist überall, München 1982, 24.

44 Ibid. 66.

45 Günther Anders, Die Antiquiertheit des Menschen, Munich 1956.

Günther Anders and the Victims of the Hiroshima and Nagasaki Bombings

Over the course of the 1950s, the protest movement began to focus on other humanitarian consequences of nuclear weapons; radiation dangers became an increasingly prominent issue. The United Nations Scientific Committee on the Effects of Atomic Radiation (UNSCEAR) published a first report to access the effects of radiation on humans and the environment in 1958.[46] American nuclear tests intensified questions about the hazards of radioactive fallout from nuclear testing. In 1954, the American tests had unexpected and terrible consequences: about three hundred people were exposed to very high radioactive radiation, and irradiated fish were caught in Japan. The crew of a Japanese fishing vessel (the name of the boat was Lucky Dragon 5) was exposed to radioactive dust, and the men suffered from serious symptoms such as burns and fever. When one of the fishermen died, the world was shocked.[47] Because it was, again, Japan that experienced the perils of the nuclear age, the transnational disarmament movement's solidarity with the country increased even more.[48]

In summer 1958, Günther Anders traveled to Japan to attend the Fourth World Conference against Atomic and Hydrogen Bombs and for Disarmament. Next to Tokyo, Anders visited Hiroshima and Nagasaki where he went to see the bombings' victims at hospitals; he also visited Yaizu, the hometown of the Lucky Dragon's crew. While there, he took part in a peace procession and met the family of the dead fisherman. During a commemoration ceremony, Anders argued that radioactive fallout knew no boundaries and that people all over the world had become neighbors.[49] He also explained why he refused to speak of "nuclear tests:" the notion of a "test" would support the illusion that nothing but a harmless experiment had happened.[50] Similarly he criticized the euphemistic use of the term "conventional weapons" in contrast to nuclear weapons.[51] He tried to unmask the dominating terms of the debate as playing down the tremendous threat. During his time in Japan Anders also worked to establish a "moral code for the nuclear age"—this idea remained central in his later antinuclear weapons activities.[52]

Anders tried to translate these experiences from Japan into the context of European peace congresses. He brought paper cranes from the hospitals of Hiroshima to the Student Congress in Berlin, where he also played the music of the Hiroshima peace march. Furthermore, Jungk and Anders brought a brick from Hiroshima to Berlin.[53] Following his journey to Japan,

---

46 Jacob Darwin Hamblin, Exorcising Ghosts in the Age of Automation: United Nations Experts and Atoms for Peace, in: Technology and Culture, No. 4, Vol. 47 (October 2006), 734–756. The full version of the report is accessible online at UNSCEAR's website: http://www.unscear.org/docs/reports/1958,%2013th%20session%20 (Suppl.%20No.17)/1958final-1_unscear.pdf.

47 For a contemporary report on the Lucky Dragon 5 see: James R. Arnold, Effects of the Recent Bomb Tests on Human Beings, in: Bulletin of the Atomic Scientists, No. 9, Vol. 10, November 1954): 347–348.

48 The history of the Japanese fishers also had a significant influence on literature, see for instance: Wolfgang Weyrauch, Die japanischen Fischer, in: Sinn und Form 8 (1956): 373–402.

49 Anders, Tagebuch aus Hiroshima und Nagasaki, 37.

50 Ibid. 38.

51 Ibid. 75.

52 Ibid.

53 Günther Anders to Werner Gessler, 10 December 1958, Anders Papers, "Konvolut Berliner Studentenkongress," Österreichisches Litertaturarchiv.

Anders published his "Journal from Hiroshima and Nagasaki," which is an impressive report of both his personal experiences with the victims of the bombings and the organizational troubles to build a transnational peace movement.

With his actions and publications, Anders made use of the symbolic power of the name Hiroshima, which he used as a pars pro toto for the overall nuclear danger. Yet, he argued several times that the dropping of a second bomb on Nagasaki was the real crime.[54]

The Vienna Context: Friends and Foes

The journalist and futurologist Robert Jungk was an early supporter of Günther Anders' nuclear disarmament activities. During the difficult beginnings of the Austrian peace movement, Anders discussed with Jungk organizational questions as well as new literature in the field. When Anders embarked on a correspondence with the so-called "Hiroshima Pilot," Claude Eatherly, he not only sought Jungk's advice, but later made him the editor of the correspondence's publication.[55] Next to the Austrian physicist Hans Thirring, who published a "History of the Atom Bomb" as early as 1946,[56] Günther Anders and Robert Jungk became the three major anti-nuclear weapons educators of Vienna. Jungk's bestselling book, *Brighter than a Thousand Suns* ("Heller als tausend Sonnen"), published in 1956, portrayed the history of the Manhattan project scientists.[57] The book received international attention, including a review by Nobel laureate John Cockcroft in the leading scientific journal, *Nature*.[58]

Notwithstanding their shared interests and goals, the intellectual friendship between Anders and Jungk was often complicated. On New Year's Eve 1959, Anders sent an angry letter to Jungk accusing him of underestimating the threat of nuclear weapons: "You have become a traveling salesman for hope," Anders wrote to his friend. He felt that Jungk had turned from someone who warned about the atom bomb into someone who believed that the greatest danger already lay behind. In the same letter Anders called Jungk "corrupt" (*bestechlich*) and explained that he would not be surprised if Jungk's fellow disarmament activists perceived him as a traitor. The conflict also had political implications. Anders worried that the West German Christian Democrat Party (CDU) would utilize Jungk's statements to support their political position. Anders' friendship with Jungk was at stake.[59]

The two writers were friends again soon after, but outbursts like this one were characteristic for Anders. As Jungk once put it, sooner or later Anders had an argument with every leading intellectual of the time, including Nobel laureates such as Erwin Schrödinger and Max Born, the Austrian peace activist Ernst Schwarcz, or the German writer Hans Magnus Enzensberger.[60] Anders' (supposedly arrogant) tone and attitude in dealing with fellow activists (for example he said to Jungk that his newspaper articles were "not at all high-quality")[61]

---

54 See: Dawsey, Nuclear Critique.
55 Anders-Jungk correspondence, Anders Papers.
56 Hans Thirring, Die Geschichte der Atombombe, Wien 1946.
57 Robert Jungk, Heller als tausend Sonnen: Das Schicksal der Atomforscher, Stuttgart 1956.
58 John Cockroft, Nuclear Physicists and Atom Bombs, in: Nature, 30 August 1958.
59 Günther Anders to Robert Jungk, 31 December 1959, Anders-Jungk correspondence, Anders Papers (translated from German, E.R.).
60 Robert Jungk to Günther Anders, 17 January 1960, Anders-Jungk correspondence, Anders Papers.
61 Günther Anders to Robert Jungk, 5 August 1961, Anders-Jungk correspondence (translated from German, E.R.)

certainly increased the problem. Nevertheless, most controversies resulted from actual differences in opinion. Whenever Anders believed "blindness towards the apocalypse" ("Apokalypseblindheit") to be at work, he was unable to accept another opinion. The philosopher Karl Jaspers was one of the major voices in the intellectual discussions on the atom bomb. He warned about their destructive power but at same time remained skeptical vis-à-vis the disarmament movement. Moreover, Jaspers still believed in a chance for world peace. For Anders this was "blindness towards the apocalypse" at its worst.[62]

In Vienna, Anders' and Jungk's greatest political opponent was the writer and journalist Friedrich Torberg, a radical anti-Communist. Torberg published the monthly journal, *Forum*, which was affiliated with the Congress for Cultural Freedom (CCF). The CCF was an influential organization of anti-Communist European intellectuals and, as became known in the late 1960s, was funded by the CIA.[63] Since the emergence of the disarmament movement in the late 1950s, Torberg had used the "Forum" to attack the transnational peace movement as being dominated by communists. These kinds of anti-Communist suspicions toward the disarmament movement were common and especially shaped the political debate surrounding the 1958 Pugwash Conference in Austria. In the same year, Torberg called Jungk "a neutralist panic monger."[64] The argument between Anders, Jungk, and Torberg reached its peak in 1964.

The cause was Günther Anders' before mentioned correspondence with the American airforce pilot Claude Eatherly. Three years after its publication, the American journalist William Bradford Huie published a book on the same subject entitled "The Hiroshima Pilot." Huie's book, however, presented an account of Eatherly's story that was very different from Anders' version. Huie argued that Eatherly was not the conscience-stricken man he declared to be. *The Hiroshima Pilot* was based on interviews with family members, former comrades, and doctors of Eatherly. According to these witnesses, Huie argued, Eatherly initially had been deeply disappointed about the fact that he was not treated as a war hero. Huie quoted Eatherly's first wife having said that her ex-husband was very disappointed about not having been chosen to drop one of the American test bombs at the Bikini atoll. Huie also criticized the fact that Eatherly was often dubbed "the Hiroshima Pilot," albeit he did not fly the aircraft that dropped the bomb but an accompanying weather reconnaissance plane. Huie thus underlined that Eatherly had not seen the actual dropping of the bomb.[65] Plenty of debate in the international press followed the release of Huie's book. In Austria and Germany, where Anders' book was well known, most leading newspapers published long reviews of Huie's *The Hiroshima Pilot*.[66]

In the eyes of Anders and Jungk, Huie's book was unacceptable. Both submitted letters to make their case to the editors of many leading German and Austrian newspapers. Anders emphasized that Eatherly had never said that he dropped the bomb on Hiroshima. Anders also held the opinion that it was of no importance whether or not Eatherly had dropped the bomb. In the weekly newspaper, *Die Zeit*, Anders explained why not: "Who, like Huie, argues that Eatherly cannot feel guilty since he did not drop the bomb does not accuse Eatherly, but

---

62 Günther Anders to Hans Werner Richter, 22 September 1959, Konvolut "Comite gegen Abrüstung" (sic).
63 Michael Hochgeschwender, Freiheit in der Offensive? Der Kongress für Kulturelle Freiheit, München 1997.
64 Forum des Lesers, in: Forum V/54, 1958: 218 (translated from German, E.R.)
65 William Bradford Huie, The Hiroshima Pilot, London 1964.
66 For a selection of media coverage see: Torberg Papers, Box 5, 5/5: Robert Jungk, Wienbibliothek, Vienna.

accuses himself. Because he argues in an Eichmann pattern, as if the one who by pure coincidence did not carry out the final step would not need to feel guilty."[67]

At around the same time of the ongoing international debate on Huie's book, the Viennese "Volkstheater" (one of the city's main theaters) staged the play "Gilda calls Mae West" that dealt with Eatherly's story. In a destructive review of the play, Torberg criticized not only the play but also attacked Anders and Jungk as the author and editor of the Eatherly correspondence. Moreover, Torberg blamed the two disarmament activists of having no real interest in Eatherly, insisting that they were only looking for publicity.[68]

The subsequent issues of Forum published the controversy between Anders, Jungk, and Torberg, which ended in court for Jungk and Torberg.[69] Torberg's insults intensified the disagreement (in one article Torberg characterized Anders with the dismissive Viennese term "Burschi") and the ideology-laden Cold War debates on Communism exacerbated the conflict. In an open letter to Anders in Forum, Torberg said that he did not know who was a communist and who was not. But, he went on, he did know who was an anti-Communist and who was not: "Mr. Jungk, you are not an anti-Communist. And neither is Mr. Anders."[70]

These anti-Communist suspicions also formed part of the background of Huie's book. Huie, a former McCarthy man and editor of the (at that time) right-wing "American Mercury," wanted to challenge the disarmament movement's hero, Eatherly. There was, however, more to Huie's criticism. Anders was indeed so impressed by Eatherly's story (and he saw him as an important guiding figure for the disarmament movement) that he kept quiet about less appropriate aspects of Eatherly's biography. In The Hiroshima Pilot, Huie said that Eatherly had prepared for further military uses of nuclear bombs after Hiroshima; Anders knew about this. In 1961, long before the Huie controversy took place, Anders wrote to Jungk that he did not want to "rub the people's noses" in Eatherly's post-Hiroshima military activities: "This is something that Eatherly himself will have to explain in his biography."[71]

Conclusion

In recent years, the history of nuclear disarmament campaigns has received increasing attention from European historians. In contrast to this new research on the German and British protest movements stands the lack of research on the beginnings of the Austrian peace movement in the 1950s and 1960s. Günter Bischof has described this as one of the main gaps in research on Austria in the first Cold War.[72]

Günther Anders exemplifies the need to address this research gap and to look into the beginnings of the Austrian disarmament movement. Anders' close exchange with like-

---

67 Günther Anders, Entlarvung des Entlarvers, in: Die Zeit, 28 August 1964 (translated from German).

68 Friedrich Torberg, "Ein Meinungsaustausch in Sachen demokratischer Gesinnung," in: Forum XI/126 (Juni/Juli 1964), 306–311.

69 Ibid.

70 Ibid. (translated from German, E.R.).

71 Günther Anders to Robert Jungk, 10 August 1961, Anders-Jungk correspondence, Anders Papers (translated from German, E.R.)

72 Günter Bischof, Eine historiographische Einführung: Die Ära des Kalten Krieges und Österreich, in: Erwin Schmidl, Österreich im frühen Kalten Krieg 1945–1958: Spione, Partisanen, Kriegspläne, Wien 2000, 19–54 (here: 51).

minded people in Austria and other countries such as Germany, the United Kingdom, the United States, and Japan, shows that Anders was indeed one of the "national internationalists" of the time. The victims of the American bombings on Hiroshima and Nagasaki, as well as those of fallout from weapons tests, were of special importance to Anders. Like many of his fellow disarmament activists he faced anti-Communist suspicions, especially from his Viennese rival Friedrich Torberg. Anders' correspondence with the so-called "Hiroshima Pilot" Claude Eatherly stood at the heart of this debate.

There is, however, one important question that existing literature on Anders has not been able to answer: If the dropping of the atom bombs on Hiroshima and Nagasaki had such a pivotal impact on Anders, why did he only start to write on the nuclear question during the 1950s? Anders argued that the news of Hiroshima left him speechless and in shock.[73]

Maybe Anders' later involvement in the peace movement offers an additional answer. The nuclear disarmament movement only gained momentum in the early to mid-1950s, following the developments of the American and Soviet hydrogen bombs, the new series of American tests, and the increasing awareness of radiation dangers. Anders' involvement in the peace movement of the 1950s gives good reason to argue that the philosopher was impacted by the emerging civil society movements of the time. Anders' nuclear critique and his anti-nuclear weapons activities show that both aspects of his work depended on each other. He was a man of thought, and a man of action.

---

73 Dawsey, Nuclear Critique.

Berthold Molden

Günther Anders as a Transnational Intellectual in the Late 1960s

Defining a Transnational Intellectual

This chapter explores Günther Anders' role as a public intellectual and political activist in the context of the transnational movement against the Vietnam War in the late 1960s. The "long 1960s"[1] were rich in writers and thinkers who did not seem to fit in the most common ideological pigeonholes of their time, many of them hailing from or having escaped the complex histories and recent bloodbaths of Central and Eastern Europe. They might be Communists who left their political camp out of frustration with Soviet power politics, like the great Vienna-born historian of the Mexican Revolution, Friedrich Katz.[2] They may have been polyglot priests and philosophers, only to transform into maverick theorists of post-authoritarian education, like Ivan Illich.[3] Or they might be philosophers who evaded the academic world and the university—viewed as an intellectual cage—to instead become activist-publicists and promoters of political change, like Günther Anders.

To quote from Russell Jacoby's famous requiem to the public intellectual in the USA and beyond, "to view the sixties exclusively through the lens of intellectuals would be a serious mistake. Nevertheless, it is equally erroneous to disregard the impact of writers, philosophers, and political theorists. [… So:] Who were the sixties intellectuals? Probably most were not American: Jean-Paul Sartre, Albert Camus, Frantz Fanon, Herbert Marcuse, Isaac Deutscher, Wilhelm Reich."[4] Although Anders does not figure explicitly among the pantheon of Jacoby's intellectuals, he surely does fit this ticket of European thinkers, writers and critical voices who had a certain repercussion in the polyphonic and conflicted public spheres of the US in the 1960s. However, the case of Anders is peculiar insofar as his tireless international activism was paired with a striking, and at times self-inflicted, marginalization within the fields of critical intellectual production.

According to Russell Jacoby and Robert Nisbet it was the university itself—the professionalization and increasing public recognition of academic social and human sciences since the 1950s—that drove public intellectuals out of business. In other words, academia cost most

---

1   This periodization is often delimited with the years 1954 and 1973, each standing for multiple impactful events in political, economic, and cultural history. Cf. Arthur Marvick, The Cultural Revolution of the Long 1960s: Voices of Reaction, Revolution, and Permeation, in: The International History Review 27 (4/2005), 780–806.

2   Javier Garciadiego/Emilio Kourí, eds., Revolución y exilio en la historia de México. Del amor de un historiador a su patria adoptiva: Homenaje a Friedrich Katz, Mexico 2010; Martina Kaller/David Mayer/Berthold Molden, eds., Friedrich Katz. Essays on the Life and Work of a Transnational Historian, Frankfurt am Main 2012.

3   Martina Kaller-Dietrich, Ivan Illich (1926–2002). Sein Leben, sein Denken, Weitra 2008.

4   Russell Jacoby, The Last Intellectuals. American Culture in the Age of Academe, New York: 2000 [1987], 114. Among the many texts on the disappearance of public intellectuals, cf. Michael Ignatieff, The Decline and Fall of the Public Intellectual, in: Queen's Quaterly 104 (1997), 395–403.

non-tenured thinkers the reputation and public prestige that makes intellectuals count, while it restrained university employees in the professional conventions of their jobs and in the economic logics of keeping these jobs.[5] In the USA in particular, from where Günther Anders moved to Vienna in 1950 after fourteen years of exile, the academic world changed in the context of the early Cold War. At a time when the witch-hunt atmosphere produced by the newly permanent status (since 1945) of the House Committee on Un-American Activities and the particularly blunt anti-Communism of Senator Joseph McCarthy shaped the political climate of the post-WWII years, academic life was influenced in a specific way. Research itself may not have been affected by a scholar's politics, and state funding may not have been either, but to speak out openly against the ideological zeitgeist of the West did have consequences. As the biologist Richard Lewontin put it, "In contrast to a highly visible legislative attack on academic radicals, there was a widespread indifference to political ideology in the research supported by agencies of the state."[6]

As a radical thinker and challenger of hegemonic opinions and Western political doctrines of the Cold War, Günther Anders remained outside institutionalized academia until his death in 1992. He also reported intellectual exclusion from the years before WWII: According to Anders, Theodor W. Adorno had vetoed his habilitation in 1929 and, in terms of line-toeing Communism, the Austrian fellow-exile and writer Manès Sperber rejected a novel of Anders' during his years in Paris in the early 1930s.[7] In short, Günther Anders could be seen as a paradigmatic intellectual outsider and yet he was part of an intensive intellectual exchange across geographic and ideological boundaries. To interpret him as a transnational intellectual allows new insights both into Anders' life and work and into the 1960s as a period of anti-hegemonic discursive transfers on a global scale.

Before going into the details of Anders' ideas and rhetoric one has yet to find a suitable definition for a 1960s public intellectual if Anders and his work shall be categorized in this fashion. At the risk of committing an act of reversed anachronism, I will first cite from what comes close to a definition of a public intellectual penned in 1969 by a contemporary and brother-in-arms of Anders, Howard Zinn:

"We might use our scholarly time and energy to sharpen the perceptions of the complacent by exposing those facts that any society tends to hide about itself: the facts about wealth and poverty, about tyranny in both communist and capitalist states, about lies told by politicians, the mass media, the church, popular leaders. We need to expose fallacious logic, spurious analogies, deceptive slogans, and those intoxicating symbols that drive people to murder (the flag, communism, capitalism, freedom). We need to dig beneath the abstractions so our fellow citizens can make judgments on the particular realities beneath political rhetoric. We need to expose inconsistencies and

5   Cf. Patrick Baert and Alan Shipman, Transformation of the Intellectual, in: Fernando Domínguez Rubio/Patrick Baert, eds., London 2012, 179–204, here: 181–182.

6   R. C. Lewontin, The Cold War and the Transformation of the Academy, in: Noam Chomsky et al., The Cold War & The University, New York 1997, 1–34, here: 18.

7   Raimund Bahr, Günther Anders: Leben und Denken im Wort, Vienna/St. Wolfgang 2010. Cf. Konrad Paul Liessmann, Wiedersehen und vergessen. Zur Biographie, in: Dirk Röpcke/Raimund Bahr, eds., Geheimagent der Masseneremiten – Günther Anders, Vienna/St. Wolfgang 2002.

double standards. In short, we need to become the critics of the culture rather than its apologists and perpetuators."[8]

Another contemporary of Anders, Jean-Paul Sartre, famously coined the term of the "engaged intellectual" that, according to the French philosopher who aspired to be just that for France, Europe, and beyond, does not content himself with "contributing to the progress of pure knowledge; the further aim upon which we fix is liberation."[9] Sarah Hammerschlag has pointed out that "the task of the engaged intellectual is not only to expose his culture's injustices but also to take part in a specific anthropological project to describe the human being in his conditions, to describe the way those conditions form him."[10] If we think of the Sartre of the late 1940s, of the analyst of the French "Jewish Question," then we encounter a writer who calls for political action among his fellow intellectuals and citizens. In the words of Patrick Baert, Sartre was a "politically engaged intellectual in the Dreyfusard tradition, [i.e.] writers who use their accomplishments within their field to speak out about political issues, who position themselves clearly at the left of the political spectrum and who are suspicious of the state and authority."[11] Moreover, Baert introduces an interesting distinction between "professional public intellectuals"—such as Foucault or Bourdieu, whose specific expertise in the prison system or the social system suddenly become sought after by politicians—and "authoritative public intellectuals, like Sartre, [who] are generalists; they might be formally educated in a certain discipline but they rely on their vast cultural resources and charisma to speak out about a wide range of topics well beyond their area of expertise."[12]

We can thus formulate six central characteristics of a transnational public intellectual in the 1960s:

- to learn from history;
- to expose untruth and promote truth;
- to be critical of authority;
- to actively contribute to liberation;
- to transcend specific fields of academic training;
- and, specifically in terms of transnationality, not to be constrained by one's respective national public sphere, but rather to intervene openly in foreign debates if they constitute global issues.

The following two observations on Günther Anders' activism against the Vietnam War, which can be interpreted as more than just a variant of the dominant rhetoric of the New Left, are intended to verify whether these qualifications apply in his case.

---

8   Howard Zinn, The Case for Radical Change, in: *The Saturday Review*, October 18, 1969, 81–82 and 94ff, here: 95.
9   Jean-Paul Sartre, Présentation, in: *Les temps modernes*, October 1, 1945, 14 (translation from: Sarah Hammerschlag, The Figural Jew. Politics and Identity in Postwar French Thought, Chicago 2010, 91).
10   Ibid., 91.
11   Patrick Baert, Jean-Paul Sartre's positioning in Anti-Semite and Jew, in: Journal of Classical Sociology 11 (4/2011), 378–397, here 383. Baert qualifies and relativizes the Dreyfusard label because of Sartre's existentialist reservations toward Enlightenment principles of universal equality.
12   Ibid., 384.

Inexact Analogies? Anders, Vietnam, and the Holocaust

The first observation focuses on Anders and his analytical entwinement of the Holocaust and the Vietnam War. One of Anders' central interests in the first two post-WWII decades was the Holocaust. In several of his texts, and sometimes linked with the issue of nuclear armament,[13] he addressed aspects of the Nazi-genocide against the European Jews.[14] Not unlike Sartre—or, on the other side of the "color curtain" across the age of decolonization, W. E. B. Du Bois in his famous "The Negro and the Warsaw Ghetto"[15]—Anders finds the reflection of the Holocaust necessary in order to understand a changed post-1945 world of social, ethnic, cultural relations. Anders gave much focus to the Nazis' industrial killing machine and its theoretical impact on the analysis of the genocidal potential of what hitherto had been considered "civilization." Besides the issue of historical guilt, of memory and repression, there was the issue of how the cruelties committed in the name of nationalism, racism, and ideology during the first half of the 20th century might be repeated or even turned to a more absolute horror in the near future. Between the two possible associations with Vietnam in Anders' intellectual map, the Austrian Anders-adept Raimund Bahr believes that "Vietnam is closer to Auschwitz than to Hiroshima," and he argues this with a biographical note: the proximity of Anders' visit to Auschwitz in 1966 and his participation in the Vietnam Tribunal in 1967.[16]

Günther Anders first published his reflections about his visit to Auschwitz in 1967,[17] the same year that he became a juror in the Vietnam War Crimes Tribunal, also known as first Russell Commission. Given the strong impact that Auschwitz had on Anders, it does not come as a surprise that the Holocaust served as a historico-political backdrop for the analysis of the Vietnam War. In fact, this non-governmental and non-institutional commission, convoked in 1966 by the British philosopher, mathematician and peace activist Bertrand Russell and presided by Jean-Paul Sartre, was designed on the basis of the International Military Tribunal against the main Nazi war criminals in Nuremberg. Sartre, and especially Russell, had published amply against the Vietnam War. Now they decided to bring together a critical and international mass of activists and intellectuals in the form of a concerned citizens' tribunal. When the commission convened in 1967, first in Stockholm and later in the Danish town of Roskilde, the list of its members and collaborators was quite diverse and included such illustrious names as: Vladimir Dedijer, Wolfgang Abendroth, Günther Anders, James Baldwin, Lelio Basso, Simone de Beauvoir, Lázaro Cárdenas, Stokely Carmichael, Isaac Deutscher,

---

13 Günther Anders, Die Toten. Rede über die drei Weltkriege, Cologne 1966. The speech "The Dead. Speech about the Three World Wars" was delivered at a peace rally in Mainz, Germany, on 24 October 1964.

14 Günther Anders, Wir Eichmannsöhne. Offener Brief an Klaus Eichmann, Munich 1964. Cf. Jason Dawsey's chapter in this book, "Fragile Apprehension: Günther Anders and the Poetics of Destruction."

15 W. E. B. Du Bois, "The Negro and the Warsaw Ghetto," in: Jewish Life (May 1952) 14–15. Also cf. Michael Rothberg, Multidirectional Memory. Remembering the Holocaust in the Age of Decolonization, Stanford: 2009, 111–134.

16 Bahr 2010.

17 Günther Anders, Die Schrift an der Wand. Tagebücher 1941–1966, Munich 1967. Anders re-published this piece thirteen years later together with an essay on the American fictional TV-miniseries "Holocaust: The Story of the Family Weiss" after its controversial broadcast in Germany and Austria: Günther Anders, Besuch im Hades. Auschwitz und Breslau 1966. Nach "Holocaust" 1979, Munich 1979. Incidentally, Anders first coincided with Claude Lanzmann, author of the most influential documentary on the Holocaust "Shoa" (1985), in their work with the Vietnam Tribunal.

Haika Grossman, Gisele Halimi, David Horowitz, Mahmud Ali Kasuri, Claude Lanzmann, Carl Oglesby, Ralph Schoenman and Peter Weiss.

It would be too simple to just invoke these fellow commissioners to prove Anders' transnational position as an intellectual, although it certainly serves as a case in point. It is even more interesting to look at the arguments of the tribunal, the historical analogies employed, as well as its juridical reference frame: the military tribunals of Nuremberg and Tokyo and the Declaration of Human Rights—all, in a way, responses to the Holocaust, even though the term was not widely used in the early post-WWII years. By 1967, however, not only had the term been in circulation for some time, but more importantly the history of Jewish suffering had become the subject of several big international (if not global) media communication events such as the Eichmann trial of 1961.

As a member of the Russell Commission, Anders did indeed, as Bahr indicated, contribute his recent impressions from Auschwitz; in fact, he advocated that the tribunal be held in Auschwitz and Krakow, and by no means in Vienna or elsewhere in Austria or Germany, where he was afraid it might fuel existing neo-Nazi sentiments by providing revisionist ideas.[18] But while these tactical implications of the historical commensurability of the Holocaust were not lost on Anders, he did not let them change his mind on the issue in general. As a left-wing intellectual and equipped with a Marxist vision of history, the historical comparison between the Holocaust and other cases of extreme state violence (whether ethnically defined or not) was no taboo for Anders. Afterall, the Frankfurt School and historians like Ernest Mandel, too, had interpreted the Holocaust as an extreme result of capitalism and imperialism.[19]

We therefore find in the protocols of the tribunal an entire terminology that stems from Holocaust and Nazi history. During the procedures, witnesses were interrogated and documents were presented into evidence to show the facts concerning two primary charges: U.S. aggression (war guilt), and genocide. The genocide claim was substantiated by the high number of victims among the civilian population, the use of chemical weapons and napalm, the destruction of resources, and obligatory resettlement in hamlets. These hamlets were repeatedly called "concentration camps."[20] Sartre himself made clear that the analogy to Nazi-practices was not lost: "Now we can recognize in those dark and misled souls the truth of the Vietnam war: it meets all of Hitler's specifications. Hitler killed the Jews because they were Jews. The armed forces of the United States torture and kill men, women and children in Vietnam merely because they are Vietnamese."[21] And he gave this accusation a global, universal twist when he stated that the USA was "consciously carrying out this admonitory war in order to use genocide as a challenge and a threat to all peoples of the world."[22]

Anders' intellectual position in this debate fits well into the argumentative framework of the Russell Commission, as we can see from his most important publications on Vietnam

---

18 Arthur Jay Klinghoffer, International Citizen's Tribunals. Mobilizing Public Opinion to Advance Human Rights, New York 2002, 114.

19 Enzo Traverso, On the edge of understanding: from the Frankfurt School to Ernest Mandel, in: Understanding the Nazi Genocide. Marxism after Auschwitz, London 1999, 42–62.

20 John Duffet, ed. Against the Crime of Silence: Proceedings of the International War Crimes Tribunal (Stockholm, Copenhagen), New York 1970, 620.

21 Ibid., 1970, 624–625.

22 Ibid., 625. Cf. Berthold Molden, Vietnam, the New Left and the Holocaust: How the Cold War changed discourse on genocide, in: Aleida Assmann/Sebastian Conrad, eds., Memory in a Global Age, Basingstoke 2010, 79–96.

published the following year.[23] As his colleagues in the debates and speeches of the Commission, Anders distinguishes between the crimes of the Nazis and the acts of US warfare in Vietnam because "it is true that the Americans in Vietnam are not primarily and programmatically interested in the extinction of the Vietnamese [...] but this question is irrelevant when answering the question whether this constitutes a genocide or not."[24] To the contrary, according to Anders, the American armed forces we re if anything more cynical towards the Vietnamese than Hitler had been towards the Jews, because the Jews did at least matter to Hitler, while the Vietnamese were just collateral damage to the Americans.[25]

As the supposed incommensurability of the Holocaust has become a common trope in historical discourse, such comparisons often appear inadmissible today. Correspondingly, the historico-political discourse of Anders and his peers is likely to be submitted to anachronistic criticism. To give one example, historian Max Friedman in his book on the history of Anti-Americanism accuses Anders of "inexact analogies." He writes that Anders felt entitled to such an argument because US politicians of the era like secretary of state Dean Rusk lumped together all enemies of America (Hitler and Ho Chi Minh) as being of the same ilk.[26] Yet Friedman seems to miss the essence of the controversy. Anders did not use the diachronic comparison as a mere tactical countermove to someone else's historical inexactness. He firmly believed that "no act of war today is non-genocidal," and thought that it was "absurd if people are outraged about the fact that the atrocities of others are equated with their own atrocities."[27]

Although Günther Anders joined other left-wing intellectuals of his time in their Marxist analysis of genocide he was rather skeptical regarding the "classical" Marxist analysis of relations of forces and their applicability to the global situation of the 1960s. In his collection of essays "Visit Beautiful Vietnam," Anders explained that pseudo-Marxist analysis building on the XI thesis on Feuerbach—"The philosophers have only interpreted the world, in various ways; the point is to change it"—was outdated, to say the least: capitalism itself was not conservative, but ever changing. Even beyond this observation, the class antagonism no longer held a promise for Anders on a transnational level as he followed, with increasing disillusionment, the complex relations between social classes and races *within* the USA and their impact on the possible movement against the Vietnam War.[28] For the better half of a century, the USA had been observed with much expectation and growing disappointment by Marxists of all camps as the most advanced capitalist society and therefore the most likely nation to pioneer a global socialist revolution, and yet, this revolution never came to pass.[29] Much to the contrary, the labor movement in the USA remained extremely underdeveloped and the specific situation of the union movement did not hold much promise for revolutionary action either. Right at the beginning of his collection of essays, Anders points out that this book was just as much about the USA as about Vietnam. This brings me to my second observation.

---

23 Günther Anders, Visit beautiful Vietnam. ABC der Aggressionen heute, Cologne 1968 (hereafter VBV); and Günther Anders, Nürnberg und Vietnam: Synoptisches Mosaik, Berlin 1968.

24 VBV, 61. Translation BM.

25 VBV, 62. Translation BM.

26 Max Paul Friedman, Rethinking Anti-Americanism. The History of an Exceptional Concept in American Foreign Relations, Cambridge 2012, 196.

27 VBV, 62. Translation BM.

28 VBV, 15.

29 Seymour Martin Lipset/Gary Marks, It Didn't Happen Here. Why Socialism Failed in the United States, New York 2000.

Minding Other People's Business:
Anders, Vietnam, and Black Power

Anders had been a severe critic of US military power politics ever since the dropping of nuclear bombs in Japan in August of 1945, when he still lived in exile in the USA. His anti-nuclear activism was therefore intrinsically connected with an interest in American politics, in the working of the wheels and engineers of cultural-political hegemony at the heart of the young superpower, in its inner contradictions, especially the social and ethnic conflicts of the 1960s that were projected outwards in different forms: from the "Cocacolonization"[30] of Western Europe to the massacre of My Lai. Just as the other European intellectuals mentioned above by Russell Jacoby, Anders entwined his criticism of American military engagement abroad in the wake of containment / imperialism with an analysis, equally critical, of the domestic situation in the USA. In doing so, he did not shy back from harsh criticism against all involved parties, both the government, the ruling classes, and the social movements fighting for Civil Rights and against the Vietnam War.

Again, the specter of the Holocaust appears as the historical screen of comparison against which his criticism is projected. This does not come as surprising, as the relations between American Jews and African Americans were very particular and reinforced through the Civil Rights movement.[31] Jewish students and intellectuals were notably active among both the movement's moderate and radical fractions. Some of the most prominent examples may be the lawyer of Black Panther leader Huey Newton, Fay Abrahams Stender, or the left writer and activist David Horowitz who would later transform into a radical conservative. The above-mentioned Eichmann trial had established the Holocaust as a reference point in the American public, with the visual images created in its unique staging and the intense news coverage especially in the USA, Europe, and Israel, but also in other parts of the world. Facts, figures, as well as the symbolic dimensions of the Holocaust had started to penetrate the minds of people who had no direct historical connection to the events. Besides Europe and Israel, it was particularly in the USA where the trial had a strong impact.[32] On the one hand, television was rapidly spreading in American households, leading up to the first global media events such as the moon landing in 1968.[33] On the other hand, immediately after Eichmann's arrest a whole number of publications appeared that disseminated basic knowledge about Eichmann and the Holocaust, often rather blatantly in the form of pulp documentaries, such as the booklet "Eichmann—Man of Slaughter," published in 1960 by the former army intelligence officer and NBC-reporter John Donovan: "The murder of 6.000,000 Jews: Hitler demanded it, Himmler ordered it—EICHMANN DID IT!"[34]

---

30 Reinhold Wagnleitner, Coca-Colonization and the Cold War: The Cultural Mission of the United States in Austria After the Second World War, Chapel Hill 1994.

31 Eric. J Sundquist, Strangers in the Land: Blacks, Jews, Post-Holocaust America, Cambridge 2005.

32 Concerning the impact of the Eichmann trial in Europe and the USA, cf. Daniel Levy/Nathan Sznaider, The Holocaust and Memory in the Global Age, Philadelphia 2006, 105–112. For the USA cf. Peter Novick, The Holocaust in American Life, Boston 1999.

33 Cf. Gary Richard Edgerton, The Columbia History of American Television, New York UP 2009, pp. 268ff. For the relevance of German TV, cf. Wulf Kansteiner, Nazis, Viewers and Statistics: Television History, Television Audience Research and Collective Memory in West Germany, in: Journal of Contemporary History 39/4 (Special Issue: Collective Memory, 2004), 575–598.

34 Printed on the cover of: John Donovan, Eichmann. Man of Slaughter, New York 1960.

All this is to say that the recent suffering of the European Jews had been sufficiently established as a marker and measuring device for state racism. Anders joined American activists like Stokely Carmichael in the strategic comparison of the Holocaust, the Vietnam War, and structural racism in the USA. In 1968, he wrote:

> "The method to console those discriminated against by admitting them the right to discriminate against others, and to even elevate this right to their national duty—this method equals precisely the method that National Socialism had introduced 35 years ago. Just like Hitler gave the Jews to the proletarians, whom he had no intention to liberate: i.e. a group to which they, the proletarians could feel superior and whose abuse and liquidation was their national duty; just like that the American government gives to the American negroes the underdeveloped peoples outside of America, right now the Vietnamese. Being bombed to death with napalm, they represent today the Jews burned in Auschwitz. One can see: today's crimes and their socio-psychological functions resemble the crimes of the past and their functions much more than is commonly assumed."[35]

This analysis closely mirrors Sartre's conclusions on the issue of genocide during the Russell Commission. It also resembles the argument of a message that Carmichael had sent to the second session of the Russell tribunal: "In order to get rid of the Blacks, they [the U.S.A.] send them to the most distant fronts in Vietnam. This makes it possible for them to commit genocide against two peoples at once without having to get their own hands dirty." Therefore Blacks in the United States had to fight to avoid being forced to "vegetate like Indians in concentration camps they call reservations."[36] It is important to keep in mind that the USA had not joined the UN's 1948 Genocide Convention precisely because it was afraid that African Americans might be using this instrument to obtain justice from their own government. Hence, the race debates in the USA had indeed been intrinsically connected with the Holocaust since the early years of the Cold War, at the very least since the petition *We Charge Genocide: The Crime of Government against the Negro People*, signed among other prominent African Americans by W. E. B. Du Bois and Paul Robeson, was presented to the United Nations in 1951.[37] But Anders goes further by claiming that the anti-war movement and Civil Rights movement could not be separated. He accused those advocates of the Civil Rights fight who didn't join the anti-war movement of betraying their own cause. The example of Joseph McNeil, who had organized the first sit-in in North Carolina in 1960, then in 1968 was proud of having flown 40 missions in Vietnam as an Airforce pilot, is a case in point. Anders writes:

> "Carmichael's understanding that the fight against the war in Vietnam and the fight for Civil Rights are the same thing; that it is morally inconsequent and unsuccessful to fight for these rights if one at the same time allows oneself to be instrumentalized by imperialism to destroy other peoples' right to live; and that one can even less advocate

---

35   VBV, 49. Translation B.M.
36   Bertrand Russell/Jean-Paul Sartre, eds., Das Vietnam-Tribunal, Oder, Amerika Vor Gericht, vol. 2, Reinbek 1968, 237. Translation B.M.
37   Cf. Anson Rabinbach, The challenge of the unprecedented: Raphael Lemkin and the concept of genocide, in: Simon Dubnow Institute Yearbook 4 (2005), 397–420.

one's own 'Civil Rights' while simultaneously threatening or destroying the rights of other peoples as a professional soldier or officer; this understanding that one cannot fight for one's own equal rights and against the rights of others at the same time, this understanding unfortunately is everything but self evident for the majority of the colored population. [...] Because as a fighter in Asia he destroys the movement he allegedly is advocating, as opposed to Carmichael who is aware of this connection. And every shot he will fire in Vietnam will backfire and hit one of his own in the United States."[38]

As mentioned before, Anders diverted from the revolutionary analysis of many of his peers because he did not trust the existence of an international class—or, as exemplified above, race—solidarity:

"Today's real front line no longer runs between the ruling and the ruled classes, but between ruling and ruled peoples. The United States prove that in the most depressing manner, because there is no other group there that would stand more loyally behind its government's war of destruction than the unions. [...] No, proletarians in Vietnam: under no circumstances should you count on the possibility that the proletarians of the countries of aggression will feel solidarity with you or much less prove it via strikes! You do not even exist for them. Even in those countries that as yet have had no direct benefit from the aggression against you and others of your kind [the proletarians] solidarize with those who attack you, even there they hate the intellectuals, the reasonable people who have made your affairs, the matter of your liberation and of peace, their own affair."[39]

These comments show Anders' paradoxical position as a European intellectual in the global entanglements of decolonization and the Cold War. On the one hand, they suggest that Anders did not trust the potential impact of the non-organic intellectual, in a Gramscian sense, who might defend the interests of the ruled classes. Nor did he believe in what Zygmunt Bauman would later describe as the interpreting role of the intellectual building bridges between different discourses. On the other hand, as this quote also indicates, Anders put himself in a paternalizing position vis-à-vis the decolonizing peoples of the then-so-called Third World. Telling the people of Vietnam that the only ones in the First World who understood them were certain critical American and European intellectuals, Anders assumes the rather Eurocentric role of Gramsci's "traditional" intellectual.[40]

A similar assessment of Anders' Eurocentrism becomes evident in the above-cited quote that "Hitler gave the Jews to the proletarians" and "the American government gives to the American negroes the underdeveloped peoples outside America."[41] The clarification "outside America" indicates that the "negroes" were the "underdeveloped people" *within* America. His

---

38 Günther Anders, Der Amerikanische Krieg in Vietnam oder Philosophisches Wörterbuch heute, in: Das Argument 45 (1967), 349–379, here: 351. Translation by B.M.
39 VBV, 15. Translation B.M.
40 Zygmunt Bauman, Legislators and Interpreters: On Modernity, Post-Modernity and Intellectuals, Cambridge 1987.
41 VBV, 49. Translation BM.

analysis ignored the solidarity that has often emerged between politicized Afro-Americans serving in Vietnam. He also pushed aside the organic intellectuals of the Black Power movement[42] who used exactly this solidarity in their internationalist discourse.[43] It is interesting to note that Michael Rothberg has found a similar sort of bias in the work of Anders' former wife and intellectual companion, Hannah Arendt. After discussing Arendt's groundbreaking study *The Origins of Totalitarianism* (1951), in which she emphasizes the connections between European colonialism and the Nazi genocide, Rothberg points out the "Eurocentric frames that, despite everything, remain in Arendt [...]."[44]

However, Anders acknowledged the cynical Hegelianism of the white US ruling class' "counterrevolutionary dialectics" that "turned things upside down" by depicting itself as the victim of a new "Black hegemony."[45] The German-Austrian intellectual Günther Anders fervently commented on the relations of social forces in the USA, as he does on the situation in South East Asia, because to him and his fellow thinkers these were all manifestations of the same common issue: repression and political violence of a global scale to which a transnational movement should respond. He therefore discursively interferes in other people's business—in this case, the African American movements—as if it were his. He does so because to him it is his business; it is the business of everyone who aspires political change, emancipation, and liberation.

Conclusion

Do these two observations about Anders' discourse on Vietnam allow us to verify or falsify the applicability of the categories formulated at the outset? Was he a public intellectual in the understanding of the 1960s, and a transnational one at that?

We can assert that his intense examination of the Holocaust gives his writings the perspective of a historically informed thinker who wants his contemporaries to learn from history, to understand the continuities and dialectics of 20th century politics and draw the necessary conclusions. It is also evident that he is critical of established authority and expresses his solidarity with specific political liberation movements while attempting to foster human liberation in the context of modernity in general. We could also see that Anders is eager to expose official propaganda and the concealing of unpopular truths, such as the war crimes committed by American troops in Vietnam. However, if we apply Zinn's high standards to Günther Anders (and to others of the well respected intellectuals of the 1940s to 1970s) then Anders, while meeting some of them, did clearly fail at others. He is occasionally guilty of steep analogies or exaggerated typifications, and thus contravenes Zinn's veto against "spurious analogies, deceptive slogans," even if they were in favor of freedom or other high ideals.

The question arises whether Zinn's ideal may not exceed the amount of intellectual heroism to be asked from any single one person. Which public intellectual can really and totally

---

42 Anders is skeptical about the "slogan Black Power" without giving any reason for it. Cf. VBV, 99.
43 Cf. Penny Marie Von Eschen, Race Against Empire: Black Americans and Anticolonialism, 1937–1957, Ithaca 1997; Joshua Bloom/Waldo E. Martin Jr, Black Against Empire. The History and Politics of the Black Panther Party, Berkeley 2013, 267–322.
44 Rothberg, Multidirectional Memory, 77.
45 VBV, 99–100. Translation BM.

renounce the rhetoric form of hyperbole? Is it possible to undermine the hegemonic *zeitgeist* of a generation's predominant worldviews without caricaturing and exaggerating them, without the recourse of extreme arguments and daring comparisons? Günther Anders did indeed criticize the discourse of the political elites of the West, but in doing so he used analogies that fifty years later may seem inappropriate and created slogans that tinted the "facts" of the Vietnam War in a partisan light.

Now the final question remains to be answered: Can Günther Anders qualify as a transnational intellectual by the terms set above? While Elisabeth Röhrlich in her chapter compellingly describes Anders' anti-nuclear activism as that of a "national internationalist,"[46] his interventions in the debates about the Vietnam War allow a different assessment. The transnational label does fit Anders not merely because of his participation in international forums and his constant exchange with other thinkers in different parts of the world. It was specifically his genuine interest in different aspects of what he analyzes as a global issue of power abuse and repression that established him as a transnational intellectual. And yet, in terms of labels, something appears to be missing when we look at Anders and his special, often marginal position within the critical discourse of his times. We might add the term "nonconformist intellectual" if it hadn't been coined to describe the Frankfurt School,[47] led by Adorno who cost Günther Anders so dearly. With this in mind, I paraphrase Enzo Traverso[48] and call Anders a marginalized transnational intellectual, a recalcitrant thinker who nonetheless formed part of a highly heterogeneous and transnational discursive community.

---

46 Cf. her chapter in this book, "To Make the End Time Endless:" The Early Years of Günther Anders' Fight against Nuclear Weapons.
47 Alex Demirović, Der nonkonformistische Intellektuelle. Die Entwicklung der Kritischen Theorie zur Frankfurter Schule, Frankfurt am Main 1999.
48 Enzo Traverso, Auschwitz denken. Die Intellektuellen und die Shoah, Hamburg: 2000, 153.

Anders—The Man of Letters

Konrad Paul Liessmann

Between the Chairs:
Günther Anders—Philosophy's Outsider

1. The Outsider

Among the thinkers of the 20th century, the one most appropriately to be cast as an outsider is Günther Anders. Like no other, he was caught between the stools. Throughout his life, he did not want to commit himself: neither to a provenance, nor to a future; neither to a style, nor to a genre; neither to a philosophical school, nor to an ideology; neither to an institution, nor to an identity; neither to a discipline, nor to a category. Although his philosophical beginnings lay in Edmund Husserl's phenomenological school he did not develop into a classical phenomenologist. Although he did study with Martin Heidegger, he knew to escape this fascination early on. While his occupation with National Socialism and his analysis of technical civilization entailed a proximity to Marxism and the Frankfurt school, he did not form an attachment either to this school nor to the political left. And even though he did strive for an academic career in philosophy, the troubled times he lived in led him into the fragile existence as a freelance author—a situation he knew to make the best of.

Failing to commit himself to either a university institution or an academic style of writing, as he did, caused him to be ignored by academic philosophy for years; although his œuvre included poems, novels, fables and tales as well as philosophical essays and treatises, literary studies hardly paid attention to him. It is the very inter- and transdisciplinarity which characterized Günther Anders that placed him outside of the established disciplines, regardless of how much these establishments like to stress their commitment to the inter- and transdisciplinarity. He also remained an outsider wherever he lived: As a Jew in Germany, as a European in America, as a remigrant in Austria. And finally, he was an outsider as an atheist in Judaism.

There is yet another aspect to Günther Anders' role as an outsider: The subjects he dealt with often ran counter to the philosophical and political mainstream debates of his time, not least because he often recognized and reflected upon issues earlier than his contemporaries did. He wrote his groundbreaking essay on television at a time when hardly anyone made use of this technology; he considered the terrible consequences of the development of the atomic bomb while others were announcing the onset of the atomic age in triumph; he spoke of the necessity of a sociology of things when a networked world was still beyond anyone's imagination. Of course, Günther Anders also suffered in his role as an outsider. He wanted to reach an audience of many, not remain the insider's choice. He wanted to be at the pulse of time, not so far ahead of it that his analyses and appeals were bound to be met with a lack of understanding.

2. Alienation and Desertion

Günther Anders' outsider role becomes apparent as early as his first philosophical efforts. From his first philosophical efforts up until his final reflections shortly before his death, Günther Anders' political philosophical interest concerned a single topic: humankind. He was an anthropologist in an eminent sense, out of passion and out of necessity, without having ever (except maybe in his beginnings) practiced the classical discipline of "philosophical anthropology." What is humankind? In Anders' works, this question gained a new dimension. He was not interested in a general definition that defined man as an intelligent, political or religious animal. For Anders, a human being entailed within it always the necessity to first define its very being. In 1929–1930, Anders held two lectures on "The Human Being's Estrangement from the World" ["*Die Weltfremdheit des Menschen*"] in which he noted that "we as humans [are not bound] to a given world or a given lifestyle" (Anders 1993b: XIV).

Günther Anders later summed up the anthropological conclusion of his lecture on *The Human Being's Estrangement from the World* in one exceptionally incisive sentence in his essay *Pathologie de la Liberté*: "The nature of humankind is artificial, its essence impermanent" (Pathologie, 22). Anders found that humans experience this liberty and alienation as a "shock of contingency"—an insight into their own existence as being random and arbitrary: "A human being experiences himself as *contingent*, as anyone, as 'just me' (who has not been chosen); as a human who is just *as* he is (although he could have been utterly different), as emanating from an origin that was not chosen but has to be identified with, as of all things 'here' and 'now'" (Anders 1936, 24). Later on, Anders called this origin the "ontic dowry" concluding that humans must make do with what they have been provided, particularly with the facts of that and how they are, their physical and mental states. Although man is free, he is not free to choose the origin of his existence (Anders 1956, 69).

For Anders, there are two ways to deal with this experience of contingency. "Nihilistic man" tries to confront the contingency, the lack of sense. "Historic man" tries to imbue his origin with a sense. The nihilist is without identity, random, free towards all and everything, without necessity. Nihilistic man thirsts for power and glory, which is nothing but omnipresence in space and time. In contrast to the nihilist man's fantasies of power and glory, historic man as defined by Anders, tries to bring himself in line with his origin. Historic man lives from memory; he finds his identity not by putting his stamp on the world but by trying to ensure himself of his provenance. He compensates for the contingency of his existence with a postulated necessity of his history. Historic man knows who he is before he can be shocked by the experience of his contingency. He has always been tied into an identifying context through his past; his own past and the past of his ancestors are the momentum and the conditions of his identity. However, this also tends to cancel out historic man's liberty. At all times, he can only stand by who he has always been after the fact.

Hence, Anders was not interested in human beings as such, but in the situation of humankind in the world. Humans, unlike animals, are not adapted to this world. They are not at home in this world; they are aliens to this world, even outsiders. This alienation, however, is a condition of human liberty. What does that mean? The "human" being, unadapted as it is, must create its own world, given the lack of a world provided for it. First, man always has to create the world he lives in. This also means, however, that there is no world as created by man that is from the outset better suited to him than any other one would have been. There are always several worlds that may be designed by man. This, then, leads to the creation of what we call history. History is the result of the human being, stranger that it is to the world, being forced to stick to a life form once created.

In these early works, Anders refused the classical anthropological questions in that he recognized the special nature of humankind in the very impossibility of defining its essence. After 1945, and after the experiences of the Second World War, the Holocaust and the detonation of the atomic bomb, however, Anders redefined the relationship between humankind and the world. He no longer focused on the human being devoid of a predefined belonging to any world due to his relentless necessity to first create a world befitting himself: From the *man without a world*, the focus of Günther Anders' philosophy moved onto one of the very worlds created by humankind, that of technology. This world, after all, not only changes humankind, it also verges on making it redundant. Anders perceived the looming danger of a *world without humankind*.

3. Humankind and Technology

It is technology, the world of devices, as created by humankind itself, that has increasingly undermined the existence of humankind since the age of industrialization. The bias of all technology, in accordance with its immanent logic, Anders says, is to say: *without us*. Technology's eventual aim is to replace and supersede humankind in a fundamental sense. Thus, Günther Anders' philosophy of technology hinged on this issue of the relationship of humankind and technology, of what it is that occurs between humans and the devices they have construed and produced. Most of all, he was interested in how the growing technologization of the human environment affects human thought, sensation and action. With this, he not only reacted earlier than many others to technological progress, but also positioned himself apart from both the Frankfurt School with its essentially technology-friendly stance and Martin Heidegger, whose criticism of technology took a different form.

This line of questioning hinges on the assumption that man is not a sovereign subject purposefully using and applying technology by its own measures, but that humankind is entering into a particularly precarious constellation via its own immersion into a technological universe it has created. Not only is man modified by his artificial technological environment, his mode of existence is increasingly questioned. One of Anders' very fundamental insights is that there is no such thing as a single apparatus. Technology may only be grasped as a system, which marks the difference between modern technology and traditional tools. This is why Anders called for a "sociology of things," anticipating a concept that would be picked up only half a century later by authors such as Bruno Latour.

For Anders, more than almost any other philosopher, the crux was what could be called the normative power of technology. To Anders, the decisive moment that set off this development is the industrial revolution, or, more precisely, that spiral of innovation beginning with the steam engine that has resulted in the replacement of the tool as an extension and improvement of human organs by the machine and its momentum: "The moment when devices were replaced by machines marked the beginning of the obsolescence of human beings" (Anders 1987, 55). Not only does the unremitting machine force its rhythm upon the worker, its capacities also far exceed human capability. Manpower, limited as it is by its own nature, becomes a stumbling block in the face of what might be technologically possible. Furthermore, the newly formed relationship between man and machine is not limited to factory halls; after all, the products created there are the very devices of increasing perfection that structure and define the learning process and daily life of modern man. Anders speaks of a "Promethean decline," an "a-synchronization of humankind with the world of its products that increases with each day." This decline can be felt on many levels: between "creating and perceiving," between "doing and feeling," between "knowledge and conscience" and, as Anders stressed, between the produced "device" and the human "body" (Anders 1980a, 16).

All of these instances of the Promethean decline share the fact that the devices have an advantage over humankind. The devices set the pace of development; humans are left with no choice but to play catch-up in what they are doing, thinking and feeling with the apparatuses' demands. This definition of the Promethean decline has one far-reaching consequence: Technology, the system of devices representing it, is not a neutral medium at the free disposal of humans for their own range of purposes, morally and politically desirable or not. To engage with a technology is to adhere to its imperatives, maxims, requisites and consequences. Technology is not impartial: "It is certainly imaginable that the danger we are facing does not emanate from a bad use of technology, but that it is embedded in the nature of the technology itself" (Anders 1980b, 126). Devices have long ceased to exist as individual instruments and have instead been united into a system of devices resulting in yet other systems; hence, each device already is its application. The intertwined nature of social community and the technological world will, at least in the developed industrial states, become the decisive, driving and structuring force of development: Technology itself, as Anders put it in a highly debated phrase, becomes the new "subject of history" (Anders 1980b, 279). "The subjects of liberty and bondage are exchanged. The things are free, humankind is in bonds" (Anders 1980a, 33).

This reversal also impacts the human emotional relationship to technology. Anders not only saw the need for a sociology of things, but also a psychology of things, which was to investigate how humans immersed in a technological universe form emotions. Anders found a rather problematic phrase for the fact that humankind has to accept the superiority of technology as created by itself: "Promethean shame," the human sensation of shame in the face of the potency and perfectibility of the devices made by humankind itself (Anders 1980a, 23f). At the same time, however, humankind submits itself to these device's requirements. In the face of the perfectibility of his own products, modern, shamed Prometheus forgets his pride, his sovereignty and his liberty. In one of his pointed and paradox formulations, Anders called this "aligned self-denigration" of humankind in the face of its own devices, a "hybrid humility" (Anders 1980a, 47).

Günther Anders demonstrated how to realize what he was calling for with regard to the overall relationship between humankind and its world of devices (a sociology and a psychology of things) with possibly the most universal machines of the age of technology: the television. This treatment of the paradigmatic electronic medium is central to Günther Anders' philosophy of technology. These reflections on television focus on the question of what the image delivered by the television represents, i.e., what is the essence of this kind of image and the reality it is based upon. "What is strange," according to Anders, "in the situation created by the transmission, is its *ontological ambiguity*" (Anders 1980a, 131). Ontological ambiguity means that the TV image cannot be placed in any of the spheres we are used to thinking in: illusion or actuality, image or reality. An event that is being transmitted (the principle of the live transmission being the paradigm for Anders' analysis, which retains its currency to this day), can be ascribed neither the pure character of a depiction, nor certainly the fictional as-if-reality of artworks, i.e., none of the forms of aesthetic illusion. However, neither is it reality, the event itself taking place in someone's living room. The transmitted events are "at the same time present *and* absent at the same time reality *and* illusion, at the same time there *and* not there." They are, in the term Anders used to capture the essence of television, phantoms: "As phantoms, after all, are nothing but shapes that appear as things" (Anders 1980a, 170). Anything watched on television can only be perceived aesthetically, as a shape, and yet it claims to be as real as little else in our world is.

The status of television productions, analogous to reality as it is, its binding nature, does not end at the construction of ontological ambiguities or vacuities and their massive solo perception: reality itself begins to measure itself by whether it was depicted or not. For Anders, this leads to one decisive consequence: "If the event gains greater social importance in its reproduction than in its original appearance, then the original must be guided by its reproduction, and thus the event be reduced to being a mere template for its reproduction" (Anders 1980a, 111). As a depiction, the TV image serves as a model for the very reality it will be claiming to be depicting: "The real—the alleged model—thus has to befit its potential depictions, has to be recreated in the image of its reproduction. Current events have to preemptively follow their copies" (Obsolescence [*Antiquiertheit*] I, 190). Television's template function does, however, make it possible for a sort of boomerang effect to occur: If the world is guided by the image, and reality becomes an image of its distorted pictures, then suddenly that which was seen on TV becomes true: The lie has lied itself into truthfulness (Anders 1980a, 179).

4. Auschwitz and Hiroshima

Günther Anders had seen the logic of making humankind superfluous that is inherent to all technology at work not least in that event that is usually dealt with under the heading of "breach of civilization" rather than in the context of an analysis and debate of the continuities of civilization: Auschwitz. Again, Anders remained an outsider with his attempts to understand what happened in the extermination camps, apart from what would later be called Holocaust research. For Anders, after all, Auschwitz was not an exception, not a relapse into barbarism, but the most extreme result of an existing trend. What irritated him was not the breach but the continuities he discovered. In other words, Anders was one of the few who supported the thesis that the incomprehensible atrocities of National Socialism were neither a unique derailment of history nor a crime like no other before, but rather that these atrocities were the assertion of an economic and technical *rationality* that had its roots in the modern process of civilization that was able to continue to develop even after the political and military dismantling of fascism: "Monstrosity having existed yesterday does not mean it did so because it was *still* there yesterday, but rather the opposite: it existed, because it was *already* there yesterday. In other words, it was there because *yesterday's actors were the predecessors to our monstrous world of today and tomorrow*" (Anders 1988, 61). "Monstrosity" was Anders' philosophical category for the Nazi crimes in all their magnitude. He used the same term for his treatment of an event that was probably more decisive than any other to his thoughts and actions after 1945: the detonation of the first atomic bombs over Hiroshima and Nagasaki.

Monstrosity, to Anders, is the most extreme expression of the Promethean decline—something that supersedes all human imagination, which can be *produced* technically, but not *imagined* in all its terrible consequences. For Anders, in the case of Auschwitz, the monstrosity consisted in the fact of an "institutional and factory-like extermination of millions of people," which could only be executed because the process of mass extermination was organized by people "who accepted this task as any other" (Anders 1988, 19). Though at first it may be disturbing, (and it may also be a reason for the silence that Anders' analyses have been met with until this day), Anders understood the mass destructions of the Nazi era to be the first cumulative *negative* eruption of the system of labor organization that we usually describe as progress in our understanding of our civilization. The work processes of a broad range of manufacturing sectors have been made so alike in their technical *form*, said Anders, that the production of a weapon of mass destruction, even for the extermination of humans, hardly differs anymore from the manufacturing of any other product. In terms of form, it has become impossible to differentiate between launching an intercontinental ballistic missile or controlling a death-delivering "drone," and playing a computer game. What was decisive for Anders, then, was that such monstrous *atrocities* as Auschwitz were no longer atrocities committed by individuals, but were comprised of a chain of perfectly "normal" actions. The great crime as a continuum of acts that are harmless by themselves, is what differentiates the barbarism of modernity from the atrocities and misdeeds of premodernity; it leads to a strange affectation of innocence among the perpetrators: As nobody committed evil, and everybody only did their work, nobody can in the end be blamed for the effect that is produced (Anders 1979, 193).

For Anders, the development and use of the atomic bomb not only made possible a new technology for the extermination of humans, but also marked humankind's entry into a new era that differs from all phases that have come before: Since Hiroshima the extermination of humankind has been technically and politically possible. This also means that humankind has achieved one of its dreams, that of being omnipotent—albeit in a negative sense: "Omnipotence, long as it has been a Promethean desire, is ours now, albeit differently from how we had hoped. As it is in our power to put and end to each other, we are the *Masters of the Apocalypse*" (Anders 1980a, 239ff). This negative omnipotence turns into impotence, radically limiting, as it does, the human scope of action. A sword of Damocles has been hanging over humankind since the invention of weapons of mass destruction: that of its self-eradication, even if no-one is currently threatening to do so and the bombs are dozing in their silos. Even after a general disarmament (no indication of which is in sight), we would never be able to erase the knowledge that it is possible to produce technologies that can exterminate mankind. This fact has separated this age from all other ages of history. Anders draws a radical historico-philosophical conclusion: "We live in an era that is, even though it may last forever, doomed to be the very final era of humanity. Because there is nothing we can unlearn" (Anders 1981, 93, 55). All that is left for humankind is a "period of grace," whatever form that might take and however long it may last. This sense of an end of times can no longer be altered, Anders said. All that is left is the desire for this "end of times to be endless" (Anders 1981, 220f).

Anders' reflections on the ability to eradicate humankind also led to his critical attitude towards traditional moral philosophy: "Religious and philosophical ethic codes that have hitherto existed have all, without any exception, grown obsolete; they also exploded in Hiroshima and were also gassed in Auschwitz" (Anders 1979, 195). That is why Günther Anders chose not to attempt to justify morality as such. He knew that the ramification of his thoughts is a moral nihilism, thus ethics must remain an impossible task for him. Morality can no more be justified than the existence of humankind. Humankind is not a privileged species who may claim any particular right to exist. Of course earth, and even more so the universe, would manage perfectly fine without humankind. The inability to provide a positive reason for the existence of humankind does not, however, mean that it ought not exist at all. Anders did not draw either practical or theoretical conclusions from his nihilism. Particularly as a nihilist, there was an "iron caprice" to his insistence on the survival of humankind (Anders 1982b, 197f).

5. Art and Truth

Günther Anders was also an outsider with regard to his language and method. Looking for a language that could comprehensibly penetrate reality while not curtailing it, Anders resorted not only to philosophical, essayistic methods, but also poetic ones. Hence one cannot separate the poet and the thinker in Günther Anders. For him, his poems and fables were also one way of philosophizing. Thus, he was already working on his novel The Molussian Catacomb [Die molussische Katakombe] as early as 1930 to 1932; in it, he lays bare the ideological mechanisms of National Socialism, its strategies of bedazzlement and maneuvers of deception. It is an ironic work with several layers of meaning, which is denoted in the preface once as a "handbook of lies" and then again as a "handbook of truth." For Anders, art was always one way to express the truth. This art is, however, being replaced by a cultural pluralism obeying the laws of the marketplace. There, where no differences are made, indifference reigns. Anders was deeply critical of this trend. For Anders, pluralism was a sign of the human lack of a world: "In the end, the truth of pluralism is the failure to have any interest at all in the truth." The result is a "polycosmism" with a multitude of worlds existing next to each other, which will eventually revert into an "acosmism." The granting of many worlds leaves no room for a single world that could be of substantial interest. Such a pluralism was nothing but mere "simultaneity" for Anders: an assortment of artistic styles, contents and forms next to each other and devoid of context, which are strange, even contradictory to each other, but apparently unable to engage in this friction. Anders was strongly critical of the enjoyment of such "cultural promiscuity" being judged a virtue, while those who take umbrage with it are derided as provincial, intolerant and uncultured. Those who "remain unable or unwilling to equally appreciate Wagner and Palestrina, Giotto and Klee, Nietzsche and St. Francis" are, he said, disgraced as barbarians or philistines. Shouldn't it be considered, though, asked Anders, whether the barbarians and philistines are not more appropriately defined by such a fundamental "simultaneity": "The almost sacred key word of our age is AND" (Anders 1993b, XVIff). Presumably, Anders would, like Sören Kierkegaard before him, have opted in politics and philosophy alike for an "either-or."

6. Reception and Impact

Günther Anders' outsider role is reflected in the way he has been received. He was considered an insider's choice for many years and he is ignored by official university philosophy. He made his greatest public impact in the course of the 1970s and 1980s anti-nuclear movements (Dries 2009, 20). Beyond the influence his early philosophy had on Jean-Paul Sartre, however, a tight personal and spiritual network has linked Anders to many of the great thinkers of the 20th century: Edmund Husserl, Martin Heidegger, Hannah Arendt, Walter Benjamin, Hans Jonas, Theodor W. Adorno, Herbert Marcuse, Ernst Bloch, Helmuth Plessner. These connections, including, for example, Anders' very early and critical confrontation of Heidegger's philosophy, are only gradually being recognized and honored. Anders' phenomenology of television also certainly had a subliminal effect on the development of media philosophy. Without Anders always being granted a mention, many considerations of media critique, such as can be found in the works of Jean Baudrillard, Paul Virilio or Neil Postman, prove to have been anticipated by him. Even current debates in the contexts of digitalization, internet and social networks would stand to gain from some surprising insights in Anders' early thoughts on a sociology and psychology of things (Dries 2009, 21). The fact that important texts from his estate may only gradually be published now means that one can expect not only an increased interest in his works, but also new impetus in the fields of philosophy of music, philosophical anthropology and political theory. The publication of further autobiographical texts and correspondence could furthermore make an important contribution to a discussion of the history of philosophy during the Second World War and the Cold War. However, the gradual academic discovery and incorporation of Anders' philosophy ought not to leave aside the insight that this philosopher's decisive intention lay in his attempt to have an impact outside of the scholarly world as a philosopher, as an author, and as a great thinker who wished to contribute his thoughts to, perhaps, an improvement, or at least a conservation, of the world.

Bibliography

1. Collected works and primary literature

Die Rolle der Situationskategorie bei den Logischen Sätzen, diss., University of Freiburg 1923. (Name: Günther Stern)

Über das Haben. Sieben Kapitel zur Ontologie der Erkenntnis. Bonn: Cohen, 1928. (Name: Günther Stern)

Philosophische Untersuchungen über musikalische Situationen [Philosophical Inquiries on Musical Situations]. Literarturarchiv der Österreichischen Nationalbibliothek [Literature Archive, Austrian National Library]: unpublished typescript, 1929. (Name: Günther Stern)

Die Weltfremdheit des Menschen [The Human Being's Estrangement from the World]. Literaturarchiv der Österreichischen Nationalbibliothek [Literature Archive, Austrian National Library]: unpublished typescript, 1930. (Name: Günther Stern)

"Une Interprétation de l'a posteriori." *Recherches Philosophiques* 4 (1934): 65–80. (Name: Günther Stern)

"Pathologie de la liberté. Essai de la non-identification." *Recherches Philosophiques* 6 (1936): 22–54. (Name: Günther Stern)

Die Antiquiertheit des Menschen [The Obsolescence of Human Beings], Vol. I: *Über die Seele im Zeitalter der zweiten industriellen Revolution;* Vol. II: *Über die Zerstörung des Lebens im Zeitalter der dritten industriellen Revolution,* Munich: Beck, [5]1980a; 1980b.

Wir Eichmannsöhne. Offener Brief an Klaus Eichmann [We Sons of Eichmann. Open Letter to Klaus Eichmann], Munich: Beck, ²1988.

Philosophische Stenogramme [Philosophical Shorthand Notes]. Munich: Beck, ²1993a.

Der Blick vom Turm [View from the Tower]: Fabeln. Munich: Beck, ²1984a.

Der Blick vom Mond [View from the Moon]: Reflexionen über Weltraumflüge. Munich: Beck, ²1994a.

Kosmologische Humoreske. Erzählungen. Frankfurt/Main: Suhrkamp, 1978.

Besuch im Hades [Visit to Hades]: Auschwitz und Breslau 1966. Nach "Holocaust" 1979. Munich: Beck, 1979.

Die atomare Drohung [The Atmoic Threat: Radikale Überlegungen. Munich: Beck, 1981. (New edition of *Endzeit und Zeitenende*, 1972)

Hiroshima ist überall [Hiroshima is Everywhere]. Munich: Beck, 1982a. (Includes an important introduction as well as: "Der Mann auf der Brücke," 1959; "Off limits für das Gewissen," 1961; "Die Toten. Rede über die drei Weltkriege," 1965).

Ketzereien [Heresies]. Munich: Beck, 1982b.

Mensch ohne Welt. Schriften zur Kunst und Literatur [Man without World. Papers on Art and Literature], Munich: Beck, 1993²b. (Includes previously unpublished texts as well as the following reprints: "Kafka—Pro und contra," 1951; "Bert Brecht," 1962; "Brechts 'Leben des Galilei'," 1966; "Bertolt Brecht. Geschichten von Herrn Keuner," 1979; "Der verwüstete Mensch," 1965; "Über Bloch," 1945/46; "George Grosz," 1961; "George Grosz," 1966).

"Mein Judentum." In *Das Günther Anders Lesebuch*. Ed. by Bernhard Lassahn. Zurich: Diogenes, 1984b.

Tagebücher und Gedichte [Diaries and Poems]. Munich: Beck, 1985.

Lieben gestern. Notizen zur Geschichte des Fühlens [Love Yesterday. Notes on a History of Sensation]. Munich: Beck, ²1989.

Günther Anders antwortet. Interviews und Erklärungen. Ed. by Elke Schubert. Berlin: Tiamat, 1987.

Mariechen. Eine Gutenachtgeschichte für Liebende, Philosophen und Angehörige anderer Berufsgruppen. Mit einer Günther-Anders-Bibliographie. Munich: Beck, ²1993c.

Die molussische Katakombe [The Molussian Catacomb]. Roman (1938). Munich: Beck, 1992.

Über philosophische Diktion und das Problem der Popularisierung [On *Philosophical Diction and the Problem of Popularisation]* (1949). Göttingen: Wallstein, 1992.

Obdachlose Skulptur. Über Rodin [Homeless Sculpture. On Rodin]. Ed. by Gerhard Oberschlick. Translated from English by Werner Reimann. Munich: Beck, 1994b.

Über Heidegger [On Heidegger]. Ed. by Gerhard Oberschlick. With an epilogue by Dieter Thomä. Munich: Beck, 2001.

Die Kirschenschlacht. Dialoge mit Hannah Arendt und ein akademisches Nachwort [The Cherry Battle. Dialogues with Hannah Arendt and an Academic Epilogue]. With an essay by Christian Dries. Ed. by Gerhard Oberschlick. Munich: Beck, 2011

2. Selected further secondary literature and supporting literature

Altbaus, Gabriele. *Leben zwischen Sein und Nichts. Drei Studien zu Günther Anders*. Berlin: Metropol Verlag, 1989.

"Günther Anders." *Text + Kritik. Zeitschrift für Literatur* 115 (1992). (Including a comprehensive bibliography of the primary and secondary literature)

Bahr, Raimund. *Günther Anders. Leben und Denken im Wort.* St. Wolfgang: Edition Art & Science, 2010.

Clemens, Detlef. *Günther Anders. Eine Studie über die Ursprünge seiner Philosophie.* Frankfurt/Main: Haag + Herchen, 1996.

Dijk, Paul van. *Anthropology in the Age of Technology: The Philosophical Contribution of Günther Anders.* Amsterdam: Rodopi BV Editions, 2000.

Dries, Christian. *Günther Anders.* Paderborn: UTB, 2009.

Fuld, Werner. "Günther Anders." *Kritisches Lexikon zur Deutschsprachigen Gegenwartsliteratur.* Ed. by Heinz Ludwig Arnold. 21. Nachlieferung. Munich: Edition Text + Kritik, 1985.

Geiger, Georg. *Der Täter und der Philosoph. Der Philosoph als Täter. Die Begegnung zwischen dem Hiroshima-Piloten Claude R. Eatherly und dem Antiatomkriegphilosophen Günther Anders oder: Schuld und Verantwortung im Atomzeitalter.* Bern: Peter Lang, 1991.

G'schrey, Oliver. Günther Anders: "Endzeit"-Diskurs und Pessimismus. Cuxhaven: Junghans Verlag, 1991.

Hildebrandt, Helmut. *Weltzustand Technik. Ein Vergleich der Technikphilosophien von Günther Anders und Martin Heidegger.* Berlin: Metropol, 1990.

Kempf, Volker. *Günther Anders. Anschlußtheoretiker an Georg Simmel?* Frankfurt/Main: Peter Lang, 2000.

Kramer, Wolfgang. *Technokratie als Entmaterialisierung der Welt. Zur Aktualität der Philosophien von Günther Anders und Jean Baudrillard.* Münster: Waxmann, 1998.

Liessmann, Konrad Paul, Hrsg. *Günther Anders kontrovers.* Munich: Beck, 1992.

Liessmann, Konrad Paul. *Günther Anders. Philosophieren im Zeitalter der technischen Revolutionen.* Munich: Beck, 2002.

Lohmann, Margret. *Philosophieren in der Endzeit. Zur Gegenwartsanalyse von Günther Anders.* Munich: Fink, 1996.

Lütkehaus, Ludger. *Philosophieren nach Hiroshima. Über Günther Anders.* Frankfurt/Main: Fischer, 1992.

Palandt, Sabine. *Die Kunst der Vorausschau. Günther Anders' methodische und psychologische Ansätze zur Technikkritik.* Berlin: Wissenschaft & Technik, 1999.

Reimann, Werner. *Verweigerte Versöhnung. Zur Philosophie von Günther Anders.* Vienna: Passagen, 1990.

Schubert, Elke. *Günther Anders.* Reinbek: Rowohlt, 1992.

Wittulski, Eckhard. *Kein Ort, Nirgends. Zur Gesellschaftskritik Günther Anders'.* Frankfurt/Main: Haag + Herchen, 1989.

Wolfgang Palaver

The Respite:
Günther Anders' Apocalyptic Vision
in Light of the Christian Virtue of Hope

It is not difficult to recognize a certain apocalyptic stage of our current world; recent incidents have contributed to the world's dangerous state. The years since the terrorist attacks that became known as 9/11 were years full of catastrophes and crises: The Indian Ocean earthquake and tsunami of 2004, Hurricane Katrina that hit New Orleans in 2005, the global financial crisis that began in 2008, the Tōhoku earthquake and tsunami of 2011 that triggered a nuclear catastrophe in Fukushima, and the increasing dangers of global warming.

It is interesting to note that today not only religious sects spread an apocalyptic world view but secular voices are also expressing apocalyptic warnings. Paradoxically, it was the agnostic writer Umberto Eco who introduced the topic of the apocalypse in his renowned letter exchange with Cardinal Martini from Milan in 1995 and 1996. Eco opened this exchange of letters in March 1995 by addressing the "Secular Obsession with the New Apocalypse":

"Revelation can be read as a promise, but also as an announcement of an end, and thus gets rewritten at every step, even by those who have never read it, as we await 2000. No more the seven trumpets, the hailstorm, the sea turned to blood, stars falling from the sky, horses rising in a cloud of smoke from the deepest abyss, the armies of Gog and Magog, the Beast emerging from the sea. In their place: the uncontrolled and uncontrollable proliferation of nuclear waste; acid rain; the disappearing Amazon; the hole in the ozone; the migrating disinherited masses knocking, often with violence, at the doors of prosperity; the hunger of entire continents; new, incurable pestilence; the selfish destruction of the soil; global warming; melting glaciers; the construction of our own clones through genetic engineering; and, according to mystical principles of ecology, the necessary suicide of humanity itself, which must perish in order to rescue those species it has already almost obliterated—Mother Earth, denatured and suffocating."[1]

Our current stage of the world justifies, to a certain degree, an apocalyptic perspective. It was born when the first nuclear bombs destroyed Hiroshima and Nagasaki. Robert Oppenheimer, the scientific director of the Manhattan Project, expressed this clearly in his William James Lecture of 1957 in which he stated that contrary to former times we are living in a world "where the possibility of an apocalypse is omnipresent."[2] A couple of years later he reiterated

---

1   Carlo Maria Martini and Umberto Eco, Belief or Nonbelief? A Confrontation, New York 2000, 21.
2   Quoted in: Silvan S. Schweber, Einstein and Oppenheimer: The Meaning of Genius, Cambridge, MA 2008, 229; cf. Josef Pieper, "Über die Kunst, nicht zu verzweifeln. Überlegungen zum Thema 'Ende der Geschichte' (1972)," in Miszellen, (Werke in acht Bänden, Bd. 8), Hamburg 2005), 486.

the apocalyptic stage that our world entered with the use of nuclear weapons: "No world has ever faced a possibility of destruction—in a relevant sense, annihilation—comparable to that which we face, nor a process of decision-making even remotely like that which is involved in this."[3] Early on, Günther Anders also understood the apocalyptic challenge we face as a result of Hiroshima. He wrote, "because we are the first men with the power to unleash a world cataclysm, we are also the first to live continually under its threat."[4] I agree with Anders' thesis that we are living in a time of the end.

In the following essay, I will reconstruct Anders' apocalyptic ideas which he himself characterized with terms like the "time of the end" (*Endzeit*) or "respite" (*Frist*).[5] Secondly, I will focus on Anders' rejection of hope in which he saw nothing but a weakening of the necessary fight against doom. Several examples will prove that Anders' skepticism in regard to hope was not unfounded. Finally, I will present a Christian type of apocalyptic by turning towards the work of the Catholic philosopher Josef Pieper whose emphasis on hope does not result in a fatalistic paralysis that was justly criticized by Anders. A closer look reveals a certain affinity between this type of a Christian apocalyptic and Anders' position.

1. Günther Anders' prophylactic apocalypse without a kingdom

According to Anders, the modern apocalyptic age began with the dropping of the first nuclear bomb on Hiroshima. It will never end because this "time of the end" is a final age that can no longer be reversed. Only an ultimate catastrophe could finish this "time of the end" but that would result in a complete and permanent annihilation of all of history:

> "*Hiroshima as World Condition*: On August 6, 1945, the Day of Hiroshima, a New Age began: the age in which at any given moment we have the power to transform any given place on our planet, and even our planet itself, into a Hiroshima. On that day we became, at least 'modo negativo,' omnipotent; but since, on the other hand, we can be wiped out at any given moment, we also became totally impotent. However long this age may last, even if it should last forever, it is 'The Last Age': for there is no possibility that its 'differentia specifica,' the possibility of our self-extinction, can ever end—but by the end itself."[6]

Anders' precise analyses of the apocalyptic stage of our world have always received special attention and increasing approval when the potential risk was on the rise or when catastrophes afflicted the world. In the middle of the 1980s when the Cold War was at its height and in 1986 after the Chernobyl disaster, Anders' philosophy was relevant, but then quickly forgotten

3   J. Robert Oppenheimer, The Flying Trapeze: Three Crises for Physicists, (The Whidden lectures), London 1964, 63; cf. Josef Pieper, Hope and History: Five Salzburg Lectures, trans., David Kipp, San Francisco 1994, 16.

4   Günther Anders, "Reflections on the H Bomb," Dissent 3, no. 2 (1956): 147; Günther Anders, Die Antiquiertheit des Menschen, Vol. 1: Über die Seele im Zeitalter der zweiten industriellen Revolution, 2 ed., München 2002, 242 (hereafter AM, Vol. 1); cf. Pieper, Hope, 16.

5   Günther Anders, "Theses for the Atomic Age," The Massachusetts Review 3, no. 3 (1962): 493; Günther Anders, Die atomare Drohung. Radikale Überlegungen zum atomaren Zeitalter, 6 ed., München 1993, 93.

6   Anders, Theses, 493; Anders, Drohung, 93.

afterwards.[7] The nuclear disaster at Fukushima brought his thinking back to the public's attention.[8] The most important ethical consideration in Anders' work is his insight that in view of the possibility of the destruction of the world, we have to strengthen our apocalyptic awareness in order to motivate humankind to initiate arrangements that may prevent the doom of the world. Anders understood himself as a "prophylactic apocalyptist," someone who must be engaged in the permanent respite of the end of the world:[9]

> "If we differ from the classic Judeo-Christian apocalyptists it is not only because we fear the end that they were hoping for but mainly because our apocalyptic passion knows no other purpose than to thwart the apocalypse. We are only apocalyptists in order to be wrong."

He sees himself as an enemy of the apocalypse: "Since we believe in the possibility of The End of Time, we are Apocalyptics, but since we fight against this man-made Apocalypse, we are— and this has never existed before—'Anti-Apocalyptics.'"[10] Anders wrote his critical "Theses for the Atomic Age" in 1959 to warn of future catastrophes so that they can be prevented or at least delayed:

> "I have published these words in order to prevent them from becoming true. If we do not stubbornly keep in mind the strong probability of the disaster, and if we do not act accordingly, we will be unable to find a way out. There is nothing more frightful than to be right."[11]

The prevention of the end of the world, which according to Anders condemns us to live a life in respite, necessitates a new understanding of time.[12] The future, with its potential dangers, has to become present in order to delay an early end. Anders decisively criticized a "future-blind" faith in progress that contributes mainly to the dominating "apocalyptic blindness."[13] Because the future is not only ahead of us but is made in the present, Anders demands a widening of our sense of time.[14] He claims that the future needs to be synchronized with the present so that it is no longer before us but with us. This emphasis on a new horizon of time is very well summarized in one of Anders' "Commandments in the Atomic Age" that he discussed with Claude Robert Eatherly, a pilot who was part of the Hiroshima bombing.

---

7   Cf. Konrad Paul Liessmann, Günther Anders. Philosophieren im Zeitalter der technologischen Revolutionen, München 2002, 119, 187–188.
8   Hans-Martin Lohmann, "Das prometheische Gefälle", *Frankfurter Rundschau*, 16.3.2011; Jean Pierre Dupuy, "Une catastrophe monstre," *Le Monde*, 20.3. 2011; Martina Heßler, "Unsere Scham vor der Maschine," *Frankfurter Allgemeine Zeitung*, 02.04.2011; Mathias Greffrath, "Zorn der Vernunft – Kämpfer, Skeptiker, Aufklärer: Erinnerungen an die Avantgardisten der Anti-Atom-Bewegung," *Die Zeit*, 19.5.2011.
9   Anders, Drohung, 179.
10 Anders, Theses, 494; Anders, Drohung, 94.
11 Anders, Theses, 505; Anders, Drohung, 104–105.
12 Anders, Drohung, 170–221.
13 Anders, AM, Vol. 1, 276–279, 282.
14 Anders, AM, Vol. 1, 283–284.

"Widen your sense of time ... the futures which only yesterday had been considered unreachably far away, have now become neighbouring regions of our present time: that we have made them into 'neighbouring communities'. This is as true for the Eastern world as for the Western. For the Eastern, because there, the times to come, to a never before dreamed of extent, are planned; and because times to come that are planned are not 'coming' futures any longer, rather products in the making, which (since provided for and foreseen) are already seen as a sector of the living space in which one is dwelling. In other words: since to-day's actions are performed for the realization of the future, the future is already throwing a shadow on the present; it already belongs, pragmatically speaking, to the present. And that is true secondly—this is the case which concerns us—for the people of the Western world, since they, although not planning it, are already affecting the remotest future. Thus deciding about the health or degeneration, perhaps the 'to be or not to be' of their sons and grandsons. Whether they, or rather we, do this intentionally or not is of no significance, for what morally counts is only the fact. And since this fact of the unplanned 'working into the distance' is known to us, we commit criminal negligence when, despite our knowledge, we continue to act as if we were not aware of it."[15]

A very illuminating literary example of this necessary reversal of time can be found in his little story "Die beweinte Zukunft" (The mourned future) that Anders created by drawing on the Biblical narrative about Noah showing us a Noah who is mourning the future's dead in order to motivate the people to build an ark that can protect them from the destructive flood.[16] Jean-Pierre Dupuy, a French social philosopher who is following Anders' insights in many ways has comprised and translated Noah's speech from this story in the following way:

"The day after tomorrow, the flood will be something that will have been. And when the flood will have been, everything that is will never have existed. When the flood will have carried off everything that is, everything that will have been, it will be too late to remember, for there will no longer be anyone alive. And so there will no longer be any difference between the dead and those who mourn them. If I have come before you, it is in order to reverse time, to mourn tomorrow's dead today. The day after tomorrow it will be too late."[17]

By partly following Anders, Dupuy developed in recent years a so-called "enlightened catastrophism" that projects humankind into the future reckoning with likely catastrophes thereby gaining the ability to act today in a way that may postpone these catastrophes.[18]

15 Claude Eatherly and Günther Anders, Burning Conscience: The Case of the Hiroshima Pilot, Claude Eatherly, Told in his Letters to Günther Anders, New York 1962, 13–14; Günther Anders, Hiroshima ist überall. Tagebuch aus Hiroshima und Nagasaki. Der Briefwechsel mit dem Hiroshima-Piloten Claude Eatherly. Rede über die drei Weltkriege, München 1995, 220.
16 Anders, Drohung, 1–10.
17 Jean-Pierre Dupuy, The Mark of the Sacred, trans., M. B. DeBevoise, (Cultural memory in the present), Stanford, Ca. 2013, 203.
18 Jean-Pierre Dupuy, Pour un catastrophisme éclairé. Quand l'impossible est certain, Paris 2002; Jean-Pierre Dupuy, Retour de Tchernobyl. Journal d'un homme en colère, Paris 2006; Jean-Pierre Dupuy, "Rational Choice before the Apocalypse," Anthropoetics: The Journal of Generative Anthropology 13, no. 3 (2008). http://www.anthropoetics.ucla.edu/ap1303/1303dupuy.htm (accessed 23.2.2013); Dupuy, The Mark of the Sacred, 175–194.

Dupuy emphasizes the necessity of a remaining uncertainty that must accompany his type of catastrophism so that it does not lead to a fatalistic paralysis.

As much as Anders turns towards apocalyptic terms in the Bible and towards Biblical images, he also emphasizes important differences between the current apocalypse and the Biblical understanding. Firstly, Anders recognizes that the apocalypse of today refers to real dangers whereas the Biblical understanding can be seen from today's point of view as a "mere metaphor" or as "fiction"[19]: "The terms have acquired their serious and non-metaphorical sense only today, or only since the year zero (= 1945), for they now describe for the first time the end of the world that is really possible."[20] The second difference cited by Anders between the Biblical understanding and the current apocalypse is the complete absence of any hope in a transcendent power that could promise salvation in the midst of catastrophe. Regarding his own time, Anders speaks about a "naked apocalypse" or an "apocalypse without a kingdom."[21] In an interview with Mathias Greffrath in 1979, Anders explicitly denies any kind of hope as a basis for his commitment. To the contrary, he emphasizes that he does not know hope and fully relies on mere human strength:

"Hope? I can only reply: out of principle, I do not know it. My principle is this. If there is even the least chance in this terrible situation that we have brought upon ourselves to intervene with a helping hand, then we must do so. ... If I should despair, then what is left? Off to work!"[22]

2. Günther Anders' secular apocalyptic and the question of hope

First of all, we have to underline that there are good reasons for not hastily relying on hope that can easily weaken our resistance against the apocalyptic dangers. Anders refers to this danger in his novel *Die molussische Katakombe* [The Molussian Catacomb]. In a dialogue between Olo and Yegussa they discuss "the old theme of hope."[23] The debate ends with a clear warning against hope that leads to inactivity:

"Hope is the activity of inactivity. It is not better than praying. And not better than despair: it is merely opinion ... don't hope and don't pray but act. Whoever is hoping, surrenders the case respectively to the others and to the enemy; and whoever is praying adores."[24]

---

19 Anders, Drohung, 214; cf. Jürgen Moltmann, The Coming of God: Christian Eschatology, trans., Margaret Kohl, Minneapolis 1996, 217.
20 Quoted in: Moltmann, The Coming of God: Christian Eschatology, 217; Anders, Drohung, 214; cf. Günther Anders, Die Antiquiertheit des Menschen, Vol. 2: Über die Zerstörung des Lebens im Zeitalter der dritten industriellen Revolution, 3 ed., München 2002, 407–410, (hereafter AM, Vol. 2).
21 Anders, Drohung, 207.
22 Quoted in: Paul van Dijk, Anthropology in the Age of Technology: The Philosophical Contribution of Günther Anders, Amsterdam 2000, 159; Günther Anders, Die Zerstörung unserer Zukunft. Ein Lesebuch, (Diogenes Taschenbuch), Zürich 2011, 328; Anders, Hiroshima, xxxii.
23 Günther Anders, Die molussische Katakombe. Roman. Mit Apokryphen und Dokumenten aus dem Nachlaß, 2 ed., München 2012, 305; cf. 105.
24 Anders, Katakombe, 306.

It is true that there are certain types of hope that result in inactivity in regards to apocalyptic dangers. This kind of hope can be found in secular and religious forms. A secular form is the optimistic faith in progress that suppresses the danger of global self-destruction; the utopian messianism of Ernst Bloch, for instance, remained blind to the apocalypse. Despite the fact that Bloch was committed to revolutionary activism he was not really concerned by the danger of doom. As much as Anders distanced himself from Jewish messianism after 1945, he also rejected Bloch's understanding of hope despite the fact that they remained friends and that Anders dedicated his book *Der Blick vom Mond* from 1970 to Bloch.[25] In Anders' eyes it was Bloch's Jewishness that gave him a positive view of hope: "In this, he was more a Jew than I. ... Attached as they are to the idea of the kingdom to come, or to be founded by ourselves, most Jews have been unable to conceive the idea of an apocalypse without a kingdom."[26] Anders' critique was not so much aimed at Bloch's famous work, *Das Prinzip Hoffnung* [The Principle of Hope], but against his particular type of hope that Anders ridiculed as *Hofferei*. "This attitude of hopelessly focusing on hope, this really cowardly attitude is what gradually came to irritate me."[27] Against Bloch's principle of hope Anders committed himself to a "Principle of Despair":

"Ernst Bloch speaks:
'we are not yet.'
More earnestly (*ernster*) than Bloch
would be: 'just yet.'
Different (*anders* in German, alluding to his own name) would be:
'no longer.'"[28]

Anders recognized in Bloch's understanding of hope a cowardly attitude—he generally identified hope with cowardice.[29] It was his thought that hope results in the renunciation of action. When he discovered a call for hope in Heidegger's use of the famous Hölderlin quote "where danger is growing, rescue is growing, too," he criticized it as an "invitation to do nothing."[30]

Christian fundamentalists are a further example for a religious attitude that vehemently trusts in God's violent intervention, so much so that every human activity is impeded. Especially in the U.S. there are quite a few Christians with such an attitude who hampered political initiatives to protect the environment or act against global warming.[31] Waiting for the "rapture" prevents any commitment to the world that may fall prey to doom like those who are not among the elected people.

---

25 Dijk, Anthropology, 55–56; Liessmann, Anders, 131–132.

26 Quoted in: Dijk, Anthropology, 55; Anders, AM, Vol. 2, 277, 452; Anders, Zerstörung, 244.

27 Quoted in: Dijk, Anthropology, 56; Günther Anders and Fritz J Raddatz, "Brecht konnte mich nicht riechen. Ein ZEIT -Gespräch mit Günther Anders," *Die Zeit*, 22.3. 1985, 65.

28 Quoted in: Dijk, Anthropology, 56; Anders, AM, Vol. 2, 452.

29 Günther Anders, Gewalt – ja oder nein. Eine notwendige Diskussion, (Knaur-Taschenbücher), München 1987, 32–33.

30 Günther Anders, Über Heidegger, trans., Werner Reimann, München 2001; cf. Anders, AM, Vol. 1, 222; Günther Anders, "Being without Time: On Beckett's Play *Waiting for Godot*," in Samuel Beckett: A Collection of Critical Essays, ed. Martin Esslin,Englewood Cliffs, N.J. 1965), 145.

31 Tim Flannery, "Endgame," New York Review of Books 52, no. 13 (2005); Bill Moyers, "Welcome to Doomsday," New York Review of Books 52, no. 5 (2005); Simon Pearson, A Brief History of the End of the World: From Revelation to Eco-Disaster, London 2006, 254–255.

While one can agree with Anders' critique of those forms of hope that impede the commitment of human beings, the question arises of whether the renunciation of all hope is not also highly problematic: can human beings really live without hope? In his novel *Die molussische Katakombe,* it is Yegussa who reckons with the people's dependence on hope and claims that it should be used for good.[32] Moreover, in his interpretation of Samuel Beckett's play *Waiting for Godot,* does Anders address the fact that the characters in this play are not able to live without hope? According to Anders, they are not nihilists but human beings that are ineradicably hoping:

> "As they do not lose hope, are even incapable of losing hope, they are naive, incurably optimistic ideologists. *What Beckett presents is not nihilism, but the inability of man to be a nihilist even in a situation of utter hopelessness.* Part of the compassionate sadness conveyed by the play springs not so much from the hopeless situation as such as from the fact that the two heroes, through their waiting, show that they are not able to cope with this situation, hence that they are *not* nihilists."[33]

Anders claims that he, like Beckett, was able to break free from this widespread need for hope.

But there are even deeper problems with a purely immanent fight against the doom of the world. Attempts to create absolute security may easily end up in a totalitarian security system. The most well-known literary example for such a counterproductive outcome is Dostoevsky's famous legend *The Grand Inquisitor.* From a theological point of view, one can also refer to the paradoxical figure of the *katechon* in the Second Letter to the Thessalonians (2 Thess 2:6–7) who, like the Grand Inquisitor, asks Jesus not to return to the world again so that he who is the restrainer (*katechon*) may not be weakened in his attempt to contain political chaos. Anders understood his own apocalyptic as a project deeply critical of society, calling into question all power relations associated with the nuclear threat. But is there not a danger that his immanent apocalyptic indirectly favors the protection of the status quo? In his interview with Mathias Greffrath, Anders claimed that, despite his preparedness for revolution, he is first of all ontologically conservative.[34] To protect the world is fundamentally more important than to change the world. The protestant theologian Ulrich Körtner justly questions the conservatism that comes along with Anders' apocalyptic:

> "This apocalyptic is negative, though no longer in the sense that the complete end is understood, if not as crisis and transition, then at least as the last means of liberation. Consequently, this apocalyptic is neither resigned nor intent on accelerating the end, but rather struggles with all its energy to preserve the apocalyptically understood world. Although politically quite progressive, viewed in this way it nonetheless fights for the preservation of the status quo: The end time from which there is no escape is to be perpetuated indefinitely."[35]

---

32 Anders, Katakombe, 306.
33 Anders, Being, 144; Anders, AM, Vol. 1, 213–231; Anders and Raddatz, Brecht, 67.
34 Anders, Zerstörung, 319–320.
35 Ulrich H. J. Körtner, The End of The World: A Theological Interpretation, trans., Douglas W. Stott, Louisville, Ky. 1995, 214.

Körnter alludes to an analogy of the medieval use of the katechon that, however, as he justly remarks, was still characterized by the traditional Christian hope in the end.[36] If we correlate Anders' apocalyptic with the specific perspectives on the katechon by the infamous law scholar Carl Schmitt and the Jewish philosopher Jacob Taubes, he is closer to Schmitt than Taubes:

"Schmitt's interest was in only one thing: that the party, that the chaos not rise to the top, that the state remain. No matter what the price. This is difficult for theologians and philosophers to follow, but as far as the jurist is concerned, as long as it is possible to find even one juridical form, by whatever hairsplitting ingenuity, this must absolutely be done, for otherwise chaos reigns. This is what he later calls the *katechon*: The retainer [*der Aufhalter*] that holds down the chaos that pushes up from below. That isn't my worldview, that isn't my experience. I can imagine as an apocalyptic: let it go down. I have no spiritual investment in the world as it is."[37]

The danger that may come along with Anders' immanent apocalypse can be seen in the current development of a security and surveillance state that began after 9/11. The anticipation of future acts of terror seems to justify more and more those security installations that limit our freedom. One of the most significant problems with this type of anticipation is the increasingly practiced form of targeted killings, the elimination of potential terrorists without any legal procedure and with the help of unmanned combat drones.[38]

3. The Christian apocalyptic emphasizes the virtue of hope

In this final section, I will use the example of the Catholic philosopher Josef Pieper to discuss a Christian apocalyptic that has clear affinities with Anders' secular apocalyptic but that simultaneously emphasizes the virtue of a form of hope that differs from those criticized by Anders. Especially in view of the virtue of hope, it is, according to Pieper, very important to understand that for a Christian apocalyptic the prediction of a catastrophe is not its final word but remains connected to the promise of a new heaven and a new earth inspiring real hope:

"Its last word, and its decisive report ... is the following: a blessed end, infinitely surpassing all expectations; triumph over evil; the conquest of death; drinking from the fountain of life; resurrection; drying of all tears; the dwelling of God among men; a New Heaven and a New Earth. What all this would appear to imply about hope, however, is that it has an invulnerability sufficient to place it beyond any possibility of being affected, or even crippled, by preparedness for an intra-historically catastrophic end—whether that end be called dying, defeat of the good, martyrdom, or world domination by evil."[39]

---

36 Körtner, End, 214.
37 Jacob Taubes, The Political Theology of Paul, trans., Dana Hollander, (Cultural memory in the present), Stanford, Calif. 2004, 103.
38 Cf. Johannes Masing, "Die Ambivalenz von Freiheit und Sicherheit," JuristenZeitung 66, no. 15–16 (2011); Zygmunt Bauman and David Lyon, Liquid Surveillance: A Conversation, (Polity conversations series), Malden, MA. 2013.
39 Pieper, Hope, 106–107.

This strong hope for a new heaven and a new earth allows a sober expectation of the catastrophe without stopping to enjoy and care for the creation:

"Therefore, despite the fact that the Christian's attitude to history includes preparation for a catastrophic end within history, it nevertheless contains as an inalienable element the affirmation of created reality. To create a vital link between these seeming irreconcilables is a task that challenges the courage of the most valiant hearts, precisely in times when the temptation to despair is strong."[40]

The martyrs in John's *Apocalypse* praise God's creation: "Great and amazing are your deeds, Lord God the Almighty!" (Rev 15:3)[41] Hoping for a new heaven and earth is not longing for a disconnected beyond as is typical of Gnosticism, but goes along with a deep concern for the creation in the here and now. According to Pieper "this created world itself is explicitly included in the supra-natural hope."[42] The "preparation for a catastrophic end" goes together with the "affirmation of the created reality."[43] Christian hope does not lead to a neglect of this world waiting in a passive fatalism for the final catastrophe. It encourages, on the contrary, our active involvement in this world: "It is … a hope that renders the believer able and willing to act here and now, within history, indeed even to see in the midst of the catastrophe itself a possibility of meaningful action within history."[44] Christians are called to act in this world and care for the creation. Even if we know that a catastrophic end is ultimately inevitable we should not despair but continue our care for this world. From this perspective one can understand a famous sentence that is attributed to Martin Luther: "If I knew that tomorrow was the end of the world, I would plant an apple tree today."[45]

For Christian apocalyptists there should be a commitment to save the world as if everything depends on them without, however, being forced to trust completely in their own strength. The commitment to the world lives on a hope that protects from a paralyzing fatalism. It was the agnostic thinker Umberto Eco who asked in his letter exchange with Cardinal Martini whether the lack of hope is not driving people to despair so that they no longer care for the world but seek a narcotizing consumerism: "One could … say that we live our fear in the spirit of *bibamus, edamus, cras moriemur* [eat, drink, for tomorrow we die], celebrating the end of ideology and solidarity in a whirlwind of irresponsible consumerism."[46] Eco asked Cardinal Martini if there is a notion of hope that believers and unbelievers could possibly share because without hope "it would be perfectly all right to accept the approach of the end, even without thinking about it, sitting in front of our TV screens (in the shelter of our electronic fortifications), waiting for someone to *entertain* us while meantime things go however

---

40 Josef Pieper, The End of Time: A Meditation on the Philosophy of History, trans., Michael Bullock, San Francisco 1999, 148.
41 Cf. Erik Peterson, Theologische Traktate, (Ausgewählte Schriften), Würzburg 1994, 116; Pieper, End, 148.
42 Pieper, End, 148.
43 Pieper, End, 148.
44 Pieper, End, 79.
45 Quoted in Hoimar von Ditfurth, So laßt uns denn ein Apfelbäumchen pflanzen. Es ist so weit, München 1988, 367.
46 Martini and Eco, Belief, 22. Cf. 1 Cor 15:32: "If with merely human hopes I fought with wild animals at Ephesus, what would I have gained by it? If the dead are not raised, 'Let us eat and drink, for tomorrow we die.'"

they go. And to hell with what will come."[47] Eco writes about a flight into consumerism that no longer cares about future generations. The spreading motto is "after us, the flood."

Anders' apocalyptic faces a similar problem. As a "professional atheist" he rejects any theological hope without compromise,[48] but when he substitutes the principle of hope with the principle of despair, he also may contribute to a fatalistic paralysis. He therefore knows very well, that out of love for human beings, he has to put despair aside. For this reason he finished his "Theses for the Atomic Age" in 1959 in the following way:

> "If some, paralyzed by the gloomy likelihood of the catastrophe, have already lost courage, they still have a chance to prove their love of man by heeding the cynical maxim: 'Let's go on working as though we had the right to hope. Our despair is none of our business.'"[49]

In a later interview Anders maintains that this attitude should not be understood as a return to hope: "This is not a 'principle of hope.' At the utmost a 'principle of defiance.'"[50] Nevertheless, the question arises whether Anders, despite all his denials, wasn't still nourished by a Judeo-Christian hope that he could only perceive as an attitude that weakens the fight against the doom of the world. Anders was not always without hope. Modifying a saying by Lessing, he once wrote: "He who doesn't lose hope over certain things, has none to lose."[51] In connection with this remark, he refers to the year 1927 in which he read Hitler's book *Mein Kampf* and lost all hope:

> "My darkening [*Verdüsterung*], which started with the beginning of National Socialism, about the year 1927, after I had read Hitler's book, and which totally poisoned many of my human relationships, even to those people who were closest and most important to me."[52]

By the way, it was Hannah Arendt, Anders' first wife, who had the trouble of dealing with his darkening and who, contrary to her husband but like Hans Jonas—a friend of both of them and another apocalyptic thinker—remained a believer in God.[53]

---

47 Martini and Eco, Belief, 26.
48 Anders and Raddatz, Brecht, 66. Concerning Anders' atheism, see: Günther Anders, Ketzereien, München 1996; Günther Anders, Tagesnotizen. Aufzeichnungen 1941–1979, Frankfurt am Main 2006, 27; Günther Anders, Die Kirschenschlacht. Dialoge mit Hannah Arendt, München 2011, 67; Anders, Zerstörung, 251, 321.
49 Anders, Theses, 505; Anders, Drohung, 46.
50 Anders and Raddatz, Brecht, 67.
51 Anders, Ketzereien, 325; cf. Eatherly and Anders, Burning, 106.
52 Anders, Ketzereien, 325.
53 Anders, Kirschenschlacht, 67–70; cf. Hans Jonas, Erinnerungen. Nach Gesprächen mit Rachel Salamander, Suhrkamp 2005, 341–342.

Andreas Oberprantacher

The Desertification of the World: Günther Anders on *Weltlosigkeit*

"The community of man is divided by uninhabitable parts of the earth's surface such as oceans and deserts, but even then, the *ship* or the *camel* (the ship of the desert) make it possible for them to approach their fellows over these ownerless tracts, and to utilise as a means of social intercourse that *right to the earth's surface* which the human race shares in common."

Immanuel Kant, *Perpetual Peace*

In one of his philosophical fables, entitled *Das verspielte Außerhalb*,[1] Anders imagines a student who, in the year 2058, comes across an incomprehensible sentence in a history book on the twentieth century. "In those moments," as the volume states, "when here and there the pressure of dictatorships became unbearable, masses of refugees were generated."[2] Because fifty years had passed since the establishment of the World State, the student of the early third millennium hardly makes sense of this sentence; he only knows of a world that is absolutely and immediately *one*, and therefore hermetically sealed. His inability to imagine "other spaces,"[3] as Foucault called them, provokes the students to eventually pose questions like: "'Masses of refugees?' What does that mean? Where could one escape to? Was there something outside?"[4] Yet, instead of commiserating his own situation, which basically amounts to that of *total* inclusion, the student finally exclaims out of contempt for his ancestors: "What *they* once called 'pressure'!"[5] And the narrator of the fable, for his part, concludes: "Where there is only *one*, there can be no remains. Thus, also no remaining site of refuge."[6]

"Interesting Times"

Anders wrote *Das verspielte Außerhalb* in 1958, the same year when Arendt published her seminal treatise *The Human Condition*.[7] A little more than fifty years later, that is, approximately in the middle of the story's fictional timeline, the following question requires attention in an

---

1   The German title of Anders' fable allows for a variety of possible translations, amongst others it could be translated as *The Wasted Exteriority* or as *The Forfeited Beyond*.
2   Günther Anders, Das verspielte Außerhalb, in: Günther Anders, Der Blick vom Turm: Fabeln von Günther Anders. Mit Bildern von A. Paul Weber, Leipzig/Weimar 1984, 53. [My translation]
3   Cf. Michel Foucault, Of Other Spaces, in: Diacritics 16/1 (Spring 1986): 22–27.
4   Anders, Das verspielte Außerhalb. [My translation]
5   Ibid. [My translation]
6   Ibid. [My translation]
7   Cf. Hannah Arendt, The Human Condition. Introduction by Margaret Canovan, Chicago/London 1998.

anthology dedicated to Anders' œuvre: what could it possibly mean to live in times that are certainly not dominated by a totalitarian World State, as envisioned in Anders' fable, but that also do not seem to promise an other "world" or, at least, a site of refuge for all those who are living under severe pressure at the moment and who all too often are confronted with misery? Only recently, Žižek published his book *Living in the End of Times*, where he argues in the Afterword of the paperback edition that "today, we are clearly approaching a new epoch of interesting times. After decades of the Welfare State, when financial cuts where limited to short periods and sustained by a promise that things would soon return to normal, we are entering a new period in which the economic crisis has become permanent, simply a way of life."[8] In other words, while Anders' fable warns its readers against the future risk of the state becoming a hypertrophic apparatus—the sole *hegemon* that tolerates nothing but itself—there is mounting evidence suggesting that at the beginning of the twenty-first century the state is neither that dominant nor an inclusive institution. More often than not, the state seems to be (or at least it acts like) a waning entity that abandons countless people in situations of insecurity, especially when there is a manifest interest to prevent public accountability by "outsourcing" and diffusing jurisdiction.

Albeit the rather improbable premise of Anders' fable, the rationale of his caveat remains intriguing. A world that is defined as one, without involving the imagination of other spaces beyond itself and the promise of an "elsewhere," is an extremely violent world for it is based on the refusal to consider anything other than what is enforced. It is, in this very sense of Anders' fable, a world resulting in an extreme in-difference and a world most probably populated by indifferent beings, too. This is also to say that as much as Anders has repeatedly characterized himself as a writer warning against a potentially devastated "world without humans,"[9] he was also aware of the various dangers that humans too may be "without world." In other words, Anders was not only a radical critic of an impending nuclear catastrophe, but also a passionate thinker repeatedly speaking out against equally dangerous situations of *Weltlosigkeit* [worldlessness], in which far too many peoples' lives are ruined. But while Arendt's critique in *The Origins of Totalitarianism*, where she evidences how former citizens were repeatedly displaced by totalitarian regimes and thus *made* worldless, and where she discusses the "historically and politically intelligible preparation of living corpses"[10] as well as the "calamity of the rightless [... who] no longer belong to any community whatsoever",[11] is well studied, comparatively less interest seems to be taken in Anders' alternative accounts of contemporary effects of worldlessness. This is rather surprising. For if it is reasonable to assume that Anders' manifold critique of modern technology is an expression of his sensibility for the menace of extreme catastrophes, it is quite possible to argue that Anders' sensibility involves not just one notion of catastrophic situations, but (at least) a double: the catastrophe as something that

---

8   Slavoj Žižek, Living in the End of Times, London/New York 2011, 403.

9   Günther Anders, Einleitung, in: Günther Anders, Mensch ohne Welt: Schriften zur Kunst und Literatur, München 1984, XI; Konrad Paul Liessmann, Günther Anders: Philosophieren im Zeitalter der technologischen Revolutionen, München 2002, 46–48; Ludger Lütkehaus, Philosophieren nach Hiroshima: Über Günther Anders, Frankfurt am Main 1992, 31.

10 Hannah Arendt, The Origins of Totalitarianism. New Edition with added prefaces, San Diego/New York/London 1976, 447. Arendt refers frequently to dangerous situations of worldlessness, not only in *The Origins of Totalitarianism*, but also in a number of other writings. See, for example, Hannah Arendt, On Humanity in Dark Times: Thoughts about Lessing, trans. Clara and Richard Winston, in: Hannah Arendt, Men in Dark Times, San Diego/New York/London 1995, 3–32.

11 Arendt, The Origins of Totalitarianism, 295.

potentially could happen and turn the world into a devastated landscape without (human) life, and the catastrophe as something that *actually* is happening for all those who are already living as if the world were a deserted space.[12] In this second sense, this article traces some of the major moments in Anders' understanding of worldlessness as an *ordinary* catastrophic situation by contrasting it with Heidegger's accounts of what it means to be in the world for humans, animals, and stones, as well as with Marx's theory of *alienation*, and by focusing on Anders' critique of simplistic uses of the term "world" that he exposed at the threshold of literature, economic theory, and technological analysis.

Of Worldless Stones

As Anders remarks in his introduction to his collection of essays entitled *Mensch ohne Welt* [*Man Without World*],[13] which was published in 1984, he first used the expression "man without world" in the 1920s, that is, in an "intermezzo" of his life that he retrospectively portrays as "absolutely apolitical."[14] Similarly to Nietzsche's dictum in the aphorism 62 of *Beyond Good and Evil*, according to which "man is the as yet undetermined animal,"[15] Anders also argues in two papers that he gave in 1929—one in front of the Kant Society of Hamburg and the other in front of the Kant Society of Frankfurt—that humans are neither defined by specific habits nor are they confined to a specific habitat. Rather as beings, they are repeatedly required to appropriate spaces and to cultivate the places they are inhabiting. In this sense, man is perhaps the only known "species-being" to date that is practically condemned to frequently re-invent its own world, writes Anders.[16] In fact, he consciously makes use of the adverb "perhaps" in his critical self-reflection to signal that the indeterminacy of human life defines no particular privilege, but rather a general defect, which man nevertheless tends to "positivize" [*positivieren*] to its own advantage.[17] While Anders is ready to concede at the time of summarizing his first anthropological efforts of coming to terms with man's worldlessness that it is quite possible that archaic cultures and their relative concepts of the world were as

---

12 The polysemy of Anders' notion of catastrophe becomes evident in passages like the following: "Large scale technology is not only catastrophic because it [...] is reifying us humans and making millions of us redundant; but also because it can suffocate resistance and protest and make some individuals almighty." [My translation] Günther Anders, Einleitung (1982), in: Günther Anders, Hiroshima ist überall, München 1995, XXXII.

13 The English standard translation of Anders' collection of essays is problematic, for the German term *Mensch* is not identical with the English "man." It rather oscillates between "man" and "human." In this sense, an alternative translation could thus be: *Human without World*. However, for the sake of terminological consistency, the standard translation shall be used in this article.

14 Anders, Einleitung, in: Mensch ohne Welt, XIV. Apart from this first, explicit use of the expression "man without world," it is important to recall, as Reinhard Ellensohn is doing, that Anders' phenomenology of music and especially his rejected habilitation project entitled *Philosophical Examinations of Musical Situations* [*Philosophische Untersuchungen über musikalische Situationen*] of the late 1920s are repeatedly referring to musical situations as situations of "not-being-in-the-world." See Reinhard Ellensohn, Der andere Anders: Günther Anders als Musikphilosoph, Frankfurt a. M. 2008, 13.

15 Friedrich Nietzsche, Beyond Good and Evil, trans. Walter Kaufmann, New York 1966, 74.

16 As Liessmann argues, Anders papers on the indeterminacy of human existence, published in French as *Une Interprétation de l'Aposteriori* (1934) and *Pathologie de la Liberté* (1936), did indeed anticipate Sartre's memorable formula that man is condemned to be free. Cf. Liessmann, Günther Anders, 30–31.

17 Anders, Einleitung, in: Mensch ohne Welt, XLIII.

fixed as those of other non-human species, he nevertheless stresses that the recent history of humanity provides ample evidence for the improvisation and multiplication of various "world-styles" [*Weltstile*] among humans. To this he adds that once he had returned from his exile in 1950, he was quite surprised to learn that in his absence a philosopher named Arnold Gehlen had become famous for coining the expression that a human being is a "deficient being" [*Mängelwesen*],[18] an expression that is very much coextensive with Anders' prior formulations.

In order to make sense of the successive politicization of Anders' use of the term "worldlessness," it might be conducive to briefly refer to a lecture, which Arendt delivered in 1954 to the American Political Science Association and which remained unpublished during her lifetime. In this lecture, entitled *Concern with Politics in Recent European Philosophical Thought*, Arendt argues that Heidegger's fundamental analysis of being human as "being-in-the-world"[19] offers unprecedented chances for the philosopher to consider the importance of a space that is (in) common and that expresses the plurality of human existence. However, as Arendt also comments in one of her footnotes to the lecture, Heidegger's phenomenological accounts "are quite apt to mislead the reader into believing he is dealing with the old prejudice of the philosopher against politics as such,"[20] or as she puts it even more frankly in the main body of her text: "[W]e find the old hostility of the philosopher toward the *polis* in Heidegger's analyses of average everyday life in terms of *das Man* (the 'they' or the rule of public opinion, as opposed to the 'self') in which the public realm has the function of hiding reality and preventing even the appearance of truth. Still, these phenomenological descriptions offer most penetrating insights into one of the basic aspects of society and, moreover, insist that these structures of human life are inherent in the human condition as such, from which there is no escape into an 'authenticity' which would be the philosopher's prerogative."[21] If passages like these support the argument that Arendt's simultaneous critique of modern worldlessness is as much the result of her becoming a stateless refugee (who eventually accepts the citizenship of the United States in 1951) as it is the result of her growing dissatisfaction with Heidegger's apolitical conceptualization of the world,[22] it may be argued that Anders' politicization of the expression "man without world" is also best understood when confronted with and discerned from Heidegger's thoughts.

Following up on his phenomenological considerations in *Being and Time*, especially on his preliminary thoughts on "the world of animal and plants,"[23] Heidegger presents a more detailed exposition of "being-in-the-world" in his Freiburg lecture of 1929/30 entitled *The Fundamental Concepts of Metaphysics: World, Finitude, Solitude*.[24] The lecture itself, which

18 Arnold Gehlen, Der Mensch: Seine Natur und seine Stellung in der Welt, in: Arnold Gehlen, Gesamtausgabe: Der Mensch. Textkritische Edition. Teilband 1, Frankfurt 1993, 16.

19 Martin Heidegger, Being and Time, trans. John Macquarrie/Edward Robinson, Oxford 2001, 78–148.

20 Hannah Arendt, Concern with Politics in Recent European Philosophical Thought, in: Hannah Arendt, Essays in Understanding, 1930–1954, ed. Jerome Kohn, New York 1994, 446.

21 Arendt, Concern with Politics, 432–433.

22 As Arendt argues, especially in her unfinished book *Introduction into Politics*, "apolitia, the indifference and contempt for the world of the city, [is] characteristic of all post-Platonic philosophy." Very likely, Arendt was also thinking of Heidegger's "philosophical" implication in the Third Reich when composing these lines. Hannah Arendt, The Promise of Politics, ed. and with an introduction by Jerome Kohn, New York 2005, 26.

23 Heidegger, Being and Time, 290.

24 At the time of Heidegger's lecture, Arendt and Anders had already moved to Berlin as a newly wed couple. Notwithstanding the geographical distance, it is quite possible that both Arendt and Anders were familiar with

is indeed one of the most "fundamental" lectures delivered by Heidegger,[25] is divided into two major sections. While the first section explores "boredom" [*Langweile*] as a fundamental mood, the second section engages with the world of *Dasein* with regards to the all-too human questions concerning *finitude* and *individuation*. In order to expose the sense of the world of *Dasein*, Heidegger resorts to a "*comparative examination*,"[26] as he calls it, of three distinct realms or kinds of beings: the *stone*, the *animal* and finally, *man*. For Heidegger the stone (standing for material objects in general) is nothing but a "*worldless*"[27] [*weltlos*] being, that is, an item with no experiences and thus with no access to the world; the animal, on the other hand, is a being "*poor in world*"[28] [*weltarm*]; in the end, only man is capable of building worlds, he alone is truly a "*world-forming*"[29] [*weltbildend*] being. The significance of this fundamental differentiation for Heidegger's metaphysical exposition is readily understood when bearing in mind that for him "the problem of world by no means lies simply in the need to provide a more exact and more rigorous interpretation of the essence of the world. On the contrary, the real task is to bring the *worldly character* of the world into view for the first time as the possible theme of a *fundamental problem* of *metaphysics*."[30] In other words, most, if not all of Heidegger's thinking before the so-called *Kehre* [turn] gravitates around the central problem of the world as the fundamental problem of metaphysics.

In the past two decades a variety of essays have been published that address and critically question Heidegger's rigid distinction between man and animal, be it Jacques Derrida's *The Animal That Therefore I am* (1997)[31] or Giorgio Agamben's *The Open: Man and Animal* (2002).[32] What is of particular relevance for the purpose of this article, however, is not so much Heidegger's account of the animal, but rather his account of the *stone*. In fact, Heidegger suggests that "worldlessness" and "poverty in world" are two distinct expressions that should not be confused. While "[p]overty in world implies a deprivation of world," according to Heidegger, "[w]orldlessness on the other hand is constitutive of the stone in the sense that the stone *cannot even be deprived* of something like world."[33] In this sense then, Heidegger draws the illustrated conclusion that the "stone lies on the path. If we throw it into the meadow then it will lie wherever it falls. We can cast it into a ditch filled with water. It sinks and ends up lying on the bottom. In each case according to circumstance the stone crops up here or there, amongst and amidst a host of other things, but always in such a way that everything present around it remains essentially *inaccessible* to the stone itself."[34] The "being-without-world" of the stone is so absolute that it is even impossible to say whether or not it is indifferent. By

---

Heidegger's effort to further define and refine "world" in metaphysical terms.

25 Cf. Giorgio Agamben, The Open: Man and Animal, trans. Kevin Attel, Stanford 2004, 49–51.

26 Martin Heidegger, The Fundamental Concepts of Metaphysics: World, Finitude, Solitude, trans. William McNeill and Nicholas Walker, Bloomington/Indianapolis 1995, 177.

27 Ibid.

28 Ibid.

29 Ibid. In *The Human Condition* Arendt argues, in turn, that the "specifically human act" is first of all the "disclosure who somebody is." In this sense, for her there is only world—between humans—as long as people speak to and act with each other. Arendt, The Human Condition, 178–179.

30 Heidegger, The Fundamental Concepts of Metaphysics, 178.

31 Cf. Jacques Derrida, The Animal that Therfore I Am, trans. David Wills, New York 2008.

32 Cf. Agamben, The Open.

33 Heidegger, The Fundamental Concepts of Metaphysics, 196.

34 Ibid., 197.

contrast, Heidegger's analysis of human capacities reveals that for him only man is *weltbildend* in the double sense of the German word: man is world-*forming* and world-*imagining*, that is, man is forming the world in his own image. The animal, for its part, has access to something, but "it does not have access to beings as such," as Heidegger states. And "[t]hus we are now in possession of a provisional delimitation of the concept of world which performs a methodological function in the sense that it prescribes for us the individual steps of our present interpretation of the phenomenon of world. World is not the totality of beings, is not the accessibility of beings as such, not the manifestness of beings as such that lies at the basis of this accessibility—world is rather the *manifestness of beings as such as a whole*."[35] This definition eventually implies, at least for Heidegger, that it is *Dasein* alone, Dasein in *man* alone, that forms world in the sense of bringing it forth, of giving an image or view of the world, but also of constituting the world.[36]

Living (and Working) in a Deserted World

In the wider context of this "provisional delimitation," which is structuring and informing Heidegger's fundamental concept of metaphysics and confers an ambiguous profile to the historical and political situation, in which Heidegger was implicated at the time of giving the lecture, it becomes comprehensible why it was literature that eventually put an end to Anders' apolitical philosophy of worldlessness. As Anders' himself recalls in 1984, it was his reading of Alfred Döblin's *Berlin Alexanderplatz*,[37] first published in the year 1929, that forced him to question his anthropological reasoning and to alter his understanding of the world inhabited by humans.[38] For the main character of this "negative novel,"[39] Franz Biberkopf, appears to be all but a "being-in-the-world," even though he apparently qualifies as a member of the human species. As Anders' puts it in his essay *Der verwüstete Mensch* *[Desolate Man]* of 1931, Biberkopf is singled out in purely negative terms: he is not living in solitude due to his individual disposition, nor is he thrown back on the world in historical or biographical terms. Rather, he is simply pushed aside by the circumstances.[40] There is, as Anders puts it, "nothing behind him: no particular custom, no bourgeois, no proletarian, no urban, no rural custom, no nature, no religion, no denegation of religion, no indifference, no milieu, no family."[41] For Anders, Biberkopf is "inhuman, because in a barbaric sense he is only human."[42]

---

35 Ibid., 284.
36 Ibid., 285.
37 Alfred Döblin, Berlin Alexanderplatz: The Story of Franz Biberkopf, trans. Eugene Jolas, New York 2005.
38 Anders, Einleitung, in: Mensch ohne Welt, XXVII–XVIII.
39 Günther Anders, Der verwüstete Mensch: Über Welt- und Sprachlosigkeit in Döblins 'Berlin Alexanderplatz,' in: Günther Anders, Mensch ohne Welt: Schriften zur Kunst und Literatur, München 1984, 4. [My translation]
40 Ibid. This image of people "being pushed around" and of losing the sense of orientation in life can also be found in another crucial essay authored by Anders. In the fictional monologue entitled Der Emigrant [The Émigré] a voice speaks up that has been pushed "from one environment to another" and that thus has no *vita* anymore, only *vitae* in a sinister plural, that is, too many lives all out of joint. See Günther Anders, Der Emigrant, in: Merkur XVI/7 (Juli 1962): 601. See transl. in this volume, pp. 171–186.
41 Anders, Der verwüstete Mensch, 5. [My translation]
42 Ibid. [My translation]

When contrasted with Heidegger's foundational exposition of the "worldhood of the world"[43] according to *Being and Time* and his subsequent differentiation between the world-lessness of the stone, the poverty in world of the animal, and the world-forming or world-picturing capacity of man, Döblin's literary world is absolutely unfounded. It is a world populated by grotesque figures like Biberkopf, figures with no sense for the world in Heidegger's terms. In other words, what intrigues Anders in *Berlin Alexanderplatz* is the surfacing of a world that is strangely *out of place* and the proliferation of a literary space in which unemployed persons, criminals, and abandoned people in general do not belong to the world in an ontological sense. Instead, they have to live "without world." And much like Heidegger's stone can be cast in a ditch filled with water, Döblin's Biberkopf can also be cast around. His irremediable indeterminacy does not allow him to become some-*one* in particular as the novel continues. He is neither a petty bourgeois nor is he a blue-collar worker. Quite the contrary, he is—like many others around him—a man without qualities and thus a "man without world," because the world as "the manifestness of beings as such as a whole" remains inaccessible to him.

And thus it was an unusual literary experience in the midst of the rapid collapse of the Weimar Republic (1919–1933) that eventually allowed or obliged Anders to reconsider his early anthropological position and to realize that there are indeed various situations in which people are forced to live as if there was no world for them. In contrast to Heidegger's definitions of "being-in-the-world" and of man as a world-forming being, Anders' subsequent reformulation of man's worldlessness is not based on a systematic metaphysical conceptualization. Rather, it is informed by Marx's thesis that the proletariat has no ownership over all those means of production that it needs to operate for the benefit of the ruling class and its exclusive interests.[44] In similar terms, Anders comes to the conclusion that Heidegger's expression "being-in-the-world" applies only to those who are actually in the position to identify themselves with their situation and thus to acknowledge the world as *their* world. Consequently, as Anders notes, "being-in-the-world" refers to a dominant attitude, and it is very unlikely that it expresses the world of those 90% of the working students who were attending Heidegger's lectures.[45] Or, to quote a slightly more drastic passage that illustrates Anders' line of argumentation in vivid colors: "The barefooted boy that I, as a bourgeois' son of the same age, observed in 1910 in front of a noble restaurant, while he was trying to peek inside by rubbing his nose on the glass panel, and that repeatedly stumbled 'nothing' when a policemen pushed him away with the question: 'what do you think you are doing here?'—this barefooted boy was indeed right: he was not thinking about anything in particular, because he didn't have anything in particular. His 'being' was certainly not a 'being-in-the-world,' but rather a remaining-outside, a 'not-being-admitted-to-the-world.'"[46] And should a "know-it-all" philosopher come to the cynical conclusion that a "world of hunger" is still a "world" after all, then Anders would remind him of those words that Marx once directed against the petty

---

43 Cf. Heidegger, Being and Time, 91–148.
44 It is, in fact, plausible to argue that Anders' entire critique of modern technology is informed by Marx's writings, especially by the so-called "Fragment on Machines" found in the *Grundrisse*. Cf. Karl Marx, Grundrisse: Foundations of the Critique of Political Economy, trans. with a foreword by Martin Nicolaus, London 1993, 704–712.
45 Anders, Einführung, in: Mensch ohne Welt, XII. [My translation]
46 Ibid., XIII. [My translation] See in this respect also Anders' thought-provoking and illuminating analyses of the "omitted hunger" in Heidegger's philosophical "realism": Günther Anders, Nihilismus und Existenz (New York 1946), in: Günther Anders, Über Heidegger, München 2001, 62–68.

bourgeois anarchist Stirner, the author of *The Ego and its Own*[47]—such a philosopher would probably not even hesitate to call a hungry person an "owner of his hunger."[48]

As much as Anders' political critique of worldlessness is evidently inspired by and even aligned with Marx's political economy, it is also more comprehensive than the classical definition of *alienation* according to Marx. Whereas Marx argues in his essay on *Estranged Labour* (1844) that the supposedly "free exchange" between the worker who is forced to sell his labor-power and the capitalist who owns the means of production involves a fourfold alienation of the worker,[49] Anders' own argument is more radical, since it refers to the loss of the world "as such," that is, the worker's very sense of "being-in-the-world." Simply put, for Anders the proletariat is forced to live and work without world. Even though Anders concedes that at first sight the proletariat could indeed be understood as a world-forming class, he eventually argues that the world formed by the proletariat through work cannot possibly be conceived as the world of the proletariat, for the workers are forming the world *for others*. This implies, in turn, that the proletariat does not really live *in* the world it is has formed so far. Quite the contrary, the proletariat lives *within* the world of others. And thus, Anders comes to the conclusion that "the expression 'man without world' designates a class truth."[50]

It designates a class truth that involves another, supplementary truth, considering that Anders' historical point of reference is not just the hard working proletariat who is being alienated in factories, but also the completely disenfranchised *lumpenproletariat* that is left without work in the shadow of the factories. In fact, Anders repeatedly mentions all those unemployed people who do not have the slightest chance to form or imagine a world for the simple reason that such people do not even count as valuable workforce. Instead, they are usually living at the very margins of all inhabited worlds and abandoned on modernity's by-roads. Yet, according to Anders, the danger of boosting worldlessness holds even more so for future situations of unemployment that will result from a "secondary unemployment"[51] due to *automation*. In his essay *The Obsolescence of Work* (1977) Anders radicalizes his initial arguments of the 1930s by suggesting that by the year 2000 the world of work will only know of unemployed people: those who are unemployed because they have lost their work to automation, and those who are unemployed because they are operating in an automated work environment. Anders calls the second kind of unemployed workers of the future "object shepherds" [*Objekthirten*],[52] that is, shepherds who will not be attending to a flock, but rather to automats. By doing so they will be condemned to an experience of "waiting" in multiple negative terms. In general, object shepherds will simply have to wait while servicing all the machines that are working automatically; more specifically, object shepherds will have to wait for something not to happen to the machines they are supposed to service. While having to

---

47 Cf. Max Stirner, The Ego and its Own, ed. by David Leopold, Cambridge/New York 2002.
48 Anders, Einführung, in: Mensch ohne Welt, XIII. [My translation]
49 According to Marx's early analyses, (a) the worker is alienated from the "fruits" of his work, (b) he is alienated from his work as activity, (c) he is alienated from his "species-being," (d) and he is also alienated from his fellow co-workers. See in this respect: Karl Marx, Estranged Labour, in: Karl Marx, Economic and Philosophic Manuscripts of 1844, trans. and ed. by Martin Milligan, New York 2007, 67–83.
50 Anders, Einführung, in: Mensch ohne Welt, XII. [My translation]
51 Günther Anders, Die Antiquiertheit der Arbeit (1977), in: Günther Anders, Die Antiquiertheit des Menschen, Vol. 2: Über die Zerstörung des Lebens im Zeitalter der dritten industriellen Revolution, München 2002, 94. [My translation]
52 Ibid., 95. [My translation]

wait for something not to happen, object shepherds will usually remain alone. In other words, according to Anders the future of work will consist of unmanned factories and unmanned offices that will be serviced by essentially useless hermits condemned to wait, while many others will be waiting outside of these automated factories and offices in the vague expectation to be—at best—employed while remaining virtually unemployed.[53]

Apart from these three major connotations of the expression "men without world" or "worldlessness," that is: (a) man's anthropological necessity to improvise different world-styles, (b) the modern proletariat as the embodiment of the experience of forming and imagining a world that is actually owned by others, and (c) the modern and ultramodern unemployed who are standing *"vis-à-vis de rien,"*[54] Anders addresses a fourth connotation that he considers to be at least as relevant. In Anders' terms that are somehow echoing Herbert Marcuse's essay *Repressive Tolerance*,[55] the formula "men without world" refers above all to "man in times of cultural pluralism."[56] Even though Anders is ready to admit that he could not live one single day without the "sweet culture-trash" [*bunten Kulturmüll*][57] that surrounds him, he is equally ready to denounce the contemporary tendency to dissolve significant differences in a generalized equivalence of cultural signs and artifacts. In this sense, contemporary man's worldlessness is not so much the consequence of a world that has exploded into a plethora of subworlds that cannot possibly be integrated into a common world, but it is instead the result of man's indifferent pluralism that reflects his *acosmic* attitude. Consequently, Anders distinguishes between a simple (primary) pluralism and an internalized (secondary) pluralism in order to expose the contemporary tendency to neutralize significant differences. While the notion "simple pluralism"[58] refers to situations where different worlds exist side-by-side, not necessarily in harmony, but also not in belligerent terms, the notion "internalized pluralism"[59] refers to contemporary man's inclination to embrace all possible cultural differences until they eventually become indifferent and insignificant. As Anders puts it, "the virtually sacred key word of our times is 'and.'"[60] This copula accurately expresses the pervasive effort to combine almost anything without simultaneously giving space to a culturally diverse world. It is certainly not a coincidence in this respect that Anders criticizes such tendencies to neutralize significant differences once more in economic terms, as the logic of cultural indifference is inextricably linked to the logic of unconditional exchange: *"We are tolerant and indifferent etc.,"* writes Anders, *"because every object […] demands the equal right to be consumed in its quality as commodity, that is, it demands the right to be equally valid."*[61] And the more the

---

53 Ibid., 95–97. [My translation] Anders' (characteristic) exaggeration of modern automation implies a further moment of worldlessness that is discussed in his "open letter" to Klaus Eichmann. As Anders argues, the world of man is also darkening because it has become impossible to "imagine" [*Bild machen*] the monstrous machinery and its effects resulting from the triumph of large scale technology. Günther Anders, Wir Eichmannsöhne, München 2002, 19–27.

54 Anders, Einführung, in: Mensch ohne Welt, XIV.

55 Cf. Herbert Marcuse, Repressive Tolerance, in: Herbert Marcuse/Barrington Moore Jr./Robert Paul Wolff, eds., A Critique of Pure Tolerance, Boston 1969, 81–123.

56 Anders, Einführung, in: Mensch ohne Welt, XV. [My translation]

57 Ibid., XXVII. [My translation]

58 Ibid, XVI. [My translation]

59 Ibid, XVII. [My translation]

60 Ibid. [My translation]

61 Ibid, XXII. [My translation]

world is reduced to a world of objects that can be commodified and consumed, the less world remains for man.

At the Margins of Today's World

After this comparatively rapid exploration of the major moments in Anders' understanding of worldlessness, some tentative conclusions shall be drawn with regard to the following two questions: what sense does Anders' philosophy of worldlessness make at times that are once again becoming "interesting" as Žižek put it? And of what use may the expression "men without world" be, which has successively been marginalized in Anders' work and, to a certain extent, replaced with the concurring formula "world without men"?

With regard to the first question it is probably fair to say that Anders' philosophy of late modern man's worldlessness presents an intriguing mix of likely and unlikely episodes of "our" common future that all question the idea that everybody is equally "in" the world. Still, Anders' speculations on the future of work seem to be quite "outdated" when confronted with the actual economic crisis and when compared with *The New Spirit of Capitalism*[62] as discussed by Luc Boltanski and Evé Chiapello for example. According to these discussions, contemporary work is not so much defined by an increasing outdatedness of man due to processes of automation, but rather by the generalized imperative of commodifying man's intellectual (and linguistic) capacities in the context of what other scholars have termed *Cognitive Capitalism*[63] or *Immaterial Labor*.[64] In other words, Anders' analyses of worldlessness seem to remain obliged to a Fordist mode of regulation that is hardly compatible with the post-Fordist discourses of creativity, innovation, spontaneity etc. that are governing, at least in normative terms, many of today's (precarious) workspaces. But apart from that, Anders' critique of modern man's worldlessness has also gained unexpected momentum with regard to the contemporary mass-production of "wasted lives" and the indifference of a benign pluralism that rests on nothing but the economic equivalence of cultural signs and artifacts, a critique that has been reenacted in a variety of contexts by Zygmunt Bauman,[65] Alain Ehrenberg,[66] and Michel Agier.[67]

With regard to the second question it is important to bear in mind that even though Anders was consciously putting the warning against a potentially devastated "world without humans" at the center of his later attention, there is also reason to argue that the two

---

62 Luc Boltanski and Ève Ciapello, The New Spirit of Capitalism, trans. Gregory Elliott, London/New York 2007.

63 As Yann Moulier Boutang argues in his book *Cognitive Capitalism*, "[n]ot only are the parameters of space and time being radically altered [in the framework of contemporary capitalism], but the radical overhaul of representations that is underway affects the conception of acting and of the agent/actor doing things, as well as concepts of producing, of the producer, of the living and of the conditions of life on earth." Yann Moulier Boutang, Cognitive Capitalism, trans. Ed Emery, Cambridge/Malden 2011, 48.

64 Cf. Maurizio Lazzarato, Immaterial Labor, in: Paolo Virno/Michael Hardt, eds., Radical Thought in Italy: A Potential Politics, Minneapolis/London 1996, 133–147.

65 Cf. Zygmunt Bauman, Wasted Lives: Modernity and its Outcasts, Cambridge/Malden 2004.

66 Cf. Alain Ehrenberg, The Weariness of the Self: Diagnosing the History of Depression in the Contemporary Age, trans. Enrico Caouette et al., Quebec 2010.

67 Cf. Michel Agier, On the Margins of the World: The Refugee Experience Today, transl. David Fernbach, Cambridge/Malden 2008.

expressions cannot be set apart easily. They both remain entangled in a complex sensibility for catastrophic situations that oscillates between *event* and *condition*. In other words, whereas the expression "world without men" is principally obliged to the devastation of the world as a future event, the expression "men without world" addresses the living conditions faced by all those who usually cannot confide in "being-in-the-world" in a privileged sense. This is also to say that Anders' later preference for the expression "world without men" needs to be problematized to the extent that it runs the risk of reproducing the dominant attitude already invested in Heidegger's term "being-in-the-world" while shifting the attention to a potential nuclear catastrophe. For a "world without men" is a catastrophic vision mainly for those who do "have" a world to lose; for all those who are already living as if the world were a deserted space it is not very different from the condition of their ordinary life.

Reinhard Ellensohn

The Art of Listening:
On a Central Motif in Günther Anders'
Early Philosophy of Music

The New Interest in Listening

If the history of occidental philosophy can be characterized as a history of an "oblivion of being" ("*Seinsvergessenheit*"),[1] then it may well be described, too, as a history of an "oblivion of listening" ("*Hörvergessenheit*").[2] Perhaps then, as it seems reasonable to suggest, oblivion of being and oblivion of listening are, if not fully identical, at least very closely related phenomena.

Since the time of Plato—according to a popular postmodern thesis and critique of traditional concepts of reason—western philosophy has been marked by a "primacy of the visual,"[3] an "ocular tyranny," one might even call it: "During its most radiant days between Plato and Hegel, this occidental philosophy of light and sight effectively had a somewhat disdainful relationship to the realities of hearing. Western metaphysics was, at its most fundamental level, an ontology of the eyes [...]."[4] Originally, however, ancient Greek culture must surely have been organized according to a paradigm of listening, as Egon Friedell has pointed out. The role of music in Greek life, Friedell explains, "cannot be overestimated. The Greeks' receptivity and sensitivity to the power of sound must have been, at least from our vantage point today, nearly pathological."[5]

Critique of the optical paradigm's predominance in metaphysics and epistemology is, of course, not new. Notably, it was Jewish intellectuals who made the case for a new culture of listening during the last century.[6] Günther Anders was among them. During the rapid expansion of work being done on the phenomenology of music during the 1920s,[7] Anders, who completed his doctorate under the supervision of Husserl in 1924, undertook studies focused

---

1 Cf. Martin Heidegger, Sein und Zeit. Gesamtausgabe, Vol. 2, Friedrich-Wilhelm Herrmann, ed., Frankfurt am Main 1977, §§ 1 and 6.

2 Cf. David Espinet, Phänomenologie des Hörens: Eine Untersuchung im Ausgang von Martin Heidegger, Tübingen 2009, 30.

3 Wolfgang Welsch, Auf dem Weg zu einer Kultur des Hörens? in: Paragrana 2 (1993), Vol. 1/2: 87–103 (90f).

4 Peter Sloterdijk, Wo sind wir, wenn wir Musik hören? in: Peter Sloterdijk, Weltfremdheit, Frankfurt am Main 1993: 294–325 (294f).

5 Egon Friedell, Kulturgeschichte Griechenlands, Munich 2009, 138; cf. Welsch, Auf dem Weg zu einer Kultur des Hörens? 90.

6 Ibid., 93.

7 Cf. Arne Blum, Phänomenologie der Musik: Die Anfänge der musikalischen Phänomenologie im ersten Drittel des 20. Jahrhunderts, PhD diss., University of Witten/Herdecke 2006; Arne Blum, Die Anfänge der Musikphänomenologie, in: Journal Phänomenologie 33 (2010): 6–19.

on questions related to anthropology and the philosophy of music. In his studies, he rigorously engaged with the phenomenon of listening and with its (musical-) aesthetic and metaphysical aspects.[8] Later remarks made by Anders himself confirm that this work had some connection with his Jewish roots.[9] Before I turn to some central aspects of his "philosophy of listening," I would like to make a few comments in the next section regarding the context in which Anders' work appeared and the fundamental principles underlying his philosophy of music.

The Failed Habilitation

During the 1920s, Günther Anders was engaged in two areas of research: philosophical anthropology and the philosophy of music. In his monograph *"Über das Haben"* ("On Having"), published in 1928, he identifies his topic as the philosophy of music and states that he "intends to present a work on musical ontology."[10] Just a year earlier, he had published an essay under the title *"Zur Phänomenologie des Zuhörens"* ("On the Phenomenology of Listening")[11] in which he criticized phenomenology's focus on optical paradigms and proposed a phenomenology of listening to impressionist music (Debussy). His magnum opus on the philosophy of music, the work on musical ontology which he had promised, was entitled *"Philosophische Untersuchungen* über *musikalische Situationen"* ("Philosophical Investigations on Musical Situations"). It remained unpublished after its completion in Frankfurt in 1930/31.[12] The text had been written by Anders in the hopes of habilitating at the university in that city. He had been encouraged in this effort by a circle of prominent figures there, including Theodor W. Adorno, Max Horkheimer, Paul Tillich, Dolf Sternberger and Hannah Arendt, after the enthusiastic reception of his lecture on "The Human Being's Estrangement from the World" (*"Die Weltfremdheit des Menschen"*), given in 1929 in front of the Kant Society of Frankfurt.[13] His attempt at habilitation, however, failed. On the one hand, the political circumstances were distinctly unfavorable: Paul Tillich attempted to console Anders by implying that a different

---

8   Anders received a comprehensive musical-aesthetic education in his childhood and teenage years and he initially considered a career as a musician. After studying philosophy and art history, he received his doctoral degree under the supervision of Husserl in 1924, but was strongly influenced by Heidegger in his earlier years and followed him to Marburg in 1925. (Cf. Konrad Paul Liessmann, Günther Anders: Philosophieren im Zeitalter der technologischen Revolutionen, Munich 2002, 14ff; Christian Dries, Günther Anders, Paderborn 2009, 10ff; Reinhard Ellensohn, Der andere Anders: Günther Anders als Musikphilosoph, Frankfurt am Main 2008, 17ff. The following remarks are predominantly based upon the last book. Further citations will not be given in the text.

9   Cf. Günther Anders, Mein Judentum, in: Das Günther Anders Lesebuch, Bernhard Lassahn, ed., 2nd edition, Zurich n.d.: 234–251 (246ff); Günther Anders, Hiroshima ist überall, Munich 1995, 125: "[…] now I know my roots. It is said: 'You shall make no graven images.' It is the source of all of my passions."

10 Günther Stern, Über das Haben: Sieben Kapitel zur Ontologie der Erkenntnis, Bonn 1928, Preface.

11 Günther Stern, Zur Phänomenologie des Zuhörens. (Erläutert am Hören impressionistischer Musik), in: Zeitschrift für Musikwissenschaft 9 (1926/27), Vol. 11/12: 610–619.

12 A bound typescript of the text (184 pages with handwritten corrections) can be found in Nachlass Günther Anders, Literature Archives, Austrian National Library, Vienna, LIT (ÖLA 237/04) [hereafter LIT (ÖLA 237/04)].

13 Günther Stern, Die Weltfremdheit des Menschen: Vortrag unter dem Titel "Freiheit und Erfahrung" gehalten in der Frankfurter Ortsgruppe der Kantgesellschaft, February 1930. Gegenüber den mündlichen Ausführungen in wesentlichen Punkten erweitert (48 pages, typescript), LIT (ÖLA 237/04).

Anders in his student days, beginning of the 1920s.
Photo: Anders Papers, Literature Archives, Austrian
National Library

outcome would be possible when the Nazis were no longer in power.[14] On the other hand, the fact that Adorno was not impressed with the work was certainly not an insignificant factor.[15] After his hopes for habilitation had been dashed, Anders and his wife at the time, Hannah Arendt, moved to Berlin in the late summer and autumn of 1931, where Anders dedicated himself to the writing of his antifascist novel "*Die molussische Katakombe*" ("The Molussian Catacomb") in addition to his journalistic work.[16]

Shortly after arriving in exile in the United States, Anders tried to have the "*Philosophische Untersuchungen*" published, but his effort met with no success.[17] And though his philosophical interests shifted in response to the technological and societal upheavals and political catastrophes of the twentieth century (World War II, Auschwitz, Hiroshima),[18] music never fully disappeared from his philosophical considerations. In 1949 (one year before his return to Europe) he gave a series of lectures on the philosophy of art at the New School for Social Research in New York in which he presented several central aspects of his philosophy of

---

14 Cf. Günther Anders antwortet: Interviews & Erklärungen, Elke Schubert, ed., Berlin 1987, 29.

15 Adorno found the work too "Heidegger-like" and not grounded enough in musical theory. Cf. Letter from Theodor W. Adorno to Günther Anders, Frankfurt am Main, 31 October 1963 (4 pages, typescript), LIT (ÖLA 237/04).

16 Cf. Liessmann, Günther Anders, 20ff; Dries, Günther Anders, 13.

17 Cf. the letter to the J. S. Guggenheim Memorial Foundation NYC, January 30, 1937 (11 pages, typescript), LIT (ÖLA 237/04).

18 Cf. Günther Anders antwortet, 41f; Günther Anders, Mensch ohne Welt: Schriften zur Kunst und Literatur, 2nd edition, Munich 1993, XIff.

music in a revised form appropriate for the lecture hall.[19] Anders' philosophy of music also found its way into the entirety of his later work. Not only does his philosophy of discrepancy take shape against the backdrop of the philosophy of identity as it relates to the philosophy of music, but musicological commentary and reflection pervade Anders' body of work. He repeatedly reveals that he "[would] much rather write about Correggio or Beethoven's late string quartets than about the last days and the end of time over and over again."[20]

A "Theory of Situations"

Anders described his philosophy of music as a "theory of situations."[21] By this he meant that he was concerned in his analysis neither with the musical work (the composition in the form of the score) nor the psychological experience of music, but with the musical situation itself. This, according to Anders, is characterized by a specific subject-object neutrality. The traditional dichotomies of subject and object or intentional act and intentional object are inadequate when it comes to music; what is specific to music is the coincidence of subject and object, performance and work.[22]

The primary philosophers from whom Anders draws his terminology and upon whose work he builds his own arguments are Kant, Hegel and Heidegger. Anders thus claims to deliver in his "*Philosophische Untersuchungen*" a musical-philosophical theory of imagination. He even declares: "This path is only available to us because of Hegel's analyses [...]."[23] It is Heidegger's existential ontology as presented in "Being and Time," however, that seems to be especially paradigmatically relevant for Anders' philosophy of music, particularly the former's concept of world and worldliness and the "Being-in-the-world" of *Dasein*. According to Anders, world and worldliness have been dispensed within the musical situation. In that form of existence, which Anders calls "musical existence," it is not only the "world" that is replaced with "music" ("Being-in-music"), but other existentialia are replaced as well, such as "Being-with" ("*Mit-sein*") with "Co-performance" ("*Mit-vollzug*") (Co-performance of musical forms of motion); "Being-one's-Self" ("*Selbstsein*") with "Transformation" ("*Verwandlung*"); "Everydayness" ("*Alltäglichkeit*") with "Being separated" ("*Abgesperrtheit*") (the musical situation as an enclave situation); Historicity with Non-historicity or "Inherent-Timeliness" ("*Eigenzeitlichkeit*"), etc. Anders bundles these phenomena together in a positive sense in the formula "Being-in-music" and in a negative sense in "Not-Being-in-the-world." While the negative descriptions of the musical situation(s) constitute the first stage of his "*Philosophische Untersuchungen*," Anders is far more interested in describing them in their positive forms.[24]

---

19 Cf. Günther Stern, Philosophy of Art (ca. 700 pages, manuscript), LIT (ÖLA 237/04); judging from the fifteen lecture manuscripts still in existence, the first through fourth deal sporadically with the philosophy of music and the tenth through fourteenth deal exclusively with the philosophy of music.

20 Günther Anders antwortet, 130, 61f.

21 Stern, Philosophische Untersuchungen über musikalische Situationen, 32.

22 Cf. ibid., 10ff.

23 Ibid., 31f.

24 Namely as situations of motion and transformation that he sought to explain in a concrete manner based on three paradigmatic situations that were each linked to concrete examples of music (Mozart, Wagner's Tristan, Schönberg's twelve tone technique) and which he named "Dissolution-into" ("Aufgelöstsein-in"), "Release" ("Gelöstsein") and "Being-separated-from" ("Abgelöstsein-von").

In this attempt to provide a "preliminary *clarification*," a "preliminary phenomenological full articulation" of the musical situation's "multiplicity of forms,"[25] Anders develops a "philosophy of listening" that is equally concerned with sensory-aesthetic listening as it is with "actual," "philosophically relevant" listening, that is to say, with metaphysical listening.[26] Finally, there is a third fundamental aspect to listening related to conditions of reception that are modern, technological and shaped by the mass media, a topic on which Anders was one of the first to critically reflect.

Musical Listening: Intentional Listening and Openness

Already in the "Phenomenology of Listening," Anders declares that "each instance of music yearns to be heard differently."[27] He differentiates at a fundamental level between three basic forms of musical listening—between two forms of "intentional listening" and a form of listening he characterizes as "openness" ("*Aufgeschlossensein*").[28] Since musical listening essentially exists in "co-performance" of musical forms of motion (and not, for instance, in a stance of passive receptivity), it is the meaning of motion inherent to each particular instance of music that determines which manner of listening is appropriate. Musical situation and type of listening correlate with one another. Thus, Anders' stipulation that on the basis of epistemological grounds one may speak of only three "relatively tangible and verifiable" paradigmatic situations applies to the types of listening as well.[29]

"Intentional listening" corresponds to the musical situation that Anders calls "release" ("*Gelöstheit*") and that he connects to the music of Viennese Classicism (Mozart). This type of listening tends to be understood as an act of (virtual) singing, as "joining in" ("*Mitmachen*")— "One listens as if one were singing."[30]

Anders locates a second form of "intentional listening" in the context of that type of situation that he describes as "separation" ("*Abgelöstheit*") and that he links with "objective" music (Schönberg, for example). This listening is no longer directed toward the succession of time— the sensory grasp of sound as it comes into existence ("*Ertönen*")—but toward an ideal object that is fully identical with itself. It "dissociates and objectifies."[31] Intentional listening (qua musical listening), however, cannot negate succession but remains bound to it. This paradoxical tension has no resolution. This music seeks to be listened to "as one regards a painting as a whole, to condense all of its moments into one, a form of simultaneity of the successive."[32]

25   Stern, Philosophische Untersuchungen über musikalische Situationen, 9.
26   Cf. Espinet, Phänomenologie des Hörens, 16f, 219.
27   Stern, Zur Phänomenologie des Zuhörens, 610. – On the research tradition regarding typologies of listening, see Helmut Rösing/Herbert Bruhn, Typologie der Musikhörer, in: Musikpsychologie: Ein Handbuch, Herbert Bruhn/Rolf Oerter/Helmut Rösing, eds., Reinbek bei Hamburg 1993, 130–136; cf. too Heinrich Besseler, Grundfragen des musikalischen Hörens, in: Jahrbuch der Musikbibliothek Peters 32/1925 (1926): 35–52; Heinrich Besseler, Das musikalische Hören der Neuzeit, Berlin 1959.
28   Stern, Zur Phänomenologie des Zuhörens, 618; Stern, Philosophische Untersuchungen über musikalische Situationen, 143.
29   Cf. ibid., 100.
30   Ibid., 70.
31   Ibid., 180.
32   Theodor W. Adorno, Der getreue Korrepetitor. Gesammelte Schriften, Vol. 15: Darmstadt 1998, 157–402 (246).

As a specific type of listening, "openness" ("*Aufgeschlossensein*") is appropriate, after all, to the situation of "dissolution" ("*Aufgelöstsein*") that Anders connects especially with impressionist music (Debussy), but also with Wagner (Tristan). Anders dedicated an entire essay to this type of listening. In "Phenomenology of Listening,"[33] he argues that the auditory concept of attention, which the listening to impressionist music requires, simply cannot be grasped by that "heretofore quintessential *concept* of attention" which "has almost always been based on the optic model." In the case of impressionist music, the specificity of listening as opposed to seeing is expressed clearly and distinctly. Impressionist music has, according to Anders, a "direction-less" and "inactive meaning inherent in its motion," a "character of motion that is decidedly not one marked by set tendencies, but nonetheless specifically non-mechanical, similar to 'letting-oneself-go,' for example." Listening to impressionist music, understood as a specific form of "inactivity" *in* which we find ourselves listening, demands a particular form of attention—one that extends beyond the binaries of activity/passivity, intentional act/object, etc.

Thus, Anders poses the question: "What does it look like, this attention that is directed toward inactivity?"[34] His response: "Openness." This pertains to an active passivity that is made reflexive when expressed in speech: "open oneself" or "let oneself go," for example, or put another way, an "inactive attention," a "Being-with" ("*Mitsein*").[35] Of course, Anders admits, one can also analyze impressionist music in its details. But he argues that this is inadequate when it comes to listening to this music: "*Though description seeks to represent exactly what has been heard, that which is heard during the act of listening is itself only there in a far less explicit way.*" Offering an analogy with visual arts, he writes, "an impressionist painting by Monet, Signac or Seurat, when viewed only in terms of its details, becomes something incomprehensible."[36]

The one feature that is shared by all types of listening is the transformation of the person who is in this state of auditory co-performance of a musical "object." In the musical situation as a situation of transformation, the listener becomes the medium. He no longer simply finds himself *in* the music; rather, he *is* the music. Music "speaks," as it were, straight through the person, the listener.

Metaphysical Listening: Musical Imagination, Hearkening and Foreknowledge

Anders considers the senses—sight, hearing, smell, taste, touch—to be "various indices of a person's relationship to the world." From these, one can discern a person's relationship with the variety of "world dimensions." At the same time, they represent the "person's various types of openness." "Do sight and hearing result in identical forms, or intimately related forms, of communication with the world? Is it the same world that he sees and hears?"[37] Anders is thoroughly convinced that each sense makes its very own sense.[38] Given these considerations,

---

33 For the following, see Stern, Zur Phänomenologie des Zuhörens, 610ff.

34 Ibid., 617.

35 Ibid., 618.

36 Ibid., 617.

37 Stern, Philosophische Untersuchungen über musikalische Situationen, 119.

38 Cf. ibid., 119, 131.

listening is, for Anders, much more than simply a form of receptivity to (musical-)acoustic stimuli.

Located precisely on the boundary between sensory listening and metaphysical listening is Anders' conception of the musical power of imagination in the form of virtual listening. Drawing especially on Kant, he describes this as "man's intuitus originarius." While the divine "intuitus originarius"[39] (intellectual intuition or an intuitive understanding) creates something from nothing, musical creation is a result of the "unstable and impermanent" element of sound and is therefore, in principle, "futile." "Musical fantasy is, so to speak, humankind's futile intuitus originarius, set into motion again and again and forced to make do with completely unsuitable materials."[40] Anders specifies that this creative moment is immanent not only in imagination but in each and every instance of resounding music. "This neutrality regarding activity and passivity in singing out (*Heraussingen*) and in acoustic internalization (*hörendes Hereinholen*) is to be found not only in instances of musical imagination, but also in those cases of complete fulfillment in which music does indeed sound."[41]

What is decisive in this context, however, is not the virtual listening that can be described as virtual singing (i.e. as an unrealized readiness to sing), but the virtual listening that testifies to something that is essentially impossible to make a (vocal) reality (essentially impossible because of the fundamental divergence between listening and the ability-to-proclaim (*Verlautbaren-können*)). This virtual listening can hear "more" than the voice can proclaim. "This 'being all ear' ('*ganz Ohr sein*') is in no way equivalent to 'being all mouth' ('*ganz Mund sein*')." This divergence is, in Anders' view, "excruciating." "Every polyphonic piece of music, the vast majority of art music in fact, draws its very life force from this divergence." This is what comprises "music's authentic 'other-worldliness' (*das 'Entrückende'*)."[42]

The acoustic neutrality regarding activity and passivity is admittedly manifested in "hearkening" ("*Lauschen*").[43] As a form of musical receptivity, this is identical to that type of listening that was described above as "openness." Hearkening is, however, a great deal more for Anders; it is a *metaphysical symptom*.

Hearkening, according to Anders, is preceded by a "foreknowledge" ("*Ahnen*"). This foreknowledge is evidence of a person's specific place in the world, his "Not-only-being-in-this-world" ("Nicht-nur-in-dieser-Welt-sein"): "The fact that a person, as someone with foreknowledge, can *mean* something other than this world that he experiences and that is available to him or something other than himself [...], that he is free to *mean past* (*vorbeimeinen*) his world is evidence of his lack of fixation on this world."

Anders is decidedly concerned here not with a hearkening "within-the-world" ("*innerweltlich*") but with a hearkening which is intent on that which is to be hearkened, that which "sounds forth from a sphere that is fundamentally separated from that in which the hearkening person is situated as a person embedded in an environment." That which is to be heark-

---

39 See Immanuel Kant, Kritik der reinen Vernunft. Gesammelte Schriften, Vol. 3 (Akademieausgabe): Berlin 1911, B 68, 72, 139, 145, 159.

40 Stern, Philosophische Untersuchungen über musikalische Situationen, 137.

41 Ibid., 138.

42 Ibid., 139.

43 I use the word "hearken" and its various forms to express the particular sense of listening carefully and attentively that is inherent in "lauschen," the German word used by Anders. – The following remarks and quotations relate to § 17 of Stern, Philosophische Untersuchungen über musikalische Situationen, 142–154.

ened is not simply available to be accessed at one's own discretion; it announces itself, it makes itself known. The stance associated with hearkening demands, much as techniques of mystical-ecstatic traditions demand, "means of catharsis, means of discharging, a detachment from life and its noise [...]." Elsewhere Anders describes this stance as a specific mode of being, a "being in an auditory state" ("*Hörendsein*") or "Being-in-listening" ("*Im-Hören-sein*"), as an "abiding in the heart" ("*Inständigkeit des Herzens*") or "abiding in prayer."[44]

The dimensions into which the hearkening person advances are those that are otherwise fundamentally hidden from him. "Inasmuch as he lives with an awareness that these fundamentally hidden dimensions exist [...], he is one with *foreknowledge*." For Anders, the "pre-acoustical hearkening-to-oneself" ("*das vorakustische Sich-selbst-lauschen*") is precisely what makes acoustical hearkening feasible in the first place. The acoustical element bestows the opportunity "to actualize as *sensory* perception the specificity of that which hearkening means to humankind."

Hearkening, which hearkens on the basis of foreknowledge, has no idea, however, to *what* it ought to hearken. It hearkens into the "nothing," or put another way, into the "silence." It is here in this hearkening into the nothing that the "specific possibility in the acoustic," which is alien to every other sense, is to be found.[45]

There is unfortunately too little space here to further explore the numerous affinities of these ideas to Martin Heidegger's phenomenology and metaphysics of listening.[46] One must add to the apposite recognition of "the deeper convergences between Anders' musical thought and Heidegger's puzzling relationship with music and the ear,"[47] that Heidegger concerned himself primarily with metaphysical, as opposed to musical, listening. It is in fact nearly impossible to find anything resembling a philosophy of music in his work.[48] Furthermore, in Heidegger's early work respectively in "Being and Time," "sight as a philosophical approach" is presented "in a still unproblematized way,"[49] and hearing is still determined by the external "world" ("the voice of the friend," "the creaking wagon," "the motorcycle," "the north wind," "the woodpecker tapping," "the crackling fire").[50]

It may be somewhat exaggerated to call Anders' philosophy of music "the most compelling attempt at rethinking musical listening since Descartes,"[51] but I find more than slightly convincing the assertion that what Anders attempts here is nothing less than "to dismantle the central position in modern Western thought of the Cartesian *fundamentum*

---

44 Hannah Arendt/Günther Stern, Rilkes "Duineser Elegien," in: Rilkes "Duineser Elegien," Ulrich Fülleborn and Manfred Engl, eds., Vol. 2: Forschungsgeschichte, Frankfurt am Main 1982, 45–65 (48).

45 Cf. Martin Heidegger's speech in 1929 upon taking up his chair in Freiburg, "Was ist Metaphysik?" in: Wegmarken. Gesamtausgabe, Vol. 9, Frankfurt am Main 1976, 103–122 (115): "Da-sein means: being held out into the nothing." ("Da-sein heißt: Hineingehaltenheit in das Nichts.") "In the Being of entities the nihilation of the Nothing occurs." ("Im Sein des Seienden geschieht das Nichten des Nichts.")

46 Cf. Espinet, Phänomenologie des Hörens.

47 Veit Erlmann, Reason and Resonance: A History of Modern Aurality, New York 2010, 333.

48 Cf. Thomas Macho, Die Kunst der Verwandlung: Notizen zur frühen Musikphilosophie von Günther Anders, in: Günther Anders kontrovers, Konrad Paul Liessmann, ed., Munich 1992, 89–102 (90). – That the chapter on sensory listening is only paid "relatively brief" attention in Espinet, Phänomenologie des Hörens, 209ff, is likely no coincidence. (Cf. Helmuth Vetter, Rezension zu Espinet, Phänomenologie des Hörens, in: Philosophischer Literaturanzeiger 64 (2011), Vol. 1: 35–40 (39)).

49 Espinet, Phänomenologie des Hörens, 191f, 194.

50 Heidegger, Sein und Zeit, 217; cf. Espinet, Phänomenologie des Hörens, 98.

51 Erlmann, Reason and Resonance, 309.

inconcussum."[52] Peter Sloterdijk explained this musicologically inspired deconstruction of modern metaphysics of subjectivity[53] with reference to Hegel and Heidegger: The "self" as *"medium percussum."*[54]

By contrast, the argument that Anders' philosophy of music is a form of coming-into-the-world ("music as a kind of midwifery")[55] appears to be highly implausible. Anders underlines that his conception of metaphysical listening does not place the primary emphasis on listening within-the-world, but far more on the *loss* of the world and worldliness instead. The hearkening subject's "world" is a *different* world, certainly not the one into which we are born and with which we, in our quotidian Being-in-the-world, seem to be so familiar.

Listening under the Conditions of Modern Technology: Music and Radio

The world's first broadcaster began regular service in 1920 in Pittsburgh. Shortly thereafter, the BBC was founded in 1922, and German broadcasting was born in 1923. On October 29, 1923, the first light entertainment program was broadcast between the evening hours of 8 and 9 o'clock from the "Vox-Haus" on Berlin's Potsdamer Straße.[56] By 1926 the United States could boast "over 5 million radio receiving sets, and Germany more than a million."[57] Vociferous debates and discussion erupted among music critics and intellectuals regarding the possibilities and potential of this new medium, its significance and the set of problems it brought with it. This was particularly urgent given the fact that nearly 40% of the programs at the time were of a "musical nature," according to a contemporary report.[58]

There was, on the one hand, a broadly held belief in the democratization of "high culture," which had previously been accessible only to a bourgeois elite, and an accompanying process of humanization.[59] But at the same time, others complained bitterly about this new "plague of music,"[60] even if it was already clear that the clock could not be turned back: "Music will [...] forever remain an object for broadcasting." As a result, the question that was more urgently posed was: "What happens to it [music] when it is broadcast?"[61]

---

52 Ibid., 312.
53 Cf. ibid., 317.
54 Sloterdijk, Wo sind wir, wenn wir Musik hören?, 313, 317ff.
55 Erlmann, Reason and Resonance, 338.
56 Cf. Konrad Dussel, Deutsche Rundfunkgeschichte, 3rd revised edition., Konstanz 2010, 30f; 50 Jahre Musik im Hörfunk, Kurt Blaukopf/Siegfried Goslich/Wilfried Scheib, eds., Vienna/Munich 1973, 8; Siegfried Goslich, Musik im Rundfunk, Tutzing 1971, 38.
57 Goslich, Musik im Rundfunk, 39.
58 Cf. Hanns Gutman, Die Rolle der Musik im Rundfunk, in: Melos 7 (1928): 295–298 (296). – A section for "Broadcasting" was added to the music journal "Melos" in 1928, for example, and expanded to "Broadcasting – Film – Phonographic Records" one year later. The journal was published at this time by the musicologist Hans Mersmann, who would become the head of the music section at "Deutsche Welle" and at "Deutschlandsender" in 1932 (cf. Hans Mersmann, Arbeitsbericht, [Berlin 1933], 6 pages, typescript).
59 Cf. Robert Hullot-Kentor, Vorwort, in: Theodor W. Adorno, Current of Music: Elements of a Radio Theory. Nachgelassene Schriften, Vol. 1/3, Robert Hullot-Kentor, ed., Frankfurt am Main 2006, 7–69 (13ff).
60 Gutman, Die Rolle der Musik im Rundfunk, 295.
61 Ibid., 297.

The music critic Heinrich Strobel (who would go on to become the director of music programming at the German Südwestfunk station) described the state of affairs in 1930: "At first, the situation was that the broadcasters, being this new instrument for the transmission of music, took over the generally accepted practices of the cultivation of music. Operas were broadcast, light music was moved from the cafes, dance halls and beer gardens, and concerts were put on by individual broadcasters according to well-founded public models. [...] Slowly the clairaudient directors of broadcasting began to realize the unsound nature of this admittedly comfortable methodology from the point of view of the broadcaster. The broadcaster was in any case creating a new sociological situation."[62]

Amid these discussions, Günther Anders published a short article in the Austrian music journal "Anbruch," of which Adorno was the (unofficial) head editor,[63] with the title "Spook and Radio."[64] In it he addressed the hotly debated topic of what it really meant to "broadcast" music. Not surprisingly, Anders criticized the relationship between music and radio, citing the radical destruction by radio of what he postulated as music's "space-neutrality." Radio not only made explicit music's *here* and *there* but—and this is where he pointed to the "spook"—it also *pluralized* music. The radio program "scattered it [music] repeatedly and afresh in its entirety across the whole of the land," meaning it became plural, quantifiable and something resembling a doppelgänger. Man's adaptation to the new technology is, according to Anders, ultimately equivalent to an act of inhumanity: "If he [the listener] attempts to wean himself from this terror, to contort himself inwardly to accommodate that which is in itself excessive, to conform to the unheard-of, and this attempt is successful, then he will himself become inhuman."[65] What Anders decries here and what sends shivers down his spine has today become a matter of course: music as a technologically produced object that can be downloaded, saved, and taken with you, which is available all the time, background music in every imaginable situation, the individual as "Divisum."[66]

In this early engagement with music and radio, Anders anticipates one of the central arguments of Adorno's critique of the music program, namely the spatialization or the visualization of music via the program.[67] In his reflections "On the Musical Uses of the Radio" ("*Über die musikalische Verwendung des Radios*"), Adorno makes only a brief reference to Anders' essay.[68] Far more illuminating in this context are the two unpublished studies that were completed in 1939[69] as part of Adorno's involvement in the "Princeton Radio Research Project,"[70]

---

62 Heinrich Strobel, Zur musikalischen Programmpolitik des Rundfunks, in: Melos 9 (1930): 178–180 (178f).

63 Cf. Stefan Müller-Dohm, Adorno: Eine Biographie, Frankfurt am Main 2003, 143, 167ff.

64 Günther Stern, Spuk und Radio, in: Anbruch: Monatsschrift für moderne Musik 12 (1930), Vol. 2: 65–66.

65 Ibid., 66.

66 Günther Anders, Die Antiquiertheit des Menschen, Vol. 1: Über die Seele im Zeitalter der zweiten industriellen Revolution, Munich 1994, 135.

67 Cf. Hullot-Kentor, Vorwort, 38.

68 Adorno, Der getreue Korrepetitor, 371.

69 Reference is made here to the studies "Radio Physiognomics," a text of central importance, and "source of Adorno's thought," which "provides something of an overview of the entirety of the theory of radio" (Hullot-Kentor, Vorwort, 58), as well as "The Radio Voice," which can be found in: Theodor W. Adorno, Current of Music: Elements of a Radio Theory. Nachgelassene Schriften, Vol. 1/3, Robert Hullot-Kentor, ed., Frankfurt am Main 2006, 73–200, 499–560.

70 The working title of the project, financed by the Rockefeller Foundation and under the leadership of Paul Lazarsfeld, was "The Essential Value of Radio to all Types of Listeners." Cf. Hullot-Kentor, Vorwort, 9ff; Müller-Dohm, Adorno, 372ff.

which prove that he had engaged quite extensively with Anders' thesis. The sixth chapter of the study "Radio Physiognomics," entitled "Space Ubiquity,"[71] comprises in its entirety a discussion of Anders' arguments: "Mr. Stern's sketch deserves careful discussion. On the one hand, it is open to criticism which may affect the ground of his interpretation. On the other hand, we think that some of his observations are well founded, and we shall have to try to bring them in line with our framework of radio physiognomics."[72] In addition to finding fault with Anders' "anthropological approach" and his concept of music's space-neutrality, what Adorno criticizes above all is the fact that at the time of its publication, Anders was "still a follower of the 'existential' philosophy of Heidegger."[73] Nevertheless, he admits that Anders had very clearly recognized the problems associated with both the pluralization of music and the disappearance of the original.[74]

There is not enough space here to examine Adorno's remarks in greater detail.[75] Instead, I will conclude with a brief look at Anders' second early text on the topic of music and radio, which provides evidence of a notable divergence not simply between Anders and Adorno, but between the earlier and the later Anders too. In his essay "The Acoustic Stereoscope,"[76] which Anders published while at the New School, he advances the surprisingly optimistic argument that the new stereo technology eliminates the character of a reproduction that otherwise marked the broadcasting of music. What we now listen to is the music itself, not just a copy of it: "Now, our acoustic stereoscope is free from this defect; […] there is no difference between the hearing of music in a concert hall and the hearing of it by means of the stereoscope. The music we hear, is not a 'view' or a 'reproduction' of a Bruckner or a Mahler symphony, but the 'symphony itself.' The distinction between original and copy (or reproduction) has lost its validity."[77] Adorno, too, admitted that stereophony allowed a "deceptively similar broadcast of any music," generally without "the acoustic equivalent of tasting like canned food," even if it was not completely without the "hear-stripe"-effect.[78] Nevertheless, as Adorno demonstrated, there are sufficient aesthetic, psychological and sociological aspects aside from technological advancement that refute Anders' early thesis.[79] In his later texts of media criticism and those engaged in critiques of technology, Anders ultimately no longer shares his own earlier optimism. The "cultural faucets (Kulturwasserhähne) of the radios,"[80] Anders declares in full, keeping with his well-known pessimistic point of view, resulted instead in the destruction of the work of art, the disintegration of the subject.

---

71   Adorno, Current of Music, 128–145.
72   Ibid., 131.
73   Ibid., 131ff.
74   Ibid., 139.
75   Reference should be made to the analogies between Anders' remarks and Benjamin's famous essay on the work of art (Walter Benjamin, Das Kunstwerk im Zeitalter seiner technischen Reproduzierbarkeit [3. Fassung]. Gesammelte Schriften, Vol. 1/2, Rolf Tiedemann, ed., Frankfurt am Main 1991, 471–508.), to which Adorno makes emphatic reference. (Adorno, Current of Music, 139ff, 551f; Adorno, Der getreue Korrepetitor, 371f)
76   Anders-Stern, The Acoustic Stereoscope, in: Philosophy and Phenomenological Research 10 (1949/50): 238–243.
77   Anders-Stern, The Acoustic Stereoscope, 242f.
78   Adorno, Der getreue Korrepetitor, 369f.
79   See ibid., 371ff; cf. too Adorno, Über den Fetischcharakter in der Musik und die Regression des Hörens. Gesammelte Schriften, Vol. 14, Darmstadt 1998, 14–50.
80   Anders, Die Antiquiertheit des Menschen, Vol. 1, 101.

This destructive character of new (media-)technologies, however, manifests itself not least in the loss of genuine opportunities for experience. In other words, music broadcast via radio is no longer *listened* to, but *consumed*. The "oblivion of listening" that had been posited from the start now assumes a new sense beyond its original epistemological meaning to encompass media criticism and critiques of technology as expounded by Anders.

Anders—The Literary Figure

Bernhard Fetz

Writing Poetry Today:
Günther Anders between Literature
and Philosophy

Günther Anders' literary work arose alongside the fault line that lies between the early philosophical anthropology of the 1930s and negative anthropology after 1945. The latter is shaped
on the one hand by the Holocaust and the experiences of emigrants, and on the other by
the irrevocable nature of the threat of nuclear catastrophe, the consequences of which had
been revealed by the bombs that were exploded over Hiroshima and Nagasaki. Having origi-
nated in this particular grouping of intellectual-biographical contexts, Anders' profile as a
writer, one who is committed to an aesthetic of effects, is best described by means of a short
genealogical excursion. This excursion winds its way back to the first half of the twentieth
century tracing the intellectual-biographical divides and branching in the metaphorical road
of German-language intellectual history. Between the years 1929 and 1937, Günther Anders
was married to Hannah Arendt. They had met in 1925 in a seminar convened by Martin Heidegger at the university in Marburg. Hannah Arendt struggled her entire life with her love for
Martin Heidegger. Anders devoted several long essays to a vehement critique of his former
teacher; these essays have been gathered together into a volume.[1]

Anders emigrated to America in 1936, whereas Hannah Arendt managed to escape the
National Socialist terror at the very last minute. On 23 May 1941, Hannah Arendt sent to her
husband, from whom she had been legally separated since 1937 and with whom she had had
little connection for years, a telegram from New York with a pithy message: "WE ARE SAFE
STAYING 317 WEST 95 HANNAH."[2] During this American exile, Arendt would become
close friends with Hermann Broch, the Austrian writer, essayist and epistemologist, who was
also in exile in the United States, living in New York, New Haven and Princeton.

Broch's major novel, *The Death of Virgil* (*Der Tod des Vergil*), which he completed in
America, was the subject of a critical response by Anders in an essay that he titled in a way
that was characteristic of Broch: "The Death of Virgil and the Diagnosis of his Illness." In it
he criticized what he called the novel's language of endlessness which, he argued, erased all
sense of difference.[3] The rejection of the high linguistic register that characterizes *The Death*

---

1   Günther Anders, Über Heidegger, ed. by Gerhard Oberschlick, Munich 2001.
2   Hannah Arendt to Günther Anders, 23 May 1941, Literature Archives of the Austrian National Library, Vienna,
    Nachlass Günther Anders (ÖLA 237/B 1480, cited hereafter as LIT); for more on Anders' and Arendt's relation-
    ship, see Christian Dries, Günther Anders und Hannah Arendt – eine Beziehungsskizze, in: Günther Anders,
    Die Kirschenschlacht: Dialoge mit Hannah Arendt, ed. by Gerhard Oberschlick, Munich 2011, 71–94.
3   Cf. Günther Anders, Der 'Tod des Vergil' und die Diagnose seiner Krankheit, in: Ibid., Mensch ohne Welt.
    Schriften zur Literatur und Kunst, Munich 1984 (cited hereafter as MoW), 195–200; cf. the letters between
    Anders and Broch in the Nachlass Günther Anders' (LIT), partially published in: Hermann Broch, Briefe, vol. 3,
    ed. by Paul Michael Lützeler, Frankfurt am Main 1981 (edition in 13 volumes, volume 13/3).

of Virgil also appears in Anders' major Kafka essay: "He who undertakes to speak to an ear when there is no hope and when he has no particular concept of any one particular listener, this person will find himself in danger of not recognizing the forcefulness of the voice, the degree of formality, etc., and he will slip unexpectedly from one register to another ... which is exactly what has happened to Hermann Broch in the worst possible way in his monumental Virgil novel."[4] Anders' reaction to *Death of Virgil* reveals the large chasm that separates Broch's utopia, based on a new secular myth, from Anders—the critical analyst of the material world of things and issuer of warnings regarding nuclear apocalypse. With a desperate insistence, Broch attempted to universalize an endangered, if not already outdated, humanism and to rescue it in the post-humanist age. In spite of Broch's skepticism regarding literature, humanism remains the conduit for all of his widely divergent, interdisciplinary efforts even after 1945. *Systematic*—classifying, hierarchizing, epistemological—thought and *aesthetic* execution were inextricably bound for this "poet against his will," as Hannah Arendt called him.[5]

This characterization of Broch could be applied to Arendt herself, slightly modified to describe her as a "philosopher against her will." In his major study on Anders, Arendt and Jaspers, Christian Dries highlights the fact that Arendt "believed her excursion into literature to be necessary," a corrective "to a genuinely scientific—and for Arendt that means tarnished by theory, predetermined—view, for seismographs that would register the coming upheavals, catastrophes and fresh starts."[6] Furthermore, he quotes Arendt specialist Barbara Hahn, who observes that there are no texts by Arendt that are not "themselves poetic, suffused with rhythm, edited with fastidious attention to the sounds of their words."[7] That is to say, these three distinguished thinkers living in American exile are all writer-philosophers or philosopher-writers. Questions of literary style are eminently important in philosophical writing. The reverse is equally true: literary writing almost always inscribes itself onto a philosophical horizon or at least rises up from one. The ability to engage in philosophical work on cognition is virtually predicated on a language that is shaped by literary models, on an adoption of literary genres and techniques—montage, dialogue and hyperbole in the case of Anders' work. Anders, Arendt and Broch belong to a group of those whom we may call, to use a word that is currently in fashion, hybrid thinkers and hybrid writers. Furthermore, all three understood literary texts to be source texts for any engagement with philosophical and epistemological questions, which can be attributed to their shared educational socialization—something that is especially evident when it comes to Arendt and Anders. One example can be found in an early essay by Anders entitled "Spook and Radio," in which he establishes a connection between modern technology and ghostly apparitions or mysticism. "French surrealist and pre-surrealist literature" provide the most apposite approaches with which to interpret the phenomenon, according to Anders.[8] One need only think of Broch's "James Joyce and the Present" ("*James Joyce und die Gegenwart*"), one of his most well-known essays, in which his

---

4 Günther Anders, Kafka, pro und contra: Die Prozeß-Unterlagen, in: MoW, 93.
5 Hannah Arendt, "Einleitung zu den Essay-Bänden von Hermann Broch," in: Paul Michael Lützeler ed., Hannah Arendt, Hermann Broch, Briefwechsel 1946 bis 1951, Frankfurt am Main 1996, 185.
6 Christian Dries, Die Welt als Vernichtungslager: Eine kritische Theorie der Moderne im Anschluss an Günther Anders, Hannah Arendt und Hans Jonas, Bielefeld 2012, 313.
7 Ibid.
8 Cf. also Karl Wagner, Adorno/Anders: Korrespondenzen und Diskrepanzen, in: Georg Gerber, Robert Leucht, Karl Wagner, eds., Transatlantische Verwerfungen: Transatlantische Verdichtungen: Kulturtransfer in Literatur und Wissenschaft 1945–1989. Göttingen 2012, 145.

literary analysis is transformed into a comprehensive diagnosis of the age. All three figures are connected on the one hand by their having written *about* others' literary work and, on the other, by their belief that *literariness* is the fundamental condition for the production of philosophy.

One of Anders' earliest published works—and Arendt's as well—is their coauthored reading of Rilke's "Duino Elegies." In a preface he wrote in 1981 for a new edition of the essay, which was originally published in 1930, Günther Anders insists that it is the product "of an epoch that disappeared a long time ago, the epoch *before* the catastrophe." The text has become so alien to him by 1981 "that I can hardly comprehend entire sections of the interpretation and, had I not more urgent things to do, I would have to interpret them all over again myself."[9] It is possible that Anders' sense of alienation from the Rilke essay is also due to the fact that the answer formulated in response to the question of poetry's communicative function is altogether different from how it would be expressed *after* the experiences of the political and economic crisis of the 1930s and *after* the rupture of civilization produced by the Holocaust and the detonation of the atom bombs over Hiroshima and Nagasaki. Right at the very beginning of the essay, Arendt and Anders write: "Confronted with poetry that is alienated from communication itself, the fundamental question necessarily arises as to what extent it even wants to be understood, to what extent it can be understood […]." The only seeming possibility is "to reveal how it came to be in that tune, reveal what is behind the tone, so to speak, which is the one and only entity."[10] Shortly after the publication of this essay, Anders' position is resolute: Literature and philosophy in the twentieth century are expressions of a comprehensive process of alienation, and it is for precisely this reason that they are obliged to function as media of communication, criticism and enlightenment.

1. Writing—For Whom?

On 1 March 1932, just two years after the Rilke essay, Günther Stern, as he was still called at that time,[11] writes the following in the *Berliner Börsen-Courier* under the title "Smart Philosophy," which sounds strangely familiar to our ears today:

> "Academic philosophy finds itself in a veritable crisis. It knows not for whom philosophy is being done; it is undecided about whether its responsibility is simply to transmit existing knowledge as a form of education, to create new theoretical material or—emulating Kierkegaard and Nietzsche—to address itself directly to the public in order to speak to a non-theoretical side of mankind. This uncertainty is of course reflected in an uncertainty of philosophical style."[12]

---

9 Günther Anders, Vorbemerkung, in: Ulrich Fülleborn, Manfred Engel, eds., Rilkes 'Duineser Elegien,' Frankfurt am Main 1982, 45.

10 Hannah Arendt, Günther Stern, Rilkes 'Duineser Elegien,' in: Ibid., 45 f. (originally in: Neue Schweizer Rundschau 23 (1939): 855–871.

11 Günther Stern became Günther Anders at the beginning of the 1930s, after Herbert Ihering, the editor of the culture desk at the Berliner Börsen Courier, complained that too many articles were bylined with "Stern". From then on, Stern called himself Anders (Different) and his life and the paths his thought took would indeed be very different from conventional ones. His name became his agenda.

12 [Günther Stern], Smarte Philosophie, in: Berliner Börsen Courier, March 1, 1932.

Anders, a student of both Heidegger and Husserl, advocated from very early on a philosophical language that resembled everyday speech. This is revealed in a review by Anders of Bertrand Russell's book *The Conquest of Happiness* that appeared on 11 December 1931 in the *Berliner Börsen-Courier*:

> "This is a case where the philosopher is not speaking to the philosopher, but to the non-philosopher [...], here one fearlessly abandons the noble sphere of Pure-Ideas [...]. The subject and language of the book is shaped by the common man. It is his life and his unhappiness that the philosopher addresses. The philosopher can simply talk about these things in a more knowledgeable way than the common man could."[13]

In spite of its dissociation from the professionalized language peculiar to philosophy, Anders's *philosophie engagée* was theoretically grounded from the very beginning. As early as 1924, he lays out his agenda stating that he wants "to be simultaneously theoretical, by which I mean stationary, and in actu, embodying momentum—to be both philosophical and topical at the same time."[14] Anders was capable of masterful playing on the keys of phenomenological philosophical language. One prominent example is the essay on Alfred Döblin's epochal novel *Berlin Alexanderplatz* that Anders wrote in 1931 and dedicated to Georg Lukács. At the same time, the essay already reveals Anders' substantive retreat from his philosophical mentors.

His plea for an active philosophy, one that was comprehensible to large numbers of people, charted the path on which Anders would remain for the rest of his philosophical life. Anders wanted to be intelligible, but for whom? In 1968, the year of the student protests, he analyzes a paradoxical phenomenon of reception, of which he sees himself a victim. Anders maintains that he has attempted since 1931 "to find a non-academic, non-esoteric, non-hermetic language" in order to reach the broadest possible readership given the threats of fascism, war and the atom bomb. Anders uses a core vocabulary that marks the crossovers between philosophy and literature. Anders further explains in this text from 1968 that he has been consistently concerned with *translating* philosophical idiom into a generally comprehensible language, and doing so in such a way that none of the "unambiguity" of philosophical language would be lost.[15] One example from the 1930s is his anti-Nazi, didactic novel *The Molussian Catacomb* (*Die molussische Katakombe*), which was profoundly influenced by Bertolt Brecht. The novel was primarily written between 1930 and 1938, and Anders began editing it during his Parisian exile, finishing it later in exile in New York. Anders relies on the effect of fable in this novel set in the fictitious country Molussia, but he emphasizes the unambiguous nature of philosophical language at the same time.[16] The book, however, reached neither those in power nor the oppressed. First published in 1992, the novel reads like a message in a bottle from a bygone era. *The Molussian Catacomb* can be read as a record of the literary engagement with the contradictory strategies embraced by the opposition to the Nazis. Their miscalculations regarding their opponents, their stubborn belief that truth and humanity would ultimately prevail, their

---

13 Günther Stern, Philosophische Tips, in: Berliner Börsen-Courier, Dec. 11, 1931.

14 Günther Stern, Aktualität, in: Das Dreieck, H. 2 (1924): 33–37, here 34.

15 Günther Anders, Dialektik des Esoterischen: Unveröffentlichtes Manuskript aus dem Nachlass. LIT (ÖLA 237/04, from the bundle: "Kunst u. Literatur. Sprache.").

16 Günther Anders, Die molussische Katakombe, Zweite, erweiterte Auflage, mit Apokryphen und Dokumenten aus dem Nachlaß herausgegeben und mit einem Nachwort versehen von Gerhard Oberschlick. Munich 2012.

corruptibility and the lifelessness of the arguments they wielded in political struggle are the object of the Molussian fables and didactic poems that are collected in the book. To be heard, truth must conduct itself like untruth; it must know its opponent as well as it knows itself and use mimicry to outwit the other. And what is true of the freedom fighters in *Molussian Catacomb* is true, too, for the author Anders. He utilizes the literary form as a vehicle. Hardly anything is simply recorded in his diaries in the exact form and on the same scale as when he first became aware of it. The diaries function like a microscope's lens in presenting their findings. This literary magnification renders things visible, hence Anders' predilection for the form of the fable, which tends to expose the truth of the situation in a most trenchant manner. Truth is never that which is there to be seen—this foundational maxim in Anders' philosophy corresponds to Bertolt Brecht's concept of realism.[17]

Translation is a genuine literary activity; it is a form of work on language. "My effort has been in vain," Anders writes in the text on the "Dialectic of the Esoteric" (*"Dialektik des Eso- terischen"*), which was quoted from above.[18] This is not because the translations are some- how unsuccessful in and of themselves, but because the translations could no longer reach those whom they wished to address. The critical public, the extra-parliamentary "opposition," is composed exclusively of students and university graduates, people who are conversant in sociological and philosophical jargon. As a result, only those who have mastered and could use this idiom themselves could count on having a widespread impact. Anders then refers to Herbert Marcuse and his success among the students in a comment that is only thinly veiled in its criticism. Because leftist university graduates are disconcerted by texts that are not formulated in an overtly academic way, Anders' texts never achieve the broader impact for which he hoped. Today, and especially in an English-speaking context, this is very much not the case. Anders' texts derive their advantage, their longevity, from the way they keep a particular philosophical jargon at arm's length. Even if many of his arguments in the *Obso- lence of Human Beings* deserve to come under scrutiny (his media philosophy, for example), the book, if not quite timeless, has remained relevant for much longer than anyone could have suspected when it was originally published, which is largely due to the way his language directly accesses philosophical issuesa quality that is also literary.

2. Anthropology in Exile: 1930—1936—1945

When Günther Anders left Paris in 1936 to emigrate to the United States, he brought with him two caches of experience that defined his habitus as an intellectual. The first was the education he had received as a musically talented child growing up in an haute-bourgeois Jewish milieu as well as his memories of this education. There is nothing exceptional in this; in more than just a few cases, emigrants' educational baggage turned into a form of resentment toward American culture, which they found to be superficial, traditionless and conformist. Only a few were able to open themselves up to the New World in a way that was both critical and

---

17 Brecht met Anders in Berlin before he emigrated. Brecht was the one who sent the manuscript for the "Molussian Catacomb" to the Kiepenheuer-Verlag publishing house where it fell into the Gestapo's hands after a raid. The agents assumed it was a collection of tales about the South Pacific since it was wrapped in a map of Indonesia. The fact that these henchmen could not see past the camouflage is itself a cynical proof of Anders' thesis.

18 Anders, Dialektik des Esoterischen.

without reservations. Hermann Broch, whom Anders criticized for his "elevated style" in spite of his favorable personal feelings toward him, could not put aside his reservations in his engagement with the New World. Broch had been too profoundly shaped by his European education, which was something most emigrants were unable to suppress, even temporarily.

It is the second aspect of Anders' intellectual and emotional baggage that is more unusual. Anders carried with him a near complete, elaborated critical commentary on the anthropological discussion during the interwar years—a model of an anthropology that would shape his later philosophy of technology and media, his political engagement and his thoughts regarding humanity in the atomic age. The fissure between pre-war anthropology and the negative anthropology after the war bears the names Auschwitz, Hiroshima and Nagasaki. Following visits to Auschwitz and to the city of his birth, Breslau/Wrocław, Anders writes in his book *Visit to Hades* (*Besuch im Hades*) that Auschwitz is "morally speaking incomparably more appalling" than both of the atom bomb detonations, whereas these are "incomparably worse than Auschwitz."[19]

The numerous notes in Anders' archive, those from his Parisian exile beginning in 1933 as well as those from his American exile after 1936, are fragments of a permanently ongoing process of reassuring himself. They are "attempts at a self-understanding," as Anders himself titled one bundle of papers.[20] A self-understanding regarding the viability of the great philosophical *and* literary conceptions of the world—Heidegger and Kafka are named here as two central philosophical and literary points of reference—in light of the conditions resulting from a completely changed reality of life. Anders' concept of the poetic arts developed out of the opposition between his socialization as a member of the educated middle-class and his intellectual socialization as well as the awareness of epochal changes in media and technology. After 1945, the desire to reterritorialize into the language of his origins those personal experiences that had been interrupted by exile, including the intellectual and cultural character of the 1920s and early 1930s, is indissolubly connected for Anders to the aesthetic-ethical question of how one can appropriately respond to the Holocaust and to Hiroshima and Nagasaki. The most accomplished literary document that emerged from this dispute with the "world of yesterday" must certainly be Anders' volume "Loving Yesterday: Notes on the History of Feeling" ("*Lieben gestern: Notizen zu Geschichte des Fühlens*"), which was originally to have been titled "Loving Today." In this book, which emerged from diary entries from 1948 and 1949, Anders reports on a peculiar encounter. Years after they had been given up as lost, seven "*Totenfässer*," "barrels of the dead" as he called them, arrived at the door of this emigrant's New York attic apartment. Included in the crates were love letters, diaries, school notebooks and other objects that had belonged to his parents and grandparents. Anders submits this material to a cultural critical analysis, the result of which is one of the best books ever to have appeared on the non-simultaneities that shape the life of the emigrant in the United States. Beyond that, it is a clear-sighted commentary of impressive literary quality that attends to the historical nature of emotions.

Günther Anders is a literary critic whose analyses of Kafka's and Döblin's work count among the best of literary criticism. Anders characterizes the work on his Döblin essay as a transla-

---

19 Günther Anders, Besuch im Hades. Auschwitz and Breslau 1966. Nach "Holocaust" 1979, Munich 1979, 203, 206.
20 Günther Anders, Versuch einer Selbstverständigung. LIT (ÖLA 237/04).

Anders in the United States during the 1940s.
Photo: Anders Papers, Literature Archives, Austrian National Library

tion of the "disintegrated language" that is used so exemplarily by Döblin's characters "into philosophical language,"[21] a translation, that is, of a genuinely literary language into the language of philosophy. A short while later, the German language itself would become a solitary, precarious home for the emigrant.[22]

A dual dissociation becomes apparent after 1945. The first is from European existentialism of the pre-war period, which is inextricably bound with Heidegger's work. The second is from post-war academic philosophy, a move in response to that philosophy's thematics as well as its style. His turn away from Heidegger is due to what Anders calls Heidegger's asceticism in relation to man's nature (his corporeality), and in relation to man's social relationships, which for Anders also include a promise of happiness.[23]

In 1930 Anders formulated a response to the question of how a person could compensate for his contingency. The specific possibility inherent in a person is "life itself; more specifically, the fact that the person not only lives, but can have his very own historical life, that he himself is this, his very own life; that this life, despite its state of never being answered and in

---

21 Günther Anders, Einleitung, in: MoW, XXVIII.
22 Cf. Günther Anders, Vita 1945, reproduced in: Klaus Kastberger, Konrad Paul Liessmann, eds., Die Dichter und das Denken. Vienna 2004, 231–236, here 236 (= Profile, vol. 11).
23 Dieter Thomä, Gegen Selbsterhitzung und Naturvergessenheit: Nachwort zur Aktualität des Philosophen Günther Anders, in: Anders, Über Heidegger, 398–433, here 422.

spite of the surfeit of contingent aspects, is still mine and only <u>mine</u>, that it is still <u>I</u>."[24] It is in this way that the person as "deficient being"— described by Anders before Arnold Gehlen as a being that has to develop his own approach to the world— can become a being of freedom, one who can forge his own happiness. The human freedom to choose, as opposed to the animal that is led solely by instinct (e.g. the whale), reaches its ironic apotheosis in Anders' long poem "Mariechen," a "bedtime story for lovers, philosophers and members of other professional groups" dating from 1946. The narrator of this story proclaims a nearly joyful anthropology in his celebration of love and in his accentuation of the corporeality and naturalness of human life. The problem of contingency receives its response in 1946, formulated slightly differently and more simply, in the following lines:

> Really there are very few things
> that are as utterly funny,
> as the fluke, that all of us
> (incl. world, Mariechen, etc.) really are there,
> of all things, each one exactly
> is as himself; and that for each
> this fluke may be so prized.
> It seems that all we are left with
> vis-à-vis this double-fact
> is *humor*: i.e.: the mix
> of bafflement and of joy,
> sense-leaving and affection, nihilism and pleasure.[25]

When viewed together with the rest of Anders' complete works, this "ethics of contingency,"[26] this literary message to fellow humankind, dilutes at least to some extent the dogmatic aspects of Anders' critique of technology as well as his fixation on nuclear apocalypse.

3. Literary Critic Under the Sign of a World in Ruins

In 1946, as Anders, from his new home in exile in New York, began to revise the lecture on Kafka that he gave in 1934 at the Institut d'Études Germaniques in Paris entitled "Theology Without God," he knew perfectly well from his own experience that of which he spoke when he analyzed Kafka's alienation in the world.

What is most captivating about his analysis is that he has found a sociological figure to match Kafka's homeless hero: the emigrant. As is signaled by its new title, "Kafka, pro and contra," Anders' essay is a fundamental critique that deals not only with Kafka's text

---

24 Günther Anders, Die Weltfremdheit des Menschen, LIT (ÖLA 237/04), 31; in Max Scheler's book "Die Stellung des Menschen im Kosmos", Darmstadt 1928, 47, there is the following stipulation: "This type of 'spiritual' being is no longer bound by drives and the environment, but is instead 'environment free' and, as we may want to call it, open to the world. This type of being has 'world.'"

25 Günther Anders, Mariechen: Eine Gutenachtgeschichte für Liebende, Philosophen und Angehörige anderer Berufsgruppen, Munich 1987, 84.

26 Dries: Günther Anders und Hannah Arendt – eine Beziehungsskizze, 114.

but with the attempt to find literature's place in this transition from *people without world* (the characters who populate Döblin's novel *Berlin Alexanderplatz*) to an abominable *world without people*.[27] Just as in his demystification of Heidegger, what Anders attempts in his Kafka essay is not a dismantling of the text's hybridity, but a grounding of it. It is to the detachment in Kafka's literature, which shocks, edifies, entertains, and can bring a reader to tears, that "Kafka's success is due in no less a degree than is Heidegger's."[28] Kafka's unreliability when it comes to the question of "where the indicative ends and the subjunctive begins [...] makes him, in spite of the wealth of his insights, a philosophically and morally unusable author."[29]

In Anders' reading, Kafka finds himself in the same double bind that characterizes Anders' thoughts on the legitimacy of art. Kafka's aesthetic practice subverts the obligation that is inherent in the religious ritual and therefore obligation in a moral codex, a position that Anders describes as "religiosity without religion."[30] At the same time, Kafka's characters wish desperately for the obligations of a value system. Kafka's name and his abbreviation K. are the keys to this paradoxical figure of modernity: Kafka "*is one of his own enemies—the most radical of them.*"[31]

And Anders? His active philosophy is profoundly rhetorical, and his poems and fables demonstrate—with a vehemence that is not always conducive to their aesthetic aims—the antiquated state of our mode of perception considering the imminent threat of total annihilation. "If we don't incorporate an analysis of perception into a general theory of communication (and resistance)," he writes in one of the notes in "Loving Yesterday," "then we will never know anything of the senses except what is superficial, unimportant or nonsensical."[32]

We believe *good* art is identifiable by virtue of its indeterminacy, its inability to be pinned down, its autonomy with respect to ideological demands. Anders invokes this aspect as well: "In Kafka, the affinity between doubt and art is made visible once more in such an exemplary way."[33] It is precisely the formula "'maybe, maybe not' that testifies to the *despairing form of works of art*."[34] This is their ineradicable defect. But this is precisely the source, as Anders frames it elsewhere,[35] of the legitimacy and quality of art. Since it means both nothing and everything, art cannot be instrumentalized in service of something definite and particular. Anders reproaches Kafka for his indecisiveness in political and social questions in order to explain his ambiguous position, which is in marked contrast with assertions of Kafka's extraordinary artistic significance. This is a diagnosis of a double bind set against the backdrop of his own double bind: Günther Anders' decisiveness with regard to political and social questions sometimes compromised the aesthetic qualities of his literary texts. At the

27 In her discussion of Hermann Broch's "Tod des Vergil", Hannah Arendt, whose opinion of the novel was diametrically opposed to that of Anders, called Kafka the author of the "not yet": "It is as though he is writing from a point in time far in the future, as if he could only be at home in a world that does 'not yet' exist." Paul Michael Lützeler, ed., Hannah Arendt, Hermann Broch, Briefwechsel 1946 bis 1951, Frankfurt am Main 1996, 170.
28 Günther Anders, Kafka, pro und contra, in: MoW, 46.
29 Ibid., 82 f.
30 Ibid., 101.
31 Ibid., 105.
32 Anders, Lieben gestern, 58.
33 Anders, Kafka, 111.
34 Ibid., 110.
35 Günther Anders, Die Antiquiertheit des Menschen, vol. 1, Munich 1983, 316.

same time, Anders is a writer of fables, one whose texts, in their best moments, call to mind Kafka's narrative short prose.[36] Only by alternately dressing his thought in literary guise and in philosophical guise, without ever giving an advantage to one or the other, is Günther Anders' criticism able to unfold.

4. Language and Truth

An instance of shadow boxing that is typical of Günther Anders' literary-philosophical logic of argumentation can be found in a largely unpublished bundle of papers from his archive (the published volume *Diaries and Poems* (*Tagebücher und Gedichte*) contained parts of this collection). This takes the form of a conversation with an increasingly silent "B" concerning the scandalous versatility of "G," an author in the most comprehensive sense of the word: poet, art critic and literary critic. He holds forth on questions of music and is a philosopher on top of that. There is one common denominator, "G" contends, that brings all of these various forms of expression into focus. This common denominator is "the truth," but:

> "The purely philosophical statement is sometimes enough to prompt a person to assimilate something into their understanding. But for that person to assimilate this new insight and transform it into a form of truth—this is beyond the powers of discursive philosophical language. This requires something else entirely."[37]

If the relationship between humanity and the world fundamentally changes, then of course there will be consequences for artistic representations of the world. If whatever has been created is too profound for our powers of imagination, then it is too profound for art, too. At the same time, the pressing need to close the gap between doing and representing is itself evidence that an alternative, that is to say artistic, way of approaching the world is needed. Perhaps art really could be the framework to give expression to what Anders saw as the state of things: molding a moral fantasy that could partner philosophical-analytical ability with an expanded sensorium to truly grasp the monstrousness of what we produce and what we do. This conviction additionally contains a biographical dimension. In the unpublished part of the collected papers entitled "Writing Poetry Today," Anders writes that the art of poetry feeds on the desire to completely assimilate that which has occurred. "I believe I need it [the writing of poetry] to memorize that which has happened."[38] He continues:

> "Man's self-destruction, the apocalypse we have made ourselves, the gas ovens: I allow all of these as motifs of horror. I make poetry of them, I tattoo them on myself, memorize them. But why? Because I cannot grasp them [...]. Since all those things that people have done to each other, those things they are doing to each other, and those they will do to each other exceeds the capacity of a single soul to understand, the horror simply cannot be understood. That which I would not otherwise hear, I scream into

---

36   See, for example, the fable "Wer zuletzt brennt," printed in: Kastberger, Liessmann, 285.
37   Günther Anders, Dichten heute. 1948. 15. Exiljahr, Archival typescript, 39 pages, LIT (ÖLA 237/04), 28 f.
38   Ibid., 22.

my very own ears. That is why I write poetry. That is the service poetry provides me. What it tries to provide."[39]

The yearning for rescue from Not-Being appears "in words" in Anders' early work in his essay on Döblin: "Simultaneity as a whole calls out in one moment and with singular justification for rescue in words."[40] Anders continues, writing in reference to *Berlin Alexanderplatz*:

> "This crying out for revelation and salvation in words is not limited to those things that lose themselves in proximity to each other or that guarantee one another no existence. The savior himself requires guarantee in these things; he seeks to make his presence felt among them all, to prove himself through them. For to be forgotten and concealed by just one single thing is, from that thing's perspective, the same as not-being."[41]

What is most significant in the essay on Döblin is that it is not just about saving the "people without world"—the unemployed, racketeers, criminals, etc.—but also about saving the saviors, as Anders increasingly sees himself. Whereas Anders' earlier uses of the terms "savior" and "word" still possess primarily ontological meanings, even implications that reveal metaphysical thinking, his perspective with regard to these terms shifts in the years following the war: the savior is now the survivor. He would like to tattoo horror onto his own skin in the form of lines of poetry and thereby bestow it with presence for himself. And he wants to impress himself upon those things that happened: as an emigrant, as a survivor and as a poet-philosopher on the threshold between Auschwitz and the atom bomb.

The real question for Anders is not whether an active philosophy should be granted an advantage over literature, whether literature, especially poetry, has lost its claim to legitimacy after Auschwitz. The question, instead, is one that asks how writing may be good. Good here means precise, truthful. And if writing is good and truthful, then it may unfurl its effects, it may reach its intended audience. After all, "'they're not so radically different,' G. began, 'these two methods of working. The philosophical and the poetical. They both come down to the same thing.'"[42] The poem, like argumentation in philosophy, must be precise.

And this is where a difference comes into play, namely one between poetry and prose. In his text entitled "On the Difficulties of Philosophical Prose," Anders explains that his poetical writing and the rules imposed on the writing of poetry consistently get in his way as a writer of philosophical prose: "My writing of poetry is exacting revenge on my prose." In contrast to the necessary circuitous paraphrasing of a situation in prose writing, the *translation* of the simultaneous into the successive, poetry seeks out the one most appropriate word that does not analyze the object but instead "evokes [it], calls it over to one or calls it out, as if it were

---

39 Ibid., 23.
40 Günther Anders, Der verwüstete Mensch: Über Welt- und Sprachlosigkeit in Döblins "Berlin Alexanderplatz," in: MoW, 19.
41 Ibid., 20; Taking this as a starting point, we could discuss an aspect that has hardly been featured thus far in research on Anders: Anders' Jewishness. The "salvation in words," the proof of an existence in the name we give to things, is evidence in the anthropology that features in Anders' early thought to an unconscious incorporation of Jewish thought on Anders' part.
42 Anders, Dichten heute, 29.

really being called its own proper name."[43] Only a short period of abstinence from writing poetry, as Anders explains elsewhere in 1950, can effect a "liberation of prose," bringing back its force, quickness, richness and breadth.[44] Whoever is looking for impact and communicability must turn to prose. It is the medium of logical argumentation, it translates the philosophical argument into stories, scenes, dialogues, fables. Anders needs one thing, poetry, as a form of reassuring himself—as proof—that what has happened truly did happen. Among the items in Anders' archive are numerous unpublished poems. Anders needs prose to make an impact and to tell the stories that precede and follow phenomena. This means freeing the phenomena from their apparent *Dasein* and revealing what they truly signify.

> "Raconter philosophement—narrate in a philosophical manner—is the advice Stendahl gave himself in the margin of one of his manuscripts. But since events cannot be shown except through narration, we would do better to note in the margin: 'Do philosophy in a narrative manner.' This maxim does not seem very trustworthy. It smacks of awkward phrasing one might read in a feuilleton. But I am unable to hit upon a more unambiguous formula for the philosophical style that is demanded by the goals we have set for ourselves. Only the text can decide if the feeling of mistrust is justified."[45]

That example of philosophical poetry, the didactic poem masquerading as a bedtime story, as a wonderfully simple text, may provide an ideal literary conclusion to this essay. Philosophers are translators—this Anders-like motto is best expressed in lyrical prose. In the long poem "Mariechen," little Mariechen (big Mariechen is a whale-girl) is told: "Since we philosophers, we who bestow phrases full-time, / always write only after the fact / *those* texts that the other, non-professional beings / thanks to their Dasein very modestly / but precisely pre-composed, / and we are in the best case scenario / nothing but accurate translators."[46]

---

43   Günther Anders, Über die Schwierigkeit philosophischer Prosa. Archival typescript, LIT (ÖLA 237/04, Konvolut Kunst und Literatur).

44   Günther Anders, zu Poetik. Archival typescript, LIT (ÖLA 237/04, Konvolut Kunst u. Literatur. Sprache.).

45   Günther Anders, Aus einem Vorwort zu Tagebuchaufzeichnungen. Archival typescript, LIT (ÖLA 237/04, Konvolut Gelegenheitsphilosophie, Halkyone 19).

46   Anders, Mariechen, 58.

Kerstin Putz

The Letters of Günther Anders: His Correspondence with Hannah Arendt

Totenpost

If letters feature in Günther Anders' literary writings, in his diaries or poems, then the "demons of memory" are never far off.[1] There are letters that evoke "encounters with the dead,"[2] ghostly letters from the dead to the living or even from the dead to the dead. There are messages that reach their recipients much too late or never reach them at all, and letters that get lost over the years while crossing the seas or during the chaos of war. In "Oh, about the Legacy" (*Ach, über das Erbe*), a passage from Anders' novel *The Molussian Catacomb* (*Die molussische Katakombe*), a sailor learns that he does not have much time left to live and so arranges to have letters he has written to his mother delivered to her over the course of several years following his death, thereby keeping the knowledge of his death from her. This "postal system" works so well that the letters continue to be delivered after the sailor's mother has died as well, from "no one to no one."[3] In Anders' didactic book-length poem *Little Mary (Mariechen)*, a single letter has a huge impact on the protagonist: a female whale swimming in the Bering Sea misses a step in evolutionary change simply because a letter is not properly delivered.[4] On the other hand, in Anders' poem "The Immortal Émigré" *(Der unsterbliche Emigrant)* (1940), undelivered letters are the key metaphor for exile and emigration. Due to their unsettled lives and ever-changing addresses, the emigrants do not receive their mail abroad. "Mountains of letters" pile up in the post offices of their former home towns and countries, each letter carrying the same note: address unknown.[5]

In his American journal, Anders describes the unexpected arrival of boxes and barrels full of letters and documents belonging to his parents and relatives at his apartment in New York. Before leaving Europe, his family members had sent them to their future address in the United States. For Anders these memorabilia come as a ghostly greeting from an estranged past. He inspects this *Totenpost*, as he calls it, these "Letters from the Dead" from his deceased family members, including:

---

1   Günther Anders, Die Totenfässer. Elegien (1949/52), typescript, Nachlass Günther Anders, Literature Archives, Austrian National Library, Vienna, LIT (ÖLA 237/04).

2   G.A., Totenpost. Elegien, typescript, LIT (ÖLA 237/04).

3   "So liefen die Nachrichten weiter von niemandem zu niemandem." – G.A., Ach über das Erbe, in: Die molussische Katakombe, 2nd edition, Munich 2012, 168–169. An early version of this story, which was originally written during the 1930s, was published in Austro American Tribune under the title "Die Freiheitspost. (Aus dem utopischen Roman 'Die molussische Katakombe')" in May 1944, Jg. II, Nr. 10, 5. Later, Die Freiheitspost was published in Anders' collection of fables: Der Blick vom Turm. Fabeln. Mit 12 Abbildungen nach Lithographien v. A. Paul Weber, Munich 1968, 77–78.

4   G.A., Mariechen. Eine Gutenachtgeschichte für Liebende, Philosophen und Angehörige anderer Berufsgruppen, Munich 1987, 12–13.

5   G.A., Der unsterbliche Emigrant (1940), Poem, LIT (ÖLA 237/04): "Also türmen sich, / seit Jahren fällig, Adressat verzogen, / Gebirge Post zuhaus im Postamt auf."

"[...] not only their own letters from their youth, love letters and letters exchanged during their engagements to be married, but diaries and correspondence and birth certificates, health certificates, death certificates, and eyeglasses and keys belonging to their long-dead parents, or others belonging to aunts, uncles and grandparents whom they themselves barely even remembered—*Totenpost, Totenpost* [...]."[6]

Furthermore, these letters reveal a bygone tradition of writing. The decline of the art of letter writing is the unfortunate result of fifty years of using the telephone, as Anders later puts it in *The Obsolescence of Human Beings (Die Antiquiertheit des Menschen)*. This decline has been so profound that letters which were written by the average educated person a hundred years ago now seem to us to be masterpieces of communication.[7]

Anders' short literary piece *Anonymous Letters (Anonyme Briefe)* (1967) recommends that writers treat every text or book they write as a letter, i.e. always to address their writing since this is the only way to reach someone and achieve something: "Because objects that don't reveal for whom they are intended, don't reveal what they are intended for either."[8] This is, in short, Anders' concept of a committed style of writing that, when practiced, would enable the writer to reach the public at large instead of an exclusive circle of academic readers.

Anders in his letters

Anders' intention to reach a non-academic public is reflected in his correspondence as well. Many of his letters are means of public discourse and intellectual intervention. Not only did he publish his correspondence with the Hiroshima pilot Claude Eatherly, he also wrote open letters to Klaus Eichmann and President Kennedy.[9] Through his letters, he spoke up for various, often small, local initiatives and projects belonging to the anti-nuclear movement and the peace movement; he sent written greetings to events abroad, signed declarations of support, and forwarded petitions or sent written requests to his contemporaries asking them for their commitment to various causes. Even at an advanced age and in bad health, Anders continued, as Paul van Dijk put it, "to wage his paper war from behind his desk in Vienna."[10]

Overall, the extensive files of Anders' correspondence held in the *Anders Nachlass* at the Literature Archives of the Austrian National Library in Vienna contain letters from over one

---

6   G.A., Lieben gestern. Notizen zur Geschichte des Fühlens, Munich 1986, 33–34, (Italics added). / "[...] nicht etwa nur ihre eigenen Jugend- und Liebes- und Brautbriefe, sondern auch Tagebücher und Korrespondenzen und Geburtsscheine und Gesundheitsatteste und Todesdokumente und Brillen und Schlüssel ihrer längst verstorbenen Eltern, sogar ihrer von ihnen selbst wohl kaum mehr erinnerten Tanten, Onkel und Großeltern – Totenpost, Totenpost [...]."

7   G.A., Die Antiquiertheit des Menschen, Vol. 1: Über die Seele im Zeitalter der zweiten industriellen Revolution, Munich, 1956, 334, (hereafter AM, Vol. 1).

8   "Weil Gegenstände, die nicht verraten, für wen sie da sind, auch nicht verraten, wofür sie gut sein sollen." – G.A., Anonyme Briefe, in: Der Blick vom Turm, 41–42.

9   Off limits für das Gewissen. Der Briefwechsel zwischen dem Hiroshima-Piloten Claude Eatherly und Günther Anders (1959–1961). Mit einem Vorwort von Bertrand Russell und einer Einleitung von Robert Jungk, in: G.A., Hiroshima ist überall, Munich 1982, 191–360. / G.A., Wir Eichmannsöhne. Offener Brief an Klaus Eichmann, Munich 1964. / G.A. to President John F. Kennedy, 13 January 1961, in: G.A., Hiroshima ist überall, 322–330.

10 Paul van Dijk, Anthropology in the Age of Technology: The Philosophical Contribution of Günther Anders, trans. Frans Kooymans, Amsterdam, Atlanta 2000, 17.

Anders portrait from the 1930s.
Photo: Anders Papers, Literature Archives, Austrian
National Library

thousand individuals and institutions as well as hundreds of copies Anders made of his own letters. Particularly interesting is Anders' correspondence with contemporary intellectuals, philosophers, scientists, and writers, including Theodor W. Adorno, Ernst Bloch, Max Born, Hermann Broch, Ernst Cassirer, Alfred Döblin, Hilde Domin, Hans Magnus Enzensberger, Oskar Maria Graf, Jürgen Habermas, Karl Löwith, Georg Lukács, Thomas and Heinrich Mann, Herbert Marcuse, Helmuth Plessner, Friedrich Pollock, Jean-Paul Sartre, Gershom Scholem, Erwin Schrödinger, Albert Schweitzer, Dolf Sternberger, Jacob Taubes, Paul Tillich, Christa Wolf, among others. Anders also stayed in touch with his (few good) friends and acquaintances over the years, such as Hans Jonas and Robert Jungk. This list of Anders' correspondents might call into question the image of Anders as an outsider, a "marginalized intellectual"[11] who had no desire to belong to any school of thought, party, or university. Anders certainly was part of an intellectual network through his correspondence and had numerous intellectual debates with those with whom he exchanged no letters. This included Brecht, for example, who had gotten him a job as a journalist at the *Berliner Börsen-Courier* in the early 1930s and with whom he would later play chess during his Californian exile. They engaged in discussions about Marx, Hegel, writing, and the theory of drama.[12] It was much the same with Walter Benjamin (his second cousin), whom he did not write at all since, as Anders explained, they saw each other regularly during their years in Paris.[13]

11 Enzo Traverso, Auschwitz und Hiroshima: Günther Anders, in: Auschwitz denken. Die Intellektuellen und die Shoah, trans. Helmut Dahmer, Hamburg 2000, 150–180; 153.

12 See G.A., Über Brecht, in: Mensch ohne Welt. Schriften zur Kunst und Literatur, 2nd Edition, Munich 1993, 135–172.

13 See G.A. to Werner Fuld, 9 November 1976, LIT (ÖLA 237/B1492). For Anders' memories of Walter Benjamin during their years in Paris, see: G.A., Brecht konnte mich nicht riechen. Interview mit Fritz J. Raddatz 1985, in: Günther Anders antwortet. Interviews und Erklärungen, ed. Elke Schubert, Berlin 1987, 97–113; 102.

For the most part, Anders' letters reveal a pragmatic writer. He rarely took the time to write detailed letters, nor did he use them to discuss philosophical questions or his own theoretical theses. Exceptions, such as his correspondence with Adorno, Jonas, Jungk, or Lukács, prove the rule. After Auschwitz and Hiroshima, it was not only that aesthetical questions were of secondary importance to Anders, but that there was simply no time for writing letters in a more expansive style—the disappearance of which Anders mourned a little as well. Because of the atrocities that marked the twentieth century, the "fine art" of writing was no longer appropriate. "Infamies keep me going," Anders once wrote in a letter dating from the late 1960s.[14] As demonstrated by the files full of his correspondences, these infamies convinced him from an early age to set aside pure theory and "desert for *praxis*," as he liked to call it.[15]

An Intellectual Couple

Before discussing the correspondence between Anders and Hannah Arendt, I would like to give a brief overview of their years together as an intellectual couple. They first got to know each other in 1925 in a graduate seminar taught by Martin Heidegger at Marburg University. In 1929 they met again at a masked ball in Berlin and married soon after in September 1929. In the years that followed, they lived together in Drewitz, near Berlin, and in Heidelberg, Frankfurt, and in Berlin itself. Their civil marriage certificate lists them both as having doctoral degrees in philosophy. Anders is additionally identified as an "independent scholar," while Arendt was described as momentarily "unemployed."[16] At this time both planned an academic career in Germany, but after Anders' failed attempt to habilitate, the couple turned to freelance work outside of academia to earn money.[17] According to Anders, together they organized a private seminar on Hitler's *Mein Kampf* in 1932 with the aim of convincing the intellectuals among their circle of friends and acquaintances of this book's deadly seriousness.[18]

During their marriage, Anders and Arendt were an intellectual couple investigating numerous subjects and working on a variety of projects together. Hans Jonas, their mutual friend, described this working relationship as "intense yet amicable" while noticing some imbalances as well. In Jonas' opinion, Anders was not quite aware of Arendt's intellectual independence or the fact that "she had outgrown him intellectually."[19] Nevertheless, the couple shared a private library and, for example, both annotated the same copy of Kant's *Critique of Practical Reason*, which is now part of the *Anders Nachlass*. Together they revised Arendt's dissertation, *Love and Saint Augustine*, which was published in 1929 as the ninth and final issue of the "Philosophical Research" series edited by Karl Jaspers.[20] In that same

---

14 G.A. to Walter Methlagl, 4 October 1968, LIT (ÖLA 237/B237).
15 G.A., Die Antiquiertheit des Menschen, Vol. 2: Über die Zerstörung des Lebens im Zeitalter der dritten industriellen Revolution, Munich, 1980, 12. ("in die Praxis desertieren")
16 Document from the Anders Nachlass, LIT (ÖLA 237/04).
17 See Antonia Grunenberg, Hannah Arendt und Martin Heidegger. Geschichte einer Liebe, Munich, Zürich 2006, 137.
18 G.A., Wenn ich verzweifelt bin, was geht's mich an? Interview mit Mathias Greffrath, 1979, in: Günther Anders antwortet, Berlin 1987, 19–53; 32.
19 Hans Jonas, Hannah Arendt: An Intimate Portrait, trans. Brian Fox and Richard Wolin, in: New England Review, Vol. 27, No. 2 (2006): 133–142; 134.
20 See Ludger Lütkehaus, Zur Edition, in: Hannah Arendt, Der Liebesbegriff bei Augustin. Versuch einer philosophischen Interpretation, ed. and with an introduction by Ludger Lütkehaus, Berlin, Vienna 2003, 9.

year, Anders delivered his lecture on anthropology, *Freedom and Experience (Freiheit und Erfahrung)*, at the Kant Society in Frankfurt in front of an audience of well-known figures, including Adorno, Horkheimer, Tillich, Max Wertheimer, and Karl Mannheim. An extended version of this unpublished paper, titled *The Human Being's Estrangement from the World (Die Weltfremdheit des Menschen)*, features a dedication to Arendt.[21]

At that time, Arendt was already involved in her research on Rahel Varnhagen and German Romanticism. She completed most of this work while still living in Germany, but unfortunately it took a long time until the "ill-fated Rahel" ("Unglücks-Rahel"), as Arendt calls the manuscript in her letters to Anders, was published in 1958.[22]

In 1930 Anders and Arendt published two separate reviews of Karl Mannheim's *Ideology and Utopia (Ideologie und Utopie)* (1929), which had been the object of much attention. Their reviews differ greatly from one another in terms of argumentation and in the styles of thinking and writing. Arendt places Mannheim's arguments in a larger context, comparing and relating them to the theses advanced by Jaspers, Heidegger, Max Weber, Lukács, and Augustine, i.e. to those with whom she was familiar from her own extensive readings in philosophy. Anders, however, chooses a different path. Though his own extensive readings of Husserl and Heidegger are equally fundamental for his review, he does not focus on situating Mannheim's theses in a philosophical or sociological tradition, but addresses the concepts of the historical situation, the historical fact, and "false consciousness" ("falsches Bewusstein").[23]

That same year, Arendt and Anders published an essay together on Rainer Maria Rilke's *Duino Elegies* in which they discuss human unworldliness and the "lack of primary affiliation" to the world of things.[24] This detachment from the world or even the state of being shunned by the world distinguishes humans from animals. The animal "belongs to this world, its rhythms, its ebb and flow in such a way that partaking in it means nothing less than being part of it."[25] This primary anthropological theme is discussed in Anders' lecture on *The Human Being's Estrangement from the World* as well, where Anders even quotes from Rilke's *Duino Elegies* in the context of his analysis of the concept of shame.[26] Anders' early anthropology is obviously

---

21 Typescript, LIT (ÖLA 237/04). – "Die Weltfremdheit des Menschen" was translated into French and published in two parts in the French Recherches Philosophiques with the titles "Une interprétation de l'a posteriori" and "Pathologie de la liberté" (see Katharine Wolfe's English translation "The Pathology of Freedom" in this volume). – In a short review of Recherches Philosophiques IV (1934) in Zeitschrift für Sozialforschung, Walter Benjamin describes Anders' "Une interprétation de l'a posteriori" as an example of a currently developing "ontologically and metaphysically defined line of thought in anthropology" ("ontologisch und metaphysisch bestimmte Richtung der Anthropologie"), which focuses—in Anders' case—on the "concept of experience" ("Begriff der Erfahrung"). See Walter Benjamin, Rezension, Recherches philosophiques IV, 1934, in: Zeitschrift für Sozialforschung. Jg. VI. 1937, H. 1, ed. by Max Horkheimer on behalf of the Institute for Social Research, Paris, 173–174.

22 See H.A. to G.A., [July 1941]; H.A. to G.A., 7 August 1941, LIT (ÖLA 237/B1480). / H.A., Rahel Varnhagen: The Life of a Jewess. English Edition 1958; Rahel Varnhagen. Lebensgeschichte einer deutschen Jüdin aus der Romantik. German Edition 1959; Rahel Varnhagen: The Life of a Jewish Woman. American Edition 1974.

23 Anders continued his discussion of Mannheim's arguments in his work as a journalist. In an article for the Berliner Börsen-Courier (Nr. 169, 12 April 1932), entitled "Aufruf zur Humanisierung," Anders mentions the controversy between Mannheim and Ernst Robert Curtius.

24 Hannah Arendt, Günther Anders [Günther Stern], Rilkes "Duineser Elegien," Neue Schweizer Rundschau 23/1930, 855–871. With a note by Günther Anders, again in: Rilkes "Duineser Elegien," ed. Ulrich Fülleborn, Manfred Engel, Vol. 2, Frankfurt am Main 1982, 45–65; 50.

25 Ibid., 60: "Das Tier […] gehört dieser Welt, ihrem Rhythmus, ihren Gezeiten so zu, daß sein Teilhaben an der Welt nichts weniger als Teilsein von ihr besagt."

26 G.A., Die Weltfremdheit des Menschen, typescript, LIT (ÖLA 237/04), 16; 27–28.

linked to his readings of Rilke.[27] Furthermore, Anders' and Arendt's interpretation of Rilke deals with acoustics, with listening in a literal sense and being listened to in a figurative sense, and is, in this respect, to be read along with Anders' studies on the philosophy of music from the same time.

In 1933 Anders left Germany for Paris, and Arendt followed him separately later that same year. By this point, their marriage had increasingly become a partnership of convenience. After years of living separately—Anders had fled to the U.S. in 1936[28]—they finally divorced in 1937, with the necessary documents mailed back and forth between Paris and New York. The English-language version of the divorce papers lists both of them as "citizens of the Reich of Jewish Religion and belonging to the Jewish community."[29] Arendt had already lost her citizenship in 1933 and was stateless until she gained American citizenship in 1951. Anders gained Austrian citizenship in the same year.[30]

The Correspondence (1939–75)

In a letter to Edith Gurian from the late 1960s Hannah Arendt insists: "Don't destroy the letters! Without access to this type of correspondence, one too that is often of a very private nature, there is little hope for future historians' work."[31] This is equally true of the correspondence between Anders and Arendt, which is a valuable historical and personal artifact.[32]

Only Arendt's letters have been preserved from the first period of the correspondence (1939–41). They contain information on the circumstances of German refugees in French exile and specifically the difficulties Arendt faced during her years in France. In the first preserved letter from September 1939, she reports from Paris on Heinrich Blücher's internment in the French detention camp Villemalard. In December 1939, Arendt received the urgently needed affidavits—the declaration of suretyship required to emigrate to the U.S.—from Anders. Arendt communicates her extreme gratitude for receiving these documents, but her euphoria is tempered

---

27   Throughout his writings Anders continually refers to Rilke, e.g. in: Kafka – Pro und Contra: Die Prozess-Unterlagen, in: Mensch ohne Welt, 87–88; AM, Vol. 1, 186; Mariechen, 76. Moreover, the Anders Nachlass contains additional material by Anders on Rilke's poetry and excerpts from Rilke's letters.

28   On 26 May 1936 the French authorities issued Anders with a "Titre d'identité et de voyage" for the purpose of leaving France for the United States. Anders' French identity card is part of the Anders Nachlass, LIT (ÖLA 237/04).

29   See the English-language divorce papers, entitled "IN THE NAME OF THE GERMAN PEOPLE," from the Anders Nachlass, LIT (ÖLA 237/04): "The two parties who are citizens of the Reich of Jewish Religion and belonging to the Jewish community, have been married since September 26, 1929, having been married in the civil courts in Nowawes. No children of this marriage. Since June, 1936, the parties have been living separate and apart. The last marital relations ceased in the summer of 1933." [English in the original] Anders' address at the time was given in the document as New York City, 70 West 69th St.

30   The official citizenship document from the Anders Nachlass dates from 28 December 1951.

31   H.A. to Edith Gurian, 5 May 1969, in: Marie Luise Knott, Veröffentlichte kleine Briefwechsel, in: Arendt Handbuch. Leben – Werk – Wirkung, ed. Wolfgang Heuer, Bernd Heiter, Stefanie Rosenmüller, Stuttgart, Weimar 2011, 177–181; 177. ("Zerstören Sie die Briefe nicht! Ohne solche Korrespondenz, oft auch ganz persönlicher Art, kann kein späterer Historiker arbeiten.")

32   LIT (ÖLA 237/B1480), Briefwechsel Günther Anders – Hannah Arendt. / Correspondence File, Hannah Arendt Papers, Manuscript Division, Library of Congress, Washington D.C., hereafter Arendt Papers. The Hannah Arendt Archive at the Carl von Ossietzky University Oldenburg, Germany, holds a complete copy of the Hannah Arendt Papers.

by new bureaucratic obstacles that delay her and Blücher's departure. In May 1940, she was arrested as an enemy alien in Paris and taken to the French detention camp Gurs.[33] She escaped at the end of June to Montauban in southwestern France, where she was in search of Blücher, whom she finally met again more or less by chance.[34] At that time, Arendt had no passport, no luggage, and was in constant need of money. Again and again, she asks Anders for financial assistance for herself and her husband, but especially for her many friends and acquaintances for whom she expresses significant and warranted concern. She worried most about Walter Benjamin, who took his own life in September 1940 while on the run from authorities. Arendt learned of Benjamin's death soon after, while she was still in the south of France.[35]

In a detailed letter from August 1940, Arendt describes her situation in Montauban, where she and Blücher persevere and await actions by the authorities.[36] Only in the spring of 1941 are they finally able to leave Europe (via Lisbon) by ship for the U.S. Immediately after their arrival in New York in May 1941, Anders received Arendt's good news via telegram: "WE ARE SAFE STAYING 317 WEST 95= / HANNAH."[37] In New York Arendt continued to work toward securing assistance for her friends who were still in Europe. But once the most urgent needs had been addressed, the everyday difficulties of being an émigré in the U.S. become more prominent. Arendt frequently talks about her troubles learning English, though she soon begins to write her letters to Anders in English, "just to have an exercise."[38] Learning foreign languages came much more naturally to her than it did to Anders, and she was soon writing and publishing in English. Anders experienced his being uprooted from his mother tongue as a painful loss, as he describes in his *Language Elegy (Sprachelegie)* (1944): "The best remain silent during these years / and talk only with a faltering voice. No one speaks / his own language. Each stutters each language. / The sentences shrink. In a heartbeat each one has to / understand the other. No dialect / remembers which tongue once shaped it."[39] On the contrary, Arendt states years later in her Sonning Prize acceptance speech that she was never really able to relate to the shared state of homesickness and nostalgia (*Heimweh*) that had been so important for the émigrés, especially for those who had come to the United States.[40]

An important issue for Arendt during the early 1940s as well as an ongoing subject of her correspondence with Anders is the publication of Walter Benjamin's posthumous writings. Benjamin had given her a manuscript version of "On the Concept of History" and Arendt, following instructions in Benjamin's will, gave the manuscript to Adorno and the Institute for Social

33 See Marie Luise Knott's notes on Arendt's essay "Wir Flüchtlinge" (1943), in: Hannah Arendt, Zur Zeit. Politische Essays, ed. and with an afterword by Marie Luise Knott, trans. Eike Geisel, Munich 1989, 188.
34 H.A. to G.A., [10 July 1940], LIT (ÖLA 237/B1480).
35 Detlev Schöttker, Erdmut Wizisla, Hannah Arendt und Walter Benjamin. Konstellationen, Debatten, Vermittlungen, in: Arendt und Benjamin. Texte, Briefe, Dokumente, ed. Detlev Schöttker, Erdmut Wizisla, Frankfurt/M. 2006, 11–44; 35.
36 H.A. to G.A., 4 August 1940, LIT (ÖLA 237/B1480).
37 "SIND GERETTET WOHNEN 317 WEST 95= / HANNAH" – H.A. to G.A., 23 May 1941, LIT (ÖLA 237/B1480).
38 H.A. to G.A., 4 June 1941, LIT (ÖLA 237/B1480).
39 G.A., Sprachelegie (1944), in: Tagebücher und Gedichte. Munich, 1985, 391–394; 392: "Die Besten bleiben stumm in diesen Jahren / und reden nur gestoßen. Niemand spricht / die eigne Sprache. Jeder stammelt jede. / Die Sätze schrumpfen. Jeder muss im Nu / den Anderen verstehen. Keine Mundart / entsinnt sich, welcher Mund sie einst geformt."
40 H.A., Die Sonning-Preis-Rede. Copenhagen 1975, trans. Ursula Ludz, in: Hannah Arendt. Text+Kritik, ed. Heinz Ludwig Arnold, H. 166/167 (2005), 3–12; 4.

Research.[41] The fact that Benjamin's theses weren't published immediately provoked harsh reactions on Arendt's part. Since their time in Frankfurt together and since Anders' failed habilitation project, Arendt and Anders shared a somewhat unfavorable attitude toward Adorno. Anders, moreover, was not terribly impressed by Benjamin's theses, and he was therefore understanding of the Institute's reluctance.[42] This caused strain in Arendt's and Anders' relationship prompting a growing distance between them for the first time. In August 1941, she tells him that no matter what one thinks of Benjamin's writings, she thinks it a matter of loyalty to a dead friend and colleague to publish everything he had intended to publish. She asks Anders to keep his ears open at the Institute and to tell her how the publication of Benjamin's works was proceeding.[43] The tensions among Adorno, Arendt, and Anders concerning Benjamin never disappeared completely. In a letter from 1963, Adorno claims that Anders had once disparagingly referred to Benjamin as a "*Caféhaus*-writer," an allegation that Anders forcefully rejects.[44]

However, the reservations they expressed regarding Adorno would be one of the few similarities between Arendt and Anders that remained constant over the years. Following a fourteen-year interruption in their correspondence, which began in November 1941, Anders writes again in November 1955: "It's sad that you don't want to write about Benj[amin]. Who should do so besides us, if the monopoly isn't be left to Adorno?"[45] Of course, what Anders feared did not come to pass. Arendt published her essay on Benjamin in 1968, and Benjamin is a recurring character in Anders' short prose. Both of them, Arendt and Anders, wrote poems in memory of their mutual friend as well.[46] But for Anders, Benjamin's writings always

---

41 H.A. to G.A., 11 June 1941, LIT (ÖLA 237/B1480).

42 Bertolt Brecht's journal entry from 9 August 1941 suggests this: "Ich lese die letzte Arbeit, die er [Benjamin; K.P.] dem Institut für Sozialforschung eingeschickt hat. Günther Stern gibt sie mir mit der Bemerkung, sie sei dunkel und verworren, ich glaube auch das Wort 'schon' kam darin vor." ("I have read the last piece of work he [Benjamin] sent to the Institute for Social Research. Günther Stern handed it to me, commenting that it was dark and confused, and I believe too that this was prefixed with the word 'quite.'") After a short synopsis of Benjamin's key arguments in "Über den Begriff der Geschichte," Brecht writes: "Kurz, die kleine Arbeit ist klar und entwirrend (trotz aller Metaphorik und Judaismen), und man denkt mit Schrecken daran, wie klein die Anzahl derer ist, die bereit sind, so was wenigstens mißzuverstehen." ("Simply put, the short piece of work is clearly written and clarifying (in spite of its profusion of metaphor and Judaic elements), and one hates to think of how small that group of people is who would be able to even misunderstand something like it.") – Bertolt Brecht, Journale 2. 1941–1955, Werke Vol. 27, Frankfurt/M. 1995, 12.
    Anders told Arendt about the Institute's attitude toward Benjamin's manuscript in an unsaved "letter of doom," as Arendt told Blücher in a letter from 2 August 1941. See: Within Four Walls. The Correspondence between Hannah Arendt and Heinrich Blücher 1936–1968, ed. and with an introduction by Lotte Kohler, trans. from the German by Peter Constantine. New York, San Diego, London 2000, 72.

43 H.A. to G.A., 7 August 1941, LIT (ÖLA 237/B1480).

44 Anders responds to Adorno's reproach from June 1963 in a detailed letter from August 1963 in which he claims that it is "absolutely impossible" that he had called Benjamin a Caféhaus-writer. – G.A. to Theodor W. Adorno, 27 August 1963, LIT (ÖLA 237/B1479).

45 G.A. to H.A., 16 November 1955, LIT (ÖLA 237/B1480): "Dass Du nicht über Benj[amin] schreiben willst, ist traurig. Wer soll denn außer uns, wenn man Adorno nicht das Monopol lassen will?"

46 H.A., Walter Benjamin, in: Men in Dark Times, New York, 1955, 153–206. / H.A.: W.B. [Poem, 1942], in: Elisabeth Young-Bruehl, Hannah Arendt: For the Love of the World, 2nd edition, New Haven 2004, 485. / Arendt's collection of essays "Fragwürdige Traditionsbestände im politischen Denken der Gegenwart" is dedicated to the memory of Walter Benjamin (Frankfurt/M. 1957).
    G.A., Das Vermächtnis [Poem, 1940], in: Aufbau, 6. Jg., Nr. 42, Oct. 18, 1940, 7; also in: Glückloser Engel. Dichtungen zu Walter Benjamin, ed. Edmunt Wizisla, Michael Opitz, Frankfurt/M. 1992, 98. / G.A., Der Defekt, in: Der Blick vom Turm, 90.

had a somewhat enigmatic status, as he once mentions to Arendt: "I've had Benji's Collected Writings at home now for two days and nights […]. I have yet to understand a word. But I'll get there."[47]

Over the years, the correspondents kept each other up to date on their ongoing projects, publications, and interests. Following Anders' return to Europe, twice they met again in Germany, in 1961 and in 1975, during Arendt's extensive travels on the continent. From Arendt's point of view both encounters were rather unfortunate, even a bit unpleasant. She reports on them in her letters to Heinrich Blücher and Mary McCarthy.[48]

Intellectual Affinities?

Besides their private issues and personal animosities over the years, Arendt and Anders shared theoretical interests, which becomes apparent in their correspondence. In the following section, I will discuss two subjects of shared interest: first, their approaches to the dangers of the nuclear age and second, their analyses of the concept of progress.

After reading Anders' essay on the atomic bomb from the first volume of *Die Antiquiertheit des Menschen*, Hannah Arendt writes an unusually euphoric letter, calling it an excellent text and the best piece written on that subject. She highlights Anders' argument that the bomb is neither a simple thing nor a means for conducting so-called "experiments," but something that has transformed the whole globe into a laboratory and which has thereby rendered the difference between experiment and emergency meaningless.[49] Arendt later refers to Anders' assumption that the term "experiment" no longer applies to nuclear experiments in a footnote in *The Human Condition* (1958).[50] In fact, she does not quote Anders in a very affirmative way in the relevant passage of her book, and her views on the nuclear age ultimately differ significantly from his. Arendt herself talks about the nuclear age as something yet to come while Anders claims it is present and absolutely urgent. Moreover, Arendt does not talk about *the* bomb, but about "various types of atom bombs" as "the first instruments of nuclear technology" instead. Although she concedes that these bombs "could destroy all organic life on earth," for her the nuclear age (that is, the age of a nuclear-based technology) lies in the future, or if it exists at this time, it does so only in the "research laboratories of nuclear physicists."[51] According to Arendt,

---

47 "Seit zwei Tagen und Nächten hab ich nun Benjis Gesammelte Schriften im Haus […]. Bis jetzt verstehe ich kein Wort. Wird aber schon." G.A. to H.A., 23 November 1955, Arendt Papers, 009955-009956.

48 H.A. to Heinrich Blücher, 28 May 1961, in: Arendt/Blücher, Within Four Walls, 374. / H.A. to Mary McCarthy, 31 May 1961 and 22 August 1975, in: Between Friends. The Correspondence of Hannah Arendt and Mary McCarthy 1949–1975, ed. and with an introduction by Carol Brightman, New York 1995, 119, 385.

49 See H.A. to G.A., 9 January 1957, LIT (ÖLA 237/B1480). / See Anders, AM, Vol. 1, 258–259: "Die Redensart: 'Angenommen, sie werde eingesetzt', bejaht nämlich implizit eine Grenzziehung, die heute nicht mehr gilt; sie macht nämlich die bis gestern in Experimentalphysik und Technik gültige Unterscheidung zwischen 'Vorbereitung' und 'Anwendung', zwischen 'Probe' und 'Ernstfall'. Das Charakteristische der Bombe besteht aber gerade darin, daß sie diese Unterscheidung auslöscht." ("This way of talking—'Suppose they are used'—implies the drawing of boundaries that simply no longer exist today. This type of talk marks a distinction in experimental physics and engineering between 'preparation' and 'use', between 'test' and 'emergency', that was valid up until yesterday. The entire point of the bomb is that it erases this distinction.")

50 See Hannah Arendt, The Human Condition, Chicago 1958, 150.

51 H.A., The Human Condition, 149–150. / For Arendt's view on the nuclear threat, see her response to the detonation of the first atomic bomb near Los Alamos, New Mexico, on 16 July 1945. In a letter to Heinrich Blücher from

the coming changes in nuclear technology and the effects they might have on our world cannot be predicted from the present point of view. In this respect, the theoretical similarities between Anders and Arendt are hardly overwhelming. This is stated most obviously, too, in a letter sent by Anders in which he describes himself and Arendt in this matter as figures standing "on two shores, none of which can be seen or understood from the other one."[52]

In a letter from 10 September 1941, Arendt responds positively to another text Anders had apparently sent her (but which has not been preserved in the files of their correspondence). This "Draft on Progress" ("Fortschritts-Entwurf") arouses Arendt's interest since she claims to be concerned with similar subjects in her own work. She asks Anders to let her know immediately when the draft has been finalized.[53] The *Anders Nachlass* contains a small typescript entitled *Disposition for The Incompleteness of the Human Being and the Concept of "Progress"* which is most likely the draft to which Arendt referred. In it, Anders sketches a project that would combine his earlier anthropological thesis with an analysis of the concept of progress. Starting from the indeterminacy and incompleteness of human beings that is the condition of their freedom, Anders describes the category of progress as a means to compensate for this anthropological inability to be determined.[54] And this is where progress' success story begins. Progress is, according to Anders, a "magic word" which is overdetermined and universalized until it is no longer simply a technical or moral category, but synonymous with the "inherent character of the world process (*Weltgeschehen*) itself as a process."[55] Anders planned to trace this universalization of progress back to antiquity and through the philosophical tradition from Stirner, Hegel, and Darwin to Nietzsche and Heidegger.

According to Anders' draft, the slow "degeneration" of the category is historically linked to the First World War, which abruptly revealed the "fraud of technology," i.e. the shift from technical progress to "new forms of slavery." This change came as a great shock, the magnitude of which reveals, especially from today's vantage point, how powerful and significant the function of the concept of progress had been as a means of providing security and stabilization. The category of progress cannot ever be eliminated, since, as Anders puts it, "nothing dies as slowly as a category." This is particularly true in the context of capitalism, where progress has only one direction—namely, "better"—but no optimum, no final state. Even if the concept of progress were to dissolve as a "speculative idea of the interpretation of history," it would lose none of its function as a regulative principle that guides our actions and plans, particularly those of collectives.[56]

August 1945 she writes: "Since the atomic devastation I feel even eerier than before. What a dangerous toy in the hands of these idiots who rule the world." – Arendt/Blücher, Within Four Walls, 78.

52   G.A. to H.A., 20 December 1959 [English in the original], Arendt Papers, 009944.

53   H.A. to G.A., 10 September 1941, LIT (ÖLA 237/B1480).

54   G.A., Disposition für Die Unfertigkeit des Menschen und der Begriff "Fortschritt," typescript, 6 pages, LIT (ÖLA 237/04), 3: "Der entscheidende moderne Versuch, mit dem Faktum der Unfertigkeit 'fertig' zu werden, ist in der Kategorie 'Fortschritt' konzentriert. Diese Kategorie ist, wie alle Kategorien, die weltgeschichtliche Mächte wurden, überdeterminiert: sie ist gespeist von Motiven ganz unterschiedlicher Provenienz, die allmählich als Beweisstücke für die Wahrheit der einen Zaubervokabel sich verdichteten." ("The critical modern attempt to 'complete' the Incomplete is focused on the category of 'progress.' This category is, as are all categories that assume world historical importance, overdetermined: it subsists on motives of various provenances that gradually converge as evidence for the validity of this one magic word.")

55   Ibid., 4.

56   Ibid., 5.

Anders' work on the concept of progress is closely linked to his observations and experiences in the United States. In 1941 he writes in the journal he kept in Los Angeles that in the U.S. there is nothing older, nothing more traditional than "good old progress."[57] After 1945 Anders' tone in this context changes radically. After the "collapse of civilization" brought about by the Second World War, after Auschwitz, Hiroshima, and Nagasaki, it has become impossible to assert that any "automatism of progress" continues to exist.[58] The confidence of earlier generations who imagined themselves walking on an "escalator of progress," leading ever upward, is nowadays—as Anders writes in 1946—completely lost.[59] Instead, an apocalyptic feeling has emerged: in the atomic age, the category of progress is replaced by the concept of the "End of Time" (Frist).

The Anders Nachlass contains an extensive collection of notes, fragments, formulated passages, and excerpts entitled Progress and Monism (Fortschritt und Monismus) which is likely the result of the work on the "Draft on Progress" Anders had begun but never completed. As is made clear in the title Progress and Monism, the belief in progress is monistic, it assumes that progress is the one and only principle of the world process, and of history. In a paragraph entitled "Progress as a 'Permanent Revolution' of the Bourgeoisie" (Progress als "permanente Revolution" des Bürgertums), Anders describes how the concept of progress was separated from the idea of an attainable goal and became something permanent and infinite, an "eternal progression" with a direction, but without an aim.

"The perpetuation of history as such is nothing more than the perpetuation of a particular historical situation, namely that of cap[italism], which has no desire to reach its end. It stabilizes itself as movement to prevent movement toward true stabilization. It adorns itself with the curve of the asymptote, because it is only ever here inasmuch as it does not arrive. Arrive, that is, at the reconciliation of the contradictions it itself created."[60]

These deliberations, and Progress and Monism in general, are preliminary work (written in American exile) for Anders' later primary work Die Antiquiertheit des Menschen, published in 1956. Anders argues therein that the concept of progress is making a restorative comeback despite the hiatus of 1945. Society at present tends to characterize any criticism of the industrial production and sale of goods as sabotage of progress and therefore labels it as "reactionary."[61]

In view of the catastrophes of the twentieth century, Hannah Arendt is also skeptical about the "superstition of progress" (Fortschrittsaberglaube), as she calls it. But at the same time, a "radical optimism" seems equally questionable to her. Arendt argues in 1946 that both an

---

57 G.A., Tagebücher und Gedichte, Munich 1985, 15. [English in the original. Date: 26 March 1941]
58 Ibid., 53.
59 Ibid., 46.
60 G.A., Fortschritt und Monismus, LIT (ÖLA 237/04), manuscript, typescript, German, Engl., French, approx. 60 pages. / "Die Verewigung der Geschichte als solcher ist nichts anderes als die Verewigung einer ganz bestimmten geschichtlichen Situation: nämlich derjenigen des Kap. [Kapitalismus], der an seinem Ende nicht ankommen will. Er stabilisiert sich als Bewegung, um die Bewegung zu einer wahren Stabilisierung zu vermeiden. Er schmückt sich mit den kurven des Asymptotischen, weil er da ist, solange er nicht ankommt. Ankommt nämlich bei der Versöhnung der durch ihn selbst geschaffenen Widersprüche."
61 G.A., AM, Vol. 1, 4.

exaggerated optimism and a "radical pessimism" originate in old, popular myths: the "myth of progress" and the "myth of decline." Since even the sciences are receptive to these myths, she strongly recommends leaving the "playground of mythology."[62] Whereas Anders practices a radical non-optimism, given the recent technological developments, and wants us to leave the comfort of optimism, Arendt thinks of contemporary technological and scientific questions first and foremost as political ones, open to discussion.[63]

Anders' and Arendt's correspondence offers new perspectives on those subjects that interested the two philosophers and theorists. On the whole, their intellectual differences outweigh their commonalities, but nevertheless they have one important thing in common, an aspiration for intellectual independence, as Anders points out in one of his letters: "But we probably don't agree on anything really, except that one should not ever devote oneself completely to someone else. And that's no small thing."[64]

---

62 See H.A., The Ivory Tower of Common Sense [Review of John Dewey's Problems of Men], in: The Nation, Oct. 19, 1946. / In her preface to "The Origins of Totalitarianism" Arendt writes in a similar tone: "This book has been written against a background of both reckless optimism and reckless despair. It holds that Progress and Doom are two sides of the same medal; that both are articles of superstition, not of faith." – H.A., The Origins of Totalitarianism, Cleveland 1958, vii.

63 See Stefano Velotti, Günther Anders: Weltbilder, "Modes of Enticement," and the Question of Praxis, Humana. Mente. Journal of Philosophical Studies, Vol. 18, 2011, 163–180; 171.

64 "Aber d'accord sind wir vermutlich über nichts, außer dass man sich niemandem verschreiben darf. Und das wäre ja nicht wenig." – G.A. to H.A., 23 November 1955, Arendt Papers, 009955-009956.

Anders—In His Own Words

Günther (Stern) Anders

The Pathology of Freedom:
An Essay on Non-Identification

Translated by Katharine Wolfe*

A Note on the Translation

In 1930, still working under his given name of Stern, Anders gave a presentation of his developing 'negative anthropology' before the Kant society of Frankfurt and Hamburg entitled 'Die Weltfremdheit des Menschen' ('The Human Being's Estrangement from the World'). This lecture, included in Anders' Nachlass housed in the Literature Archives of the National Library in Vienna, was the basis for the first French translation of Anders' work, by Emmanuel Levinas, published in Recherches Philosophiques IV (1934–35) under the title 'Une interpretation de l'a posteriori' ('An interpretation of the A Posteriori'). Levinas translated the first 24 pages of the manuscript. The essay which appears here–first published in Volume VI of Recherches Philosophiques (1936–37), and translated by P.-A. Stéphanopoli under the title 'Pathologie de la Liberté' ('The Pathology of Freedom')–shares some content with passages from 'Die Weltfremdheit des Menschen' but does not have a clear predecessor in this text.

Incomplete and inaccurate citations in the French suggest that the piece Stéphanopoli worked with remained very rough. Here, citations have been corrected and completed for readability, with reference to English-language editions of sources where available, and hopefully without too great a harm done to the feel of the text. German passages and terms preserved in the French have been carried over into the English. All endnotes are my own. Anders's original footnotes have been incorporated into the body of the text, in parentheses {} and introduced with 'Note'. Although any shortcomings are my own, I wish to thank both Anne O'Byrne and Marcus Michelsen for their assistance in revising and improving early drafts of this translation.

****

An analysis of the situation of man in the world has revealed to us, in broad strokes, the following conclusions [see Stern 1934–35: 65]:[1] In contrast to the animal that instinctively knows [*connaît*] the material world belonging to it and necessary for it—like the bird migration south, and the wasp her prey—man does not foresee his world. He has but one *formal a*

*   Katharine Wolfe translated Anders' "Pathologie de la liberté" from French for *Deleuze Studies* (2009). She would like to thank Gerhard Oberschlick, who holds the rights for the Anders *Nachlass* Papers deposited at the *Literaturarchiv* of the Austrian National Library, for his kindness in granting permission to reprint this essay.

priori. He is not cut out for any material world, cannot anticipate it in its determination, and instead must learn to know it [*connaître*] 'after the fact',[2] *a posteriori*; he needs *experience*. His relation with a factual determination of the world is relatively weak, and he is in the awaiting of the possible and the indeterminate [*le quelconque*].[3] Likewise, no world is in fact imposed on him (as, for example, on every animal a specific milieu), and instead he transforms the world and builds over it according to a thousand historical variants and in a way as a super-structure; sometimes as a 'second world', sometimes as another. For, to put it paradoxically, *artificiality is the nature of man and his essence is instability.* The practical constructions of man and his theoretical faculties of representation testify equally to his *abstraction*. He can and must disregard the fact that the world is such as it is for he is himself an 'abstract' being; not only part of the world (it is this aspect that materialism treats) but also 'excluded' from it, 'not of this world'. *Abstraction*—thus meaning freedom vis-à-vis the world, the fact of being cut out for generality and the indeterminate, the retreat from the world, and the practice and the transformation of this world—is the fundamental anthropological category, which shows the metaphysical condition of man as well as his λόγος, his productivity, his interiority, his free will, and his historicity.

Man proves his freedom vis-à-vis the world with all his acts, but in none so expressly as in the act of retreating within himself. For by this act he now takes in hand the destiny of his rupture with the world, he intensifies it until a gateway to the world is made, and he offsets the world by himself. What will follow proceeds from this self-experience and from the adven-tures of the 'unhappy consciousness', as Hegel calls it. This will be reduced in the first part to a description simply of the *nihilist*—of the man who, because sometimes free and sometimes not, sometimes of this world and sometimes 'not of this world', loses the possibility of self-identification. This failure of identification will be brought to light through an analysis of the nihilist *states of the soul*. In the second part, an antithesis will be opposed to the picture of the nihilist, that of the historical man. In conclusion, in place of a synthesis, the problematic will be put in question as such, and we will attempt to determine if the question, relative to philosophical anthropology, of knowing what man in general could be is justified according to this formula.

I. Thesis: Picture of the Nihilist

1. The shock of the contingent: 'That I am precisely myself'.
   The identification of the 'I' and its failure.

It is not necessary for man to accomplish a deliberate act of 'self-positing' or 'self-determina-tion' (expressions that constantly recur in transcendental philosophy, particularly in Fichte) in order to secure the guarantee and the coronation of his freedom.[4] Man's retreat within him-self reveals the ability to disregard the world and is already sufficient proof of freedom. But the expressions persist with all their excessive pretension. And they conceal the ensemble of dif-ficulties and antinomies that lead to this free act of retreat into oneself: *i.e., the paradoxical fact that only if man discovers himself freely, by an act emanating freely from him, then he discovers himself precisely as non-free, and as non-self-determined.* The character of the 'non-positing by oneself' has a double aspect. On the one hand, the man who finds himself in the state of freedom discovers himself as 'existing there beforehand', as 'delivered' and 'condemned' to himself, as non-'self-constituted', as a real, irrevocable presupposition of himself, as a part of the world, as an *a priori* of oneself defying all subsequent freedom; as all that which the term '*Amor fati*' attempts to rise above. On the other hand, and this is in close correlation with the previous point, this irrevocable presupposition appears qualitatively as something absolutely indeterminate. Man experiences himself as *contingent* [Troeltsch 1951: 87–9], as indeterminate, as 'me precisely' (such as he has not chosen), as one who is precisely as he is (although he could be entirely different), as coming from an origin to which he does not answer and with which he nevertheless has to be identified; as precisely 'here' and as 'now'. This deepening paradox of freedom and contingency's reciprocal belonging, this paradox that is an imposture, freedom's fatal gift, is elucidated in the following way.

To be free, this means: to be strange [*étranger*],[5] to be bound to nothing specific, to be cut out for nothing specific, to be within the horizon of the indeterminate and in an attitude such that the indeterminate can *also* be encountered amongst other indeterminates. In the indeterminate, which I am able to find thanks to my freedom, it is also my own self that I encounter; by the same token, for as much as it is of the world it is strange to itself. Encountered as contingent, the self is, so to speak, the victim of its own liberty. The term 'contingent' must consequently designate these two characteristics: the self's 'non-constitution of itself by itself' and its 'existence precisely such as it is' [*telle et ainsi*].[6] This holds for all that will follow. {Note: Hegel has presented a dialectic that we have totally neglected; it also relates to the insistence of the *I* on its own formalisation. The expression 'I' designates something precise, stripped of all contingent reality; but it does not only designate only the self. The expression is misleading, for everyone can say 'I', and the 'I' is everyone; thus, in existence there is moreover the general. If we put the Hegelian antinomy together with our own, it can be said that the self searches in vain to take place between its contingencies, the attributes that are accidental for it (but that always belong to it), and the form *I* in general [*Ichheit*] (that is not its alone). A painful position.}

2. Formulation of the shock of the contingent; falsification thereof.

'Why', demands Schopenhauer in his *Tagebüchern*, 'is the now precisely now?' [*sic*] [Schopenhauer 1969: 279].[7] This type of question is characteristic of the shock of the contingent. In so far as Schopenhauer does not intend to answer it, the question is nothing other than a formulation of this shock.

Nonetheless, the translation of the shock ('that I am precisely myself') into an interrogative proposition—and it is only under this form that the problem of contingency appears in the history of philosophy—seems to us to emanate already from a theoretical point of view, and appears falsified. The real shock can be formulated only in a subordinate anacoluthon; it is much too fundamental and much too absurd for one to be able to answer it. For alone susceptible to answers are the questions that arise as formulations of the lacunae that a context, unquestionable in itself, may comprise. And in the case of the shock of the contingent this context and its non-problematic state are precisely shaken. Even more illegitimate than to translate the shock into an interrogative statement would be to transform it into a judgement—to return it, for example, to the proposition 'I am not myself', the like of which may be encountered in numerous formulas imitating Hegel. All judgement, even dialectical judgement, observes [*constate*].[8] But the observation [*constatation*] at the base of the shock is precisely this one: that however unhappily, I am nevertheless myself. Translation: 'I am myself.'

Without fail, judgement also knows the distinction between Subject and Predicate as such a rupture. But although it is possible to transform or to exchange the predicate, this cut presupposes the identity of the subject with itself. It is precisely this identity that will be shaken in the subordinate. For what shocks in the shock of the contingent is not even primarily the fact 'that I am thus or not', but precisely the fact that 'myself, I am myself'. The intention to formulate this state of affairs by a dialectical formula runs up against the fact that in dialectical logic 'is' almost always means 'becomes', the transformation of one determination into another by the intermediary of a phase of transition ambiguous in itself. There can be no question of it in our case. What is there only a more or less ambiguous phase of transition becomes the theme of our research.

3. An extension of the matter of contingency.

The contingency that the *I* discovers within itself must not decrease when it enters into relation with the world. Although by this route the *I* loses itself in the world most of the time, to such an extent that the internal division of this free and contingent *I* is only a neutralised element of consciousness, it can happen, conversely, that the relation with the world and the encounter with anything whatsoever can hold the 'being-precisely-me' [Gerade-ichsein] in suspense, further still than before and in a continuous way. Astonishment [*étonnement*][9] before the contingent—formulated initially in the proposition 'that I am precisely myself'—now discovers in every thing and in every place an occasion to show itself and a source of nourishment, and is expressed thus: 'that I am neither this one here nor that one there, but precisely myself'. {Note: The many forms of Pantheism that convey fraternisation and identification with the All are revealed on more in-depth examination as no more than opportunist dissimulations and a deficiency of self-identification. See the following implications of contingency and of Pantheism in Hölderin's *Empedocles*.} This possibility of being everything thus signifies neither the unity nor the affinity of the *I* with man and with world, but, conversely, its perfect strangeness: *it can be all, because it is as strange and as contingent to itself as to any other part of the world.* Each contingent thing that I am not increases once more the weight of the fact of being that which I am precisely. The *I* and the world complement each other, reciprocally rising up in their fortuitousness. If the *I*, itself contingent, seizes the occasion of the world to confirm its own contingency once more, that of the world will be likewise made more radical. From now on the accident of self-identity and the uselessness of 'self-identification' will be attributed to each fragment of the world as such, that is, outside of human contingency: the one who is astonished now pronounces 'that this, which is here, is precisely here and nothing

148

else'. Likewise in this new phase, nothing contingent, an accident, will be observed [*constat-era*] starting from something non-contingent, a substrate; astonishment will still remain in a way within the field of the validity of the principle of contradiction, with the pathology of this astonishment characterised precisely by constantly breaking such frameworks. And what this boils down to is that any *Hoc* and *Illud* is really itself. {Note: Thus formulated, this paralysis of things and this nihilist stage of freedom appears completely contrived. Nevertheless, we are acquainted [*connâit*] with it in pictorial art. The majority of still-life paintings make it their theme. For in these paintings, man not only depicts the thing that has lost its relations with others and has become strange to them—as if it were not 'his' thing, the thing that is no longer either man's neighbour or handled by him, and which, isolated in a space without atmosphere, is simply there (Chardin)—but also the thing as contingent, as if it were blameworthy in its own mode of existence, and which, fixed now in the painting, can no longer escape from the shame of its contingent existence (for example, the chairs and the shoes in the first Van Gogh). It is not by accident that this ridicule and strangeness can be represented by art. For isolation is not only characteristic of strangeness, but is also an important condition of the beautiful (cf., for example, the function of the frame). Painting that fixes the aspect of a man or a thing in a picture seems as it were to repeat the act by which each thing is already condemned to itself.}

Hölderlin, in his first outlines for Empedocles, described contingency and what is unbear-able in it in the following way: Empedocles would be unsatisfied, inconstant, suffering simply because (these relations) would be *particular* relations [*sic*].[10] Each determined relation is thus for him the loss of all the others; each being-itself the loss of all the beings whose form it could take.

But Empedocles' contingency is not the most radical. Empedocles searches and finds deliver-ance anew from his 'Being-precisely-this', the pantheistic salvation: total being, to which he entrusts himself while leaping in the crater and in which his personal being, the being that he is precisely, is sublimated, remains for him the non-contingent, the last absolute. It is certainly understandable that one reserves such a salvation, a non-contingent residue. But this goes against the nihilist's classical principles. For the radical nihilist, in his fury at contingency, renounces not only the unique, the particular, and the indeterminate, not only the being that he is personally, but the being of the existent itself, which falls now under the curse of indeter-minate contingency, as if it were any existence whatsoever. 'That there exists a world in gen-eral', 'that there exists a "there is something"', 'that I am quite simply', 'that there is something in general which I am'; such are the formulas that the nihilist employs.

In truth, the henceforth unlimited astonishment that is expressed in these expressions and the shaking of being's simple existence have their deepest foundation in this state of things: that man at bottom is not cut out for any mode of existence whatsoever, but for himself, in so far as he is also of the world. He reaches a pathological extreme in so far as he remains within theory alone, in so far as he does not realise his freedom in practice, in the constitu-tion of *his* world. {Note: This goes for all the forms of freedom that are here discussed. They all belong to the domain of reason, described by Kant, that deceives itself and that, in place of being understandable as praxis, in place of transforming itself into practical reason, remains theoretical, and so moving and tragic that it is possible for the antinomies and pathological forms of freedom born henceforth to arise. These antinomies, insoluble within the framework of theoretical reason, will be resolved by practical reason; further still, they will no longer be posed.}

4. Digression on the general validity of the statements concerning philosophical anthropology.

These first formulations of the non-identification of man with himself are exaggerations. But they are, if it will be allowed, *philosophical exaggerations*. The principle indicated is at the root of the facts, but, taken as such, it appears more radical than reality and seems pathological. If man dwelled perpetually on the impossibility of self-identification, there would remain for him no other solution [*issue*],[11] to put it bluntly, than suicide—the only one the Stoics perceived; no other means to abolish what one is in the state of non-freedom, to cancel contingency. However, what we are calling 'philosophical exaggeration' is not falsification; if consciousness of contingency is, admittedly, almost always less precise and more illusory than the formulas claimed to express it, these formulas are nevertheless born of the nihilist life itself, and must be once again, as it were, there transposed. They are thus not only statements concerning the life that unfolds in the paradoxical, but documents emanating from this life itself. The exaggeration stems from what these statements in principle only express in situations of exception, of which, moreover, certain formulations complete and specify actual [*effectifs*] states, and lead them only then to their actual truth [*effective*]. What is 'exaggerated', that is to say, pushed to an extreme of acuity and to a bare truth, is in the first place the situation of contingency itself, and in the second place only the statement of which it is the object. The formulations are thus not only expressions of this existence but they 'inform' it, and in such a way that they *become* real.

Although we take them to be rare, situations of non-identification are probably not. They are only rarely expressed and rarely communicated because their formulas are not the starting point of anything and because they come from a socially non-existent point of view (for they are neither questions nor answers; they reveal only astonishment). Even if it will be admitted that such situations are extremely rare, this will say nothing against their philosophical value or against their utility in philosophical anthropology. It should be noted, moreover, that philosophy preserves a certain antipathy towards treating the infrequent philosophically, be it due to the identification of the general and the essential, fatal in many respects to Western philosophy, or because the verifiable in general is accepted as criteria of the scientific. It is very characteristic of this state of things that Jaspers dealt with his theory of 'limit situations', which are certainly rare, in a 'psychology of conceptions of the world'. It was not quite obvious in his eyes—still wholly confused by a naturalist conception of science—that he was philosophising in treating despair, death, ecstasy, etc. . . . . It is necessary to uphold, on the contrary, that the rarest human situations and the least familiar human types can play a part in an interpretation which would aim at the general on the condition of considering and interpreting the very fact of their rarity. To return to our case, we can say that an extremely precise state of shock of the contingent is rare, because, in the first place, the duplicity of the *I* is not experienced in practice—the man who discovers himself as already existing can really *make* something of himself—and because, in the second place, the mortal shock is resolved into attitudes that already constitute a *modus vivendi*, attitudes that conceal their character of contingency. The study that is attempted here can thus only have for its theme a subject whose life continues, and thus of such compromise attitudes. {Note: What goes for these exceptional human situations goes for all the phenomena and human types that must be explored in philosophical anthropology, this being something that must not remain perfectly empty out of consideration for the concept of validity in general. Such an account, which seems directed against scientific 'rigor', and just as easily justifies precisely those who depend on the fixation of general traits, that, more often than not, must admit of statements that are valid in general, does not sufficiently question the philosophical significance of the term 'generality', and does not hesitate to take 'generality' for a purely logical category that could be indifferently applied to all classes of objects. These statements are false. For the general plays different roles in different places (different in the domain of the animal, for example, than in that of man); it becomes in each case significant only in relation to individuation and specification, in such a way that, consequently, these general statements have for each class of objects a different essentiality and dignity. *Man is general in a very specific [spécial] way*; he is not realised according to a single form foreseen in principle and valid in general, but, as daily life and history indicate, according to many different types. Man is in plural 'men' in an entirely different way than the animal is in plural 'animals'. In the latter case the plural signifies the generality of the specific [spécial]; in the former, the set of the multiple specifications of the general. Such a plural represents much more than just empirical variants of an *a priori* 'humanity' in itself. It is the fact of the variation, and not the constancy of the variable, that defines the specifically human in philosophical anthropology. Therein, it is true, something of the general is likewise still expressed. To what extent is a general determination valid?

The fact of not being fixed on any *a priori* material world, of not being settled on any world, of not having any foreseen determination, thus of being *indeterminate*, defines man essentially (as we have shown elsewhere, *Recherches philosophiques*, IV).

It is thus only to the point of specific indetermination that the general determinability of man is possible. What comes from this indetermination, what man makes of it, can no longer be determined from the point of view of the general if one does not want to affirm and deny indetermination simultaneously. The case of the nihilist who perpetuates the instability and the indetermination of his role, who does not decide in favour of any determination and who ceaselessly confuses the indicative 'can' with the conditional 'could', and who does not want anything other than to find himself in his most formal *I*, is a special case. We will not hesitate in what follows to introduce a different type of man, equally 'held up' to philosophical anthropology.

We are aware of thus making ourselves advocates of the concept of the type, employed and rejected in an equally vague way. The criticism addressed to this concept, namely, that it does not have the univocal structure of γένος, should be handed over to another court. The famous 'accusation of the good Lord' with which the biologist set an end to the ideas of his colleague, the mathematician, is also applicable here. If the essential is not essential through its generality, the question of knowing if a thing will be general or specific [*spécial*] could be rejected as non-philosophic. Undoubtedly, the philosophical enterprise, accustomed to an average generality, becomes unstable in renouncing its claim to the general; it does not know to just what specific [*spécial*] and to just what concrete it can and must advance. When it deepens into the specific [*spécial*], an external limit of its competence is not prescribed in advance. Instead, as in historical research, the thing that one discovers and the documents by which one discovers it are mutually conditioned and corrected; it is the result of this working together, which decides the degree of specification [*spécialisation*] and this decides the result.[12]}

5. Shame as the reality of the consciousness of the contingent, and as the classical form of its concealment.

{Note added by Stéphanopoli: The states of the soul to be treated further, and encompassed in the German term 'Scham', are exhausted neither by what we call 'shame' nor 'modesty' considered independently of one another. Sometimes expressed as shame and sometimes as modesty, it is a matter of shame of being such as one is, of one's own origin, and thus of something pre-existing which serves as the foundation of these expressions, and of others as well, to which a nuanced analysis might appeal. (It is thus a matter of an affective state inherent to an existence, not to an action. Shame of the act is remorse. Shame of being diversifies up to the point of regret and sometimes reaches shame of the Act. The 'shame' in question goes thus from regret of the Act from which I arose, and which is not mine, to modesty in unveiling my self, which is not as I would have liked.)}

Thus we return to contingency.

The state of shock of the contingent, as an attitude within life, and stripped to the fullest extent possible of all shocking character, is called *shame*. Shame is not originally shame of having done this or that, even though this form of shame already signifies that I do not identify myself with something that emanates from me, my action, and that nevertheless I must, that is, by constraint, identify with it. The fact of being capable of this special moral shame itself already requires that I am at the same time identical and non-identical with myself as a formal condition; *that I can not get out of my skin, even though I can conceive of it as such*, which I meet in the freedom of the experience of myself—but as non-free. Shame is not born of this incongruity; this incongruity is itself already shame. In shame the self wants to free itself, in so far as it feels definitely and irrevocably delivered to itself, but where it escapes it remains in a deadlock; it remains at the mercy of the irrevocable, and thus of itself.

Nevertheless, man makes in this a discovery: precisely whilst he experiences himself as not-self-made, he has a presentment for the first time that he comes from something that is not him, he has a presentment for the first time of the *past*; not, however, of what we are accustomed to calling the 'past', not our own, familiar, and historical past, but precisely the completely strange, irrevocable, and transcendent past; that of the *origin*. Man has a presentment of the world from which he comes but to which he no longer belongs as himself. *Thus shame is above all shame of the origin.* We defer to the first biblical examples of shame: to the coin-

152

cidence of shame and the fall, and to the example of the sons of Noah who, 'the face turned away from shame' [sic],[13] covered the nudity of their father. {Note: In the case of historical man, *Scheu* (*veneratio respectus*), that is, timid respect, is the piety that replaces shame. It is the circumspect approach of one's own past and of the one that precedes it, which is undoubtedly further off, but which is no longer beyond.}

Although the origin arises as what one *is not* as free, and what one could not elect by a free choice, the category of the origin is a characteristic category of human existence. The animal has not accomplished the definitive leap from the origin [*Sprung aus dem Ursprung*] into freedom. It remains constantly bound to the reality from which it comes and confused with it in such a way that the origin can no more be considered as anterior reality than the animal can be considered *qua individuum*.

For this being only, separated from the reality from which he comes, and for whom it *is not* there for him alone, this reality is something unique; it is the *origin* and as such it is to some extent endowed with a transcendence that presents itself under the aspect of anteriority [*Transzendenz nach rückwärts*]. In man alone, the liaison with that from which one comes can be maintained.

What starts as shame [*Schande*] ends as honour:[14] the one who is ashamed undoubtedly returns to himself. The power to not remain in the grips of the world, with its heritage of being-precisely-oneself and being-also-of-the-world, and the power to refer yet again to oneself, testifies already to the double condition of man: although he is something other than himself, he is nevertheless himself. The one who is in the state of shame undoubtedly flees, but only towards himself. He would like through shame to retreat underground, but he only retreats into himself up to the point where he forgets, proud of the power to escape (in himself), the motive that he had for fleeing (from not being himself). *Then the one who is in the state of shame prides himself on his power of concealment.* He sublimates and falsifies his genuine motive, which has been presented as the scandal of shame in the failure of identification. *He now makes the misery of shame a virtue.* In the concealing, he rehabilitates the concealed under the aspect of the secret, or alternatively holds it in reserve as his most intimate and deliberate self, and as what belongs to the self expressly and belongs only to the self. In concealing, he appropriates what he must conceal, what is of the world, what is 'common' in the world, and what there is in 'common' with the world, in such a way that it now becomes 'private' and one's 'own'. The weariness of being-precisely-myself and the original motives of concealment are now not only stifled and disowned but are also the occasion of a strengthening of oneself and of a positive pride. The man who has so transformed shame is no longer engaged in this world, it is no longer offered to him. And he denies afterwards, while abstaining from the world through callousness and through purity, the fact of having come into the world through contingency and the imposture of 'worldliness'.[15]

Precisely because of this moral *happy ending*, shame is the most typical symptom. In it, since life continues, the antinomy is transformed into a *modus vivendi*. Among many other equally instructive symptoms the most important is *self-disgust* because it presupposes the habituation of the *I* to itself, which is fulfilled in the course of life, and thus its *identification* 'despite

153

itself'. Self-disgust is the occasional protest against this automatic habituation of the *I* 'precisely to itself'. At the moment when disgust occurs, life takes on, as it were, the function of an external milieu in which the *I* is misled in perpetuity. In self-disgust, one is not strange to oneself and astonished, as in the shock of the contingent but, on the contrary, is *too* familiar to oneself. Yet this self-habituation proves next to nothing against contingency. 'Why', asks the I in disgust, 'is this self precisely so familiar to me?' 'Why does all this concern me?' And it returns so-called 'normal' self-identity to the simple habituation of the parts of the self to each other.

The thousand forms of hypocrisy, of disguise, and of comedy positively exemplify the negative proof of shame and disgust: the instability of man in relation to himself, his vagueness. The self succeeds only provisionally at abandoning its precise existence as such and thus at taking the form of another and making itself, as it were, the occasion and the matter of multiple personifications. The provisional is itself conclusive: among all the species, man is the one who has the least character.

6. The future perfect; the spirit of escape [fugue];[16] man in the subjunctive.

In shame, man discovers himself as delivered to himself, as a being that was already there before the act of self-experience. The imperfect 'I was there' is in a sense already a disavowal of my self as free [*mon moi en tant que je libre*]; even more so is the past perfect, as far back as one can go. For the past perfect announces that 'what had been there, that was not me'.

This dubious freedom to proceed as far as the past perfect, and to act as if one reached what is underneath the self, has a parallel in man's possibility of reaching the future perfect. This possibility is equally the sign of his freedom and his non-freedom; it also leads to the failure of self-identification.

For a start, the simple future is the most common symptom of human freedom. It is no more than a cliché that the future is the dimension of indeterminacy, the dimension within which I can act. It is no surprise that philosophies that spring from the Kantian theory of freedom, from Hegel's to Heidegger's, are philosophies of time.

But in so far as man does not realise this freedom in the practical—in so far as he uses the dimension of the future to override his contingent 'being-precisely-now' [gerade-jetzt-Sein], as he reserves all the energy required by the demands of the hour, as he spends it in order to realise this dimension as such and is committed more and more, hands tied, to the positive direction of time, *ad infinitum*—*he compromises his freedom*: for the more he proceeds, abandoning his ties, in the direction of the future that this freedom makes him glimpse, the more he is led astray in the domain of the indeterminate [*l'indéterminé*]. The future thus prolonged is qualitatively transformed, it is dialectically reversed, and all of a sudden it is no longer the future that is man's own. This is mislaid in something that is no longer available to him. To this 'time' not even the specific direction of time, its forward sense, applies; it is reduced to something that will no longer be of the future, to an αἰών irrelevant to the self. Man can surely still think and indicate the existence of this αἰών, but in a sterile way, without comprehending or realising it; it is too far beyond the horizon of life that is close and one's own.

The 'I will be' is henceforth changed into a 'what will be, I will not be'. The positive expression of this formula is the future perfect: 'I will have been'.[17]

That man can declare 'I will have been' and that he can outlive himself in thought constitutes an astonishing act of freedom and of self-abstraction. In anticipating memory, he returns to himself as if he were not imprisoned in the framework of his present life, as if he were able to live his life in advance, to be transported beyond it, and to preserve its memory; a memory to which he is nevertheless referred in the time of his present life, for which the future is henceforth neutral. But what he discovers in these acts of free self-transposition is once again something negative; he sees himself pushed back into the deepest past and already sees his death—still future—as past, like his birth. Everything is already seen as past, and, as in *Ecclesiastes*, everything that does not accidentally express its nihilism in the future perfect is understood as 'vanity'. To those that will be, no memory will be granted by those that will come after them, because they will have simply been. And already the future becomes past.

This freedom to exceed oneself (of which the future anterior is both the triumph and the failure) has its analogue in the *spatial freedom* of man. This is particularly important because space, more than anything else, represents a possibility of evading the being that I am precisely. This degenerates into spatial panic and the spirit of escape.

One can envisage space, as does Max Scheler, as a milieu, seeing it as the product of the freedom characteristic of motility [*liberté motrice*], as the independence of the here and the there, and as their permutability.[18] This freedom can now go astray, veering off into areas of complete irrelevance to me. If it sets its course according to its own impulse, a moment comes where it exceeds the limits of its own domain. Countless 'also-theres' [auch-dort] arise without any differentiation: they are there simultaneously and claim to be there singularly, without this simultaneity being fulfilled in such a way that man could be there-and-there at the same time. *Together these points remain in the subjunctive.* Since 'I could have been here, but also there and there', every here is changed into a 'precisely-here', whose contingency makes it unbearable. No 'here' is preferred to another.[19] The original sense of spatial freedom, in so far as it consists of a power [*pouvoir*] to pass from a certain here to a certain there, is neutralised by the fact that free movement [*liberté motrice*] is on the wrong track. This neutralisation can present itself as inertia or as the spirit of escape. The one to whom space presents itself under the aspect of the pathological and who falls into the contingency of the 'here' no longer attempts any movement because this would be entirely useless; or, indeed, the anxiety of 'never being able to be here precisely and of having, nevertheless, to be precisely here' will become identified with the panic of the nihilist in the paradox of freedom: to want never to be precisely-me and to be nevertheless perpetually restrained to the precisely-me. Space appears now as the ensemble of the possibilities of fleeing the precisely-there and the Being-precisely-me. But all emigration ends nevertheless in a new here and pushes the wanderer from one contingency to another, and from one subjunctive to another.

Pulled from one side to the other by the excessive possibilities of the world and of things that he knows simultaneously, and of which he knows that to experience them is to lose them, the one who is sick with the sense of Space, snatched from the place that he has just given up, does not arrive at nothing; he remains, in the strong sense of the term, always himself, because he is the only constant within the change. Nevertheless, he never actually [*effectivement*] returns to himself. At bottom, he searches for nothing. If he seeks something, it is not the determinate, but precisely the end of determinations. He wants to impose the *equivalence* of this 'there' and another 'there' in order to *occupy* it with his own present, because, in another way, this would remain an imaginary dimension. This equivalence, however, can never be verified through an omnipresent existence. It oscillates thusly, seeking over every thing the indetermination of everywhere; but it is deceived at every step of the way by the determination of the precisely-here.

Nothing can stop this pursuit; it comes to its end only there where the sick fall blind and dizzy. The points reached, then lost again, and all those not even reached, are reduced to each other and interchanged. Omnipresence finally seems achieved because during the short duration of vertigo, they enkindle the indetermination sought. But this is only an appearance for this indetermination costs too much. It cannot be preserved because we have ourselves been struck by indetermination at the moment where it sprung up in space, and as guarantee of our own existence, there is nothing more than the uneasiness of vertigo. Just like the fundamental panic of being-precisely-me, this wandering is condemned to a perpetual repetition: the pursuit begins again. This attempt to make Being-precisely-there disappear is once again overcome:

That is, the specific precisely-Here loses its significance, and the pursuit of other heres and other theres becomes unmotivated and superfluous, as soon as the space of all heres—*the space of the world* itself—gathers in one and the same *precisely-Here*. One is now the *prisoner* of the *precisely-Here*, in spite of the incalculable number of fragments of the world still unrealised; in whatever direction one turns, one always remains precisely-here—that is, *in this world*—and the attempt to steal away from this world, to escape from it through any other place, is thus revealed as impossible, for there is no wall surrounding the Here that could lend itself to any effraction. One is prisoner of the precisely-Here not despite but because it is precisely without limits. The terror is transformed into torpor.

It is necessary to explain once more why being-precisely-here is identified with being-precisely-me, and why, in the impulse that determines the escape from the self, in the flight before the being-precisely-me, the *Here* is abandoned in the place where it is oneself. For the man who possesses κινησις κατα τοπον, the system of spatial positions appears as the very principle of immobility and contingency: no point can transform into another, none concerns the other, each is nothing but itself. Space is thus the *Principium individuationis*. This reciprocal indifference will undoubtedly only be manifest for the being who can pass from one point to another, for the being that can go out of the element to which it is accustomed. This the animal cannot achieve because, despite its κινησις, it remains in its specific vital space, its own milieu, and never transports itself in what is strange as such. This only man can do. He *can abandon 'his' place, and he hopes that by losing it he can forget the principle of individuation and his own belongings. And in losing what belongs to him—the 'his'—he hopes to lose himself.*

7. Thirst for power and search for glory.

The one ill from the sickness of space wants the contingency of where he is precisely to be neutralised. He wants to be *everywhere at the same time*; he wants to *seize* totality in one fell swoop. But the desire to possess is only one specification of a deeper thirst for power: the desire to render the world congruent with oneself, more exactly, to force the world to become the *I*. It can at most become *mine* instead of becoming *I*; for the thirst for power, this is the first scandal and the first compromise.

Although a symptom of the shock of the contingent, the thirst for power also strives to neutralise the fact of contingency. In the fact that man is given to himself in advance, that he can only discover himself without being able to invent himself, and that the world and the Other are always ahead of him, the weakness of man is ceaselessly demonstrated to him and reproached. He cannot bear that there is still something outside of him that is not him. He cannot bear to be in the world superfluously, like 'a fifth wheel on a car', for it works just as well without him, or that once condemned to being, he must content himself with being only one being among others. The total absence of limitation to the thirst for power which wants to hold everything under its thumb, even beyond all necessity, is only the expression of the absolute disappointment that the *I* feels when it realises that once in existence it is confined to *share it with* other beings and that the totality of existence is not its alone. A word from Nietzsche, 'If there was a God, how could I endure not to be God' [*sic*], constitutes the definitive formulation of this painful state.[20] In the desire for power, man seeks to make up for the advance that the world has on him; since already he *is not* all, he must *have* all. He gets his revenge on the world by spreading his contingent self over the world, by incorporating it within himself and by representing it. For the one who is powerful is no longer only *himself*, such as he was in his miserable condition, but this one and that one, himself and the other, an ensemble. He is simultaneously here and there and there again. For he is, in domination, in representation, and in glory, to employ an expression from theology, *omnipresent*.

So he wants to be now and always. That is, he attempts to be immortalised in time, just as he worked to be glorified in space; he attempts to subsequently refute the contingency of the now to which he is abandoned. And he endeavours to set up his authentic being in the form of a permanent monument, in relation to the Memory and in the Renown of which his actual and incomplete form stands merely as the phenomenon to the Idea. His being is still only the unfaithful and temporal copy of this glorious monument. Here is the paradox: the more its glory increases, the less he 'himself' seems to have to do with his own monument. It has usurped his name and will reap the glory in his place even long after his death. Crushed and devastated, he is now envious of his own great name.

It is not by chance that we have entitled the preceding the 'pathology of freedom'. It would undoubtedly be vain to think that the goal of this designation is to draw a portrait of the complete man. The descriptions that correspond to it are, as we said, philosophical exaggerations. But the pictures that we have presented, considered in themselves, are not absurd. They represent the radical dangers that man can be subject to, and they are better known to each of us than one usually thinks; dangers which are here pushed to their ultimate, catastrophic aspect, compromising life itself. The forms of shame, disgust, desire for glory, depict compromises that are all too familiar to us. And if, in these ordinary phenomena, we are not in the habit of discerning the shock of the contingent, it is because of their 'ambivalence'. They all present themselves, as it were, in positive disguises; they constitute the *refuges* where one escapes from the threat of the contingent, and, compared to suicide, they are already *modi vivendi*. Shame, disgust and desire for glory take place, in the final analysis, in the course of contingent life; since practical life is a self-affirmation, they are already constant compromises with life accused of contingency; they are protests and insults. They are the protests and injuries that splinter on the back of the insulted enemy, and which are nevertheless made for him to carry, less in order to constantly devastate him by their sarcasms than in order to remain purely and simply with him in order to live. Antinomies are rarely stronger than the love of life. The Nihilists also want to live.

II. Antithesis: Picture of The Historical Man

8. Life continues. The shock of the contingent repeats itself unwillingly.

'One thing alone can cure us from being ourselves.'
'Yes, but at bottom, it is less important to be cured than to be able to live.' [*sic*]
(Conrad, *Lord Jim*[21])

The man who gets lost ceaselessly and futilely in the deadlock of his own contingency, and who finds his way in his 'being-precisely-me', as if he did not have life behind him, and precisely as if each time he had just been born, *pursues his life*. This is to say that paradox does not spring forth suddenly, from an imaginary point of departure situated 'before' life. It is rather in the middle of life itself, of life as it goes on in defiance of paradox and from under it, in so far as man does not make paradox a pretext for putting an end to himself. To whatever extent he compromises and impedes the course of life with his fanatical formalism and constant interruption, alleging that it is not itself, and that it cannot continue because it can take place in *iteration* and indeed must take place in iteration if it wants to remain effective [*efficace*], he concedes the possibility of life that perseveres in spite of him and he yields to it. The possibility of its repetition thus drives paradox *ad absurdum*; this is itself paradox and contradicts its own destructive claim. Consequently, the condition of paradox is iteration. The latter is itself paradox anew; for paradox should never be repeated within this life which it claims can never have a positive outcome. In fact, that paradox repeats does not mean that it repeats itself on its own initiative. Its movement is neutral from a temporal point of view; neither would it want nor would it be able to generate the temporal mode of repetition on its own. Repetition is rather the paradoxical temporal mode of life itself as it is realised in duration *against all* paradox: life hastens against the resistance of paradox opposed to its course, and at each point of this current of life paradox is experienced in so far as it plays the part of a barricade. It is thus not paradox that repeats but life that repeats the experience of paradox at every moment. From the point of view of the resistance which paradox represents, it is always the same life that collides with it in order to afterwards continue its course from under it. Repetition only takes place for the life that goes on; it thus develops as the permanence of its arrest. It always represents the *specific* negation of life carried out in time.

As iteration of the identical, 'movement opposed to memory' [sic], repetition is thus the principle of the neutralisation of historical time within a life that can continue its course even outside historicity [cf. Kierkegaard 1941: 33].[22] *That is, the nihilist paradox of the experience of freedom characterises non-historical existence, or more exactly, existence against history; this [existence] consequently heightens its own difficulty and attempts with so much obstinacy to attack the walls of the antinomy that contains it as it is deprived of time, which alone, in so far as it could be historical, would pass for an answer to paradox.* The man henceforth deeply engaged in the idea of the antinomy is actually non-historical. What so falls due to him in division— and this necessarily since he now pursues his life once and for all—that is, what he is and what he was, is not in a strict sense a life; it is at bottom only an event arriving accidentally, an event that in relation to the constancy of paradox remains something simply possible and does not lend itself to recollection [cf. Simmel 1971: 190].[23] The shock of the contingent thus destroys the strict possibility of experience itself, of appropriating life lived *de facto*. Everything happens as if it took place 'for nothing'; even the fact that it has been lived is constantly repudiated by paradox. Since he has been exposed to the accidental change of his fortuitous experiences, if man tried to return to himself, he could no longer capture his life *in concreto*. For there is no life, strictly speaking. Not because of but despite the paradoxical nature of man's situation at large, at the moment when paradox takes place at 'the interior of life', it becomes increasingly stringent, and all the more stringent as it neutralises life and makes it unfit for memory. Yet it becomes in the end the one and only real. That is to say, it is not only paradox that is disavowed by the life that continues, but life is in its turn disavowed by paradox; because it is unfit for recollection, and because it has yielded its vital force and its reality to paradox, it passes by as if it were not there.

It is only an apparent contradiction that both life and paradox are at once the conquered and the conqueror. If life merely goes on, it is defeated; paradox loses out in turn because it is constrained precisely to repetition, constrained to ceaselessly seek to overcome. This ambiguity and oscillation between victor and vanquished, never finding the equilibrium of indifference, preserves precisely the paradox 'of life'; and the duration of what is lived in life in spite of paradox determines paradox's pride. For the larger the field in which man continues, the more paradox proves that it was right. Thereby man in despair finally 'grabs hold' of himself and of the contingent fact of his being-precisely-me, and remains suspended in this situation, without having succeeded at discovering himself or at unifying himself through a positive experience.

Here already, with man in the grips of paradox, the historical path takes shape as the power [*puissance*] opposing paradox. This fact expresses that historical life is itself placed outside of paradox, but also that the man opposed to history, instead of simply meeting paradox, brings it to light as his characteristic property. It maintains, fixes and tyrannises man, acquiring for him a sort of retro-active truth. That is to say, paradox is only valid for the man who experiences it in its acuity, and who does not easily come to the end of it. Thus paradox expresses the troublesome character of the very one who questions; it is not the sign of a 'question in itself' which would exist apart from the one who questions or which would apply to man in general. The special situation corresponding to the paradox of identification is thus determined. But if we now cross over to a new type, the historical man, we can no longer conceive of man as a fugitive before the shock of the contingent; it is necessary to consider him as a type *sui generis* which is already beyond the state of contingency, and of which the principle traits, such as memory and the ability to experience, do not represent ulterior acts carried out with an eye to salvation, but original *modi vivendi*. {Note: admittedly, these are still *modi vivendi* that do not yet reveal man in full possession of himself and in the free exercise of his freedom. We do not quite reach to the highest degree of self-concretisation. It is a matter of a return to the concrete, the steps of which have already been marked out in the history of the philosophy of freedom: between the Kantian philosophy of the *I* and the Marxian theory of practice and of action, there is a Hegelian philosophy of history.}

9. The 'I remember, therefore I am myself' as the minimum of identification.

The nihilist who expresses himself in the proposition 'that I am precisely myself', when he wants to escape from himself, turns in circles or only encounters a contingent stranger who bears his name. It is difficult to positively determine the mode of identification that such an I awaits and claims. The proposition that he states expresses at bottom his indignation in the face of the fact that the various parts of his self do not coincide through the miracle of a pre-established harmony. He does not realise that identity can be stabilised subsequently by memory. This can be brought to light by a kind of *Cartesian argumentation*.

From the point of view of memory, the antinomy and the difficulties of identification that have just been described are inconceivable. *Because what I discover as myself in memory does not only contain the 'strange', but also precisely me, the subject itself that is affirmed. The man of yesterday whom I remember already contains the two I's in an indissoluble union.* For the same reason, the very man who is astonished today by his contingency has the possibility of remembering his being astonished yesterday.

Thereby, a minimum of identification is achieved, so to speak, in a Cartesian manner: the *I* now no longer insists on its being-here and its being-now; he has suddenly discovered in himself a determination (i.e. yesterday's shock of the contingent) with which he can identify in good conscience today. He no longer discovers only the contingent man that he avoided, but the one who avoided contingency. But here is what is strange: both are already unified in memory. It is not only the act of recollection that confuses them. The object of memory is already an identity in memory. This will be further interrogated. Speaking first of the forms of identification: they are thus not immediately expressed by the formula 'I am myself', but by the alternatives, *'that which I was, I am'*, and *'I remember, therefore I am myself'.*

This argument appears somewhat complicated. Two different types of identification intersect; it is firstly today's *I* that is identified with yesterday's; then in yesterday's *I*, the formal and contingent I merge. The second point is the most important: in yesterday's I, all that happened to it, all that it experienced, is confused. For yesterday's I is not exactly an 'I' but a *fragment of life*—at least in the eyes of today's memory.

10. Identification and the possessive.

For what does one remember? {Note: This question has not been posed despite the imposing number of monographs devoted to the psychology of memory; for this psychology is nearly always interested in the quantum and duration of memory. Philosophy, for its part, barely caught sight of the question. It accepted as a matter of course that memory agreed in its object with perception, that only their acts and their temporal value differed. An analysis along the lines of ours, which is even phenomenological in the sense of the school, has been curiously neglected in thorough analyses of phenomenological time.} This seemingly crude question is decisive for philosophical anthropology. Unlike perception which has its object in front of it, a fragment of the world, memory is memory of a *situation* in which the perceiving and the perceived, the *I* and the world, are already confused to such an extent that neither the *I* without the world nor the world without the *I* can be abstracted as such from this single given.

I see, for example, a misfortune approaching me; it is still strange to me. It fills me with anguish: this anguish is nothing other than the stupefaction of the *I* before a radically strange object. But in memory, the misfortune is already *mine*. Not only do I remember its approach and my subjective reaction, but I remember the whole of the situation, which consists of the two preceding aspects, and thus presents itself as a fragment of life. It is henceforth impossible in the face of this fragment of life to fall back into astonishment that 'as myself I must be myself', because, in the case of painful experiences, it is in truth no longer the *I* that recalls memory and which arranges that which is recollected, but memory itself that forewarns the I and arranges it. In identical cases it is not the I that defines the self but lived experience; and now the I is no longer as indeterminate as before. From this point of view the shock of the contingent, in spite of the terror that accompanies it, even seems to be a kind of supplementary element: this terror of being precisely myself, disappearing because of a really unpleasant memory, can be postponed to a subsequent epoch and appears futile.

In memory, the contingent events that one has lived, those which occurred by accident, are thus already confused with the *I*. Identity was established before the terror of identification could rush to the surface. From this, one can draw very important conclusions for the notion of experience. Memory thus abolishes what we have recognised of the indeterminate and of the contingent in experience. In memory man discovers himself as a situation and not as an I; what he experienced, he now *is*; and if he disregarded the experience of his 'being such as it is' [*tel et ainsi*] [sosein], as well as everything he experienced and the modalities of his entire history, nothing of him would remain, not even his former *I*.

But this is not enough. For it is not only particular situations and fragmentary experiences which appear in memory, but life as a totality; life in the sense of bibliographical life. But it does not present itself as a 'Gestalt', or as the unity of a thing; it is there as a 'medium': one is at home in one's own life, this life is *my* life, in spite of and through the multiplicity of beings and of things experienced. It is furthermore the field of all particular experiences wherein each is identified as '*mine*'; and I can run through it at any time. Through his history, which becomes one with him and envelops him, man escapes from the strangeness of the world and from the contingency of his 'being-precisely-me'. The identical proposition 'I am myself', analytical at its origin, and contradicted by the shock of the contingent, is transformed into this more meaningful proposition 'I am my life' or 'the self is life', and thus into a proposition of identification that is *'synthetic'* in the true sense of the term. It is completely characteristic that the 'am' and the 'is' of the two preceding statements are interchangeable. Life is not only the first person (I) nor only the third person (something strange and contingent), but is a possessive: it is *mine*, it is MY LIFE.

In truth, this *'my'* does not indicate the presupposition of the I as the proprietor to which life belongs. This would be to argue against history from a nihilist point of view of existence all over again. *The possessive pronoun does not ordinarily designate only the fact of possession but also the fact of 'being possessed'; neutrally, it designates the general fact of belonging. 'My' life thus equally signifies the fact that I belong to my life, as I, and that my life belongs to me, as mine.* {Note: It is only now that we reach the concept of authentically human experience. It represents here 'the having of the experience of life', a concept that indicates a knowledge of what there was to experience in life, a complete mode of man: this concept of experience could not have arisen earlier. Originally, that is, for the man against history, experience is not. For originally, that is, for the man against history, experience is not in itself 'experience of life', but rather announces a need for experiences. Experience thus becomes experience of life only from the point of life recollected and already lived as such. Curiously, in this situation, man finds not only himself, and even less the contingent things that he has experienced, but he extends his experiences to a characteristic generality that one can neither define nor refute theoretically. In any case, this generality signifies that the type of experience in question is not simply the subsequent result of experiences previously undergone, but that it is qualitatively more than the sum of these specific experiences. In so far as man can continue his life and grow old, and consequently no longer remains, like the nihilist, in the perpetual repetition of the now, this type of experience can become the specific character of the stage he reaches.}

The most diverse traits of historical man testify to the self-identity memory reveals under its formal aspect. He no longer knows the surprise of 'being such as it is' [*tel et ainsi*], of 'being-precisely-me'; he no longer knows the concrete faces of the shock of the contingent. The historical man would consider absurd the ideas of the nihilist on an indeterminate *transcendent* origin, and on his being placed here below thanks to a strange design. He is beyond the polarity of the present and the transcendent past that the nihilist, on the contrary, felt with such acuity. For he has his *own* past, a past in which he is not only united with his experiences, but with other beings and other persons. Even the time of his ancestors is not, in truth, strange to him; it is only distant. He can 'approach it with piety'. And if piety, like shame, is at the same time respect and fear, it does not compromise identification, as shame did. Piety consists instead of recognising the distance that the act of identification must cross when it realises the identification of a being with his ancestors.

11. What today is called 'I' as of tomorrow will be 'life'; of what the I's formality consists.

If the *'I'* nevertheless restores these a posteriori and contingent original experiences to its life through memory, this subsequent identification does not present any incorporation 'nor any organisation of the matter of life by an already *formal I*. For this *I* is nothing other than the vanguard of the plenitude of material life itself. If the *I* is formal, it is thanks to life; it is because life laid out and forced to consider all the possibilities, to experience the new, and to show presence of mind, formalises itself in an *I*, and ends at the point of an acute and lucid present, in such a way that it puts an end to its material richness at the point where it culminates. Whereas the nihilist I believes he chances to be precisely this man or that, and claims: 'Me, I am called man', it is, on the contrary, man who gives himself the 'name' of I, and who actually formalises himself as an I. *Man is not the rear-guard of the fact named 'I', but the I is the vanguard of the state of affairs named 'man'.* What is I today, so as to introduce life to experience and the world, constitutes my life as of tomorrow, joined together with all that was present; and a part of what is my life today was the 'I' yesterday.

The alternative between the *I* and contingent determination that ceaselessly shocked the nihilist is, so to speak, a mistake the I makes about its own role: it emphasised its conditioned formality and its presence as positivity and freedom; it opposed this to life 'which is only material', and which sinks into the past. *This mistake about the self*, which brings the *I* to *actually [effectivement]* break with life in the case of counter-historical existence, does not take place in the case of historical man.

The conception of the *I* 'as a constitutive element' of life (at once in a logical and a temporal way) must yet not be understood as if there were no difference between the form of life and of the I. Certainly, they form but one in memory; yet memory itself is not an indifference, but a perpetual identification. A certain duality is incontestable; a certain hiatus remains, ventured through life between itself and the I. It is only when it gets ahead in the freedom of its possibilities and when it wants to be 'in the know' [*au courant*] that it takes precisely the form of the I. This hiatus admittedly always disappears in memory, and identity is restored anew.

We said above that memory 'informs'. We understand by this not only that the *I* remembers, and not only that the I 'keeps its life in the know', but that *life* draws its I close to it and into itself. This type of memory is even more frequent than the first. It has commonly been neglected in theories of memory, for this relapse of self within life does not present itself as an act, and psychology, like philosophy, is quite elementary when it comes to the vocabulary of the I's passivity. The conditions of normal memory are such, in any case, that the I yields to life's gravitational force ['Schwerkraft'], where it is then charged with melancholia ['Schwermut'] and drawn to life's interior: it thus disappears as the I and as the terminal present.[24] For memory, life is no longer *its* own life, for life and I are now confused, there is no longer between them this distinction, this separation, which alone allows the use of the possessive pronoun. The life that is thus at home in memory no longer has need of particular representations, of the realisation of former situations, of the precise repetition of past experiences. It can fully suffice with the states of the soul of another time, of which images and realisations constitute a secondary process. {Note: Cf. the classical example of Proust (*A la recherche du temps perdu,* I, ch. I) [*sic*].}

12. Identity in certain stable situations.

The presentation of the problem of identity and of identification would be incomplete without mention of the situation in which the panic of identity does not break forth, and where no problem of identification arises.

If in order to be at home, man is forced to superimpose on the natural world an artificial world, arrested and constructed by him—that is, the social and economic world with its customs and its laws—he shows undoubtedly that he is not cut out for the natural world. But this second world, ever varied according to historical conditions, can nevertheless succeed and stabilise, to such an extent that man is in his element there and the problems and pathological attitudes of identity fade into the background, just as identification does through history. In these stable social states, *it is the world itself that takes care of identifying* the self before auto-identification is necessary.

The social world already realises a minimum of identification in the *name.* Once man is baptised—and no one can baptise himself—the name persists as a constant in life; and it is a constant so natural that the one who is named, without worrying about the debate between nominalism and realism, not only claims *to be called* John or James, but *to be* James or John. Conversely, in the case where the name is changed (as is, for example, the name of the woman who becomes a wife), a real [*effectif*] change takes place.

James is thus named James today and tomorrow, and is regarded as James yesterday. Identification thus seems assured. But as we have said, it is only so when the milieu remains relatively identical and identifiable. *For the identity of the self is a function of the identity of the world which is its correlate.*

In this world, we thus exceed the minimum guaranteed by the name and the I now plays a determined role. This role can be so stable and so natural that it obstructs the *role of man* (the judge, the professor, the general, etc.), and disregards it. Thus it is conceived of as independent of him, as his simple substrate, and as simple 'role overload'; thus as an *empty* 'I'. This ensures that man sees neither difference nor antinomy between himself and his function, and that he cannot restrict his authentic existence to an abstract self. In these stable situations, the phenomenon of the role of 'what' and 'that which' one is, is no less a 'primary phenomenon' than the phenomenon I. That the role represents the accident and the I the substrate—a distinction which undoubtedly applies to the situation that we experience in this day and age, in which the social world ceaselessly transforms itself and in which man continually changes position, as well as to a great number of social and historical situations—is not *a priori* and is not demonstrated by the philosophy of the I. *In stable or stationary epochs, it is entirely possible that it is not the self that 'has' a role, but conversely the role that 'has' a self; at the very least it is possible that the tension and the non-identity* that were treated in the portrait of the nihilist *are not realised.*

In the situation outlined here, the relation between man and the world differs essentially from the one that has been described up to now. Under the form of the role, belonging to the social world, 'social worldliness' [soziale Weltlichkeit], is already in place. That here the world is not something 'exterior', something that is added on to me, shows the uselessness of terror in the face of the contingent as well as the necessity of its interiorisation by memory and its subsequent assimilation. One might think that in the stable situation where man is identified through the world, he is discharged of and exempted from all collaboration with identification. This is not the case. Rather, even in stable situations, man must comply with and answer to the claim to identity that the world places in him. This correspondence consists, in truth, of other acts than the simple acts of recollection that are the means of historical identification. It consists of moral acts, of acts of 'responsibility' above all. Today I must answer before the world for what I did yesterday. This identity is clearly no longer of a historical nature, but is of a juridical and moral nature. It is historical only when, on the one hand, the place and the role of man, and on the other hand, the claim and the authority of the world in him, become so vague that man is forced to call himself by his name so that he can answer to it through identity and so be put back 'in himself'. Just as it is from the heart that one obeys for his part the call of duty according to Kant, the call of identification now springs up from the heart of the historical man. When he answers his own call and when called by his name, when he pulls himself together and is put back in himself, he resembles, from the point of view of the stable situation, the Münchhausen knight who pulls himself out of a marsh by his own hair.

From the point of view of this identity guaranteeing the social, the two types that we have described up till now, the nihilist who does not succeed in identifying with himself, and the historical man who takes charge of his own identification, no longer appear so far from one another as it seemed before. For both *need* identification. And the forced staging of the rescue of the historical man together with the unconcealed catastrophe of the nihilist testify to their identical position: strangeness in relation to the world.

Despite this similitude, the portrait of the nihilist appears philosophically much more important to us than that of the man placed in historical existence. If the essence of man actually [*effectivement*] consists of his non-fixity, and thus of his propensity for a thousand incarnations, it is the nihilist who makes of this instability *as such* his definitive destiny, and who is determined by indetermination; he does not profit from specifying in this or that manner. The nihilist, indetermination incarnate, paints *an exaggerated portrait of man* through his manner of flaunting his faults without the least concealment.

Next to this the portrait of historical man appears of dubious ease. Man as historical presents himself as a being who is worthy of [*à la hauteur de*]²⁵ what happens to him, of his contingency, and as a man who has the courage to risk *amor fati* because he follows *fatum* closely and always calls it 'myself', who thus, to employ a famous Hegelian formula in a non-orthodox sense, makes all that is in him, and in him by contingence, 'reasonable' after the fact [*après coup*]. Certainly, he takes pride in saying in the face of all that happens to him 'this is mine'. But he cannot dispose of what has become 'mine': this identification is thus suspect.

13. Calling into question the problem of philosophical anthropology.

Identification is not so simple. Undoubtedly, it is necessary, when one is not identified and situated by the world itself, to be identified through oneself. Nevertheless, it is not enough to be situated in oneself. Without the world, identification is impossible. *The one who acts* (disregarding the socially identified self) is alone set apart from the difficulties of the terror of contingency; for he does not insist on his ceaselessly assimilated past but on his task, which relates him to the world. Although the world did not assign him a determinate place anymore than the nihilist and the historical man, he actually [*effectivement*] achieves identity.

In the eyes of the one who wills, what is willed is thus, compared to everything which is only encountered and to his empirical existence, something non-contingent. This non-contingent, in contrast to experiences, goes without being assimilated; it is the will that must assimilate the world. {Note: It is not by chance that many *want* to will simply in order to escape from contingency, and that the fact of having a task is a solution for them.}

It is true that there is a good possibility that the world appears contingent to the one who seeks to transform it. But it is beyond all contingency that it is *him* who has the will to transform it. If one now wants to attempt to mimic the proposition we have stated 'that I am precisely me' in the formula 'that I will precisely this', the latter would be revealed as a pure construction: it is absolutely inconceivable starting from the will. And if one accepted this formula in the situation of will, it would neutralise it. The man who seeks something precise can be against the world, and although the world did not assign him a determinate place, can thus achieve an actual [*effective*] identification. This would be expressed by a formula that is neither that of the nihilist—'I am myself'—nor that of the historical man—'I am that which was'—but which is stated as follows: 'what I willed, I will'. In the concept of the task, the constant is already there; it is thus not necessary that it be maintained as such, in the form of a memory or of any experience. For the task disappears only once the result is achieved. {Note: It is entirely characteristic to observe that from the permanence of the will results, without the least secret intent, *a* life, and that few biographies, and even few autobiographies, offer a unity as clear as those of the life of great men of State or revolutionaries, whose will aimed at everything but identity. This unity is thus a kind of 'bonus', unlike that of autobiographical existence.}

Through this recourse to action, it is true that philosophical anthropology reaches the limits of its legitimacy, its capacities and its competence. From the point of view of what man *does*, the question 'what is he and who is he authentically?' seems wrongly posed. *For acting is not being.*

It was Hegel who made the act disappear in considering it as already both developing and to come (and it becomes an actual [*effectif*] being subsequently and as past). In making it already engulfed by being itself, he transformed it in any event into a kind of 'being', and a kind of being not specifically human, for it is not by chance that it is called 'organic'. This attempt, the consequences of which are unlimited, now obscures the phenomenon of action. It was Kant, however, who treated the question as such and without any mask, although Hegel more explicitly than Kant gave an expression to the problem of self-identification. (He characterises history as the fact of coming to itself for the spirit that is not identical with itself). Self-identification through 'Aufklärung' and through the critique is an action for Kant: there is no question for him of observing [constater] what reason *is* (and for him it is equivalent to man), but of constituting it through the critical operation.

Hegel asks himself on the contrary what it *is* in order to answer dialectically that it is not *Being*; thus, although proceeding by negation, the answer that he gives remains within the framework of the theoretical. It recoups the qualitative leap from the theoretical to the practical from the term 'genesis', and replaces it in the theoretical domain itself. Historical materialism gets credit for having formulated anew the specific sense of Kantian idealism, that is, the transformation of theoretical reason into practical reason.

The aims of Kant are ours also. And we presume that they carry a much greater significance than we had supposed at the start. Philosophical anthropology and its problem of the definition of man must consider itself opposite human action as a productive misunderstanding, and put an end to itself.

The question of knowing what man is authentically [eigentlich] *is consequentially wrongly posed. For the theoretical definition is only a shadow that decision rejects in the theoretical realm* [sic].[26] '[W]hat I am in an authentic sense', 'what I discover in me', is always already decided, whether by myself or by another. What is opposed to the definition of man is thus not the irrational but the fact of human action; the action whereby man is constantly defined in fact, and whereby he determines what he is on each occasion. In this perpetual definition of himself that man presents in acting, is it useless to appeal to the principle of order, to demand a moment's pause to pose questions of 'authentic' definition, and to establish what man is in an 'authentic' sense. There is nothing more suspect than this 'authenticity' [Eigentlichkeit]. It is no accident that the German term *feststellen [constater]* signifies both to state something [konstatieren] and to fix something. And it is not by chance that the problem of definition (for example 'what is authentic to a German?' and also 'what is man authentically?') presents itself in conditions of reaction; in particular, in the state of incertitude and of crisis where one is no longer anything precise. The one who poses the problem of definition is now the inactive one, the one who compromises the real transformation and poses this problem retroactively, so to speak. 'Who am I authentically?', he asks, in place of being actually [effectivement] defined and of making someone of himself. While he poses the question and as he poses it, to put it hyperbolically, he is nothing at all; he is thus whatever he or another has made of him with the aid of an outdated practical definition. This is what he can consequently discover and define as his authentic existence. The question of knowing who I am is not of the sort that it is sufficient to pose, but of the sort that it is necessary to answer.

We finish with this consideration. The problematic of philosophical anthropology, which explored in the first part the pathological specifications of human freedom, appears from this point on as itself a contaminated form that denatures its problems. It makes of autonomy a definition of oneself; and while it teaches man to run after his 'authenticity' [Eigentlichkeit], it abandons him to those who have an interest in putting him in his place, and makes him lose his freedom.

Notes

1. The reference is to Emmanuel Levinas' translation of the first part of (Stern) Anders' presentation before the Kant society of Frankfurt and Hamburg in 1930, entitled 'Die Weltfremdheit des Menschen' (Stern 1934–35). 'Pathologie de la Liberté' shares some content with the later half of the same lecture.
2. Stéphanopoli's quotation marks suggest that Anders' term is 'Nachträglichkeit', from Freud. The term is conventionally translated as 'après-coup' in the French, and is translated as 'deferred action' in James Strachey's English translations of Freud. Jean Laplanche suggests 'afterwardness' as a preferable English rendition. See the editor's introduction to Laplanche (1999).
3. Alternative translations of 'le quelconque' include 'the whatsoever', 'being whatsoever', 'anything whatever', and 'the indefinite'. I have chosen to translate 'le quelconque' as 'the indeterminate' throughout, due to its adequacy in every context. Where noted, 'the indeterminate' translates 'indéterminé' rather than 'quelconque'.
4. Stéphanopoli's translation uses the terms 'auto-position' and 'auto-production'. In the English scholarship, 'self-positing' carries the significance of Fichte's 'setzen', which means to position or place as well as to posit.
5. I have translated 'étranger' as 'strange' throughout the text.
6. Alternatively, 'telle et ainsi' might be translated 'in such a way'. Literally, it translates as 'such and so', 'such and thus', or 'such and in this way'. Stéphanopoli may be translating the German 'sosein'—'suchness' o'essence'—with this locution.
7. 'Why is this now, his [the questioner's] now, precisely now and *was* not long ago? Since he asks such strange questions, he regards his existence and his time as independent of one another, and the former as projected into the later. He really assumes two nows, one belonging to the object and the other to the subject, and marvels at the happy accident of their coincidence' (Schopenhauer 1969: 279).
8. See Anders' remarks below on the dual meaning of the term *feststellen* in German which Stéphanopoli's *constater* is likely translating here.
9. I have translated 'étonnement' as 'astonishment' throughout the text.
10. The early sketch for Empedocles, called 'The Frankfurt Plan', opens with this passage: 'Empedocles, by temperament and through his philosophy long since destined to despise his culture, to scorn all neatly circumscribed affairs, every interest directed to sundry objects; an enemy to the death of all one-sided existence, and therefore also in actually beautiful relations unsatisfied, restive, suffering, simply because they are *special* relations, ones that fill him utterly only when they are felt in magnificent accord with all living things, simply because he cannot live in them and love them intimately, with omnipresent heart, like a god, and freely and expansively, like a god; simply because as soon as his heart and his thought embrace

anything at hand he finds himself bound to the law of succession . . .' (Hölderlin 2008: 29).

11. 'Issue' also translates as 'exit'.

12. The French term 'spécial' carries the Latin speciālis's sense of being of a given species.

13. See Genesis 9: 23: 'But Shem and Japheth took a garment and laid it upon both their shoulders and walked backward and covered the nakedness of their father; and their faces were turned away, so that they did not see their father's nakedness' (New American Standard Bible 1995).

14. The German term 'Schande' carries the sense of both shame and dishonour.

15. The term here is 'mondanité', which is the standard French translation of Heidegger's 'Weltlichkeit'.

16. The term 'fugue' can also be translated as 'flight' and, like 'fuite', comes from the Latin term 'fugere'.

17. My translation of the preceding three lines in part follows and in part differs from Mark Lester's translation in The Logic of Sense (Deleuze 1990: 349, n. 5). The most signification difference is that I have translated 'le sens positif' as time's 'forward sense', whereas Lester translates it as 'positive sense or direction'.

18. The term 'liberté motrice' may be a play on Scheler's notion of 'motor intention', subsequently developed in the work of Maurice Merleau-Ponty, and possibility also on the phrase 'freedom of movement'—liberté de mouvement.

19. Stéphanoli's text reads: 'Puisque "que j'aurais sément" que sa contingence rend insupportable. Aucun "ici" n'est prépu être là, mais aussi là et là', tout ici se transforme en un 'ici-précifére à un autre'. My translation follows the changes suggested on the site Les Amis de Némésis, with the difference that I change the first 'la' in their '[p] uisque "que j'aurais pu être là, mais aussi là et là"' to an 'ici' in light of the context. See http://www.geocities.com/nemesisite/anders.patholib.htm

20. Nietzsche (1961: 110): 'If there were Gods, how could I endure not to a be God!'

21. 'One thing alone can us from being ourselves cure / Yes . . . strictly speaking, the question is not how to get cured, but how to live' (Conrad 2002: 153). This passage is notable not only for its significance but for its unconventional and improper grammar, possibly intended to demonstrate one language moving—bumpily—into another. See Sylvére Monad, 'Joseph Conrad's Polyglot Wordplay', available at: http://www.mhra.org.uk/ojs/index.php/MLR/ article/view/2/30

22. 'Repetition and memory are the same movement, only in opposite directions; for what is recollected has been, is repeated backwards, whereas repetition properly so called is recollected forwards' (Kierkegaard 1941: 33). In the French, the passage in quotation marks reads: 'mouvement opposé au souvenir' (literally: movement opposed to memory), but Kierkegaard's text suggests that the sense Anders' intended is something more like 'movement in the opposite direction of memory'.

23. In his original note, Anders' references page 14 of Simmel's Philosophie der Kultur. The actual title of this text is Philosophische Kultur: Gesammelte Essais (Leipzig: W. Klinkhardt, 1911). 'Das Abenteuer', or 'The Adventurer', spans pages 7–24 of this volume. Simmel conceptualises the adventure thusly: 'The most general form of adventure is its dropping out of the continuity of life. 'Wholeness of

life', after all, refers to the fact that a consistent process runs through the individual components of life, however crassly and irreconcilably distinct they may be. What we call an adventure stands in contrast to that interlocking of life-links, to that feeling that those countercurrents, turnings, and knots still, after all, spin forth a continuous thread. An adventure is certainly a part of our existence, directly contiguous with other parts which precede and follow it; at the same time, however, in its deeper meaning, it occurs outside the usual continuity of this life' (Simmel 1971: 187–8). On the corresponding page in the English translation, Simmel adds: 'the adventurer is also the extreme example of the ahistorical individual, of the man who lives in the present. On the one hand, he is not determined by any past . . . nor, on the other hand, does the future exist for him' (Simmel 1971: 190).

24. *Schwerkraft* is the force of gravity; *schwermut* is melancholia. Their shared root, *schwer*, can be translated as 'heavy', indicative of the weightiness and overwhelming force that marks both the force of gravity within nature and of melancholia within an individual life. *Les Amis de Némésis* note this; see http://www.geocities.com/nemesisite/anders.patholib.htm

25. '*À la hauteur de*' can also be translated as 'equal to'.

26. 'Car la définition théorique n'est qu'une ombre que la decision rejette dans le domaine du théorique'. It seems that the second 'théorique' should read 'practique' (practical).

References

Conrad, Joseph (2002) *Lord Jim*, ed. Jacques Berthoud, Oxford: Oxford University Press.

Hölderlin, Friedrich (2008) *The Death of Empedocles*, trans. David Farrell Krell, Albany, New York: SUNY Press.

Kierkegaard, Søren (1941) *Repetition: An Essay in Experimental Psychology*, trans. Walter Lowrie, New York: Harper and Row.

Laplanche, Jean (1999) *Essays on Otherness*, ed. Jean Fletcher, London and New York: Routledge.

Monad, Sylvére (n.d.) 'Lord Jim's Polyglot Wordplay', available at: http://www.mhra.org.uk/ojs/index.php/MLR/article/view/2/30

Nietzsche, Friedrich (1961) *Zarathustra*, trans. R. J. Hollingdale, London: Penguin Classics.

Simmel, Georg (1971) 'The Adventurer', in *On Individuality and Social Forms*, ed. Donald N. Levine, Chicago and London: University of Chicago Press, pp. 187–98.

Schopenhauer, Arthur (1969) *The World as Will and Representation*, Vol. 1, trans. E. F. J. Payne, New York: Dover Publications, Inc.

Stern, Günther (1934–35) 'Une interprétation de l'a posteriori', trans. Emmanuel Levinas, *Recherches Philosophiques*, IV, pp. 65–80.

Troeltsch, Ernst (1951) 'Contingency', in *Encyclopedia of Religion and Ethics*, Vol. IV, ed. James Hastings, New York: Charles Scribner's Sons, pp. 87–9.

Günther Anders

The Émigré[1]

Vitae, not vita

Your request for a CV leaves me feeling utterly perplexed. I have no "vita." Not as far as I can remember. Émigrés are prone to being unable to remember. Hunted by world history, we have been cheated of "life" in the singular.

I can hear you raising objections: no life can ever be conceived in the singular; no one can lay claim to a single "vita;" there is no such thing as a curriculum vitae that does not disintegrate into phases; what "life" refers to is no more than the unity of these discrete phases; and the fact that life is subdivided into phases is not something that renders memory ineffective. I will concede this—with one caveat: normally moving from one phase to another takes place against the backdrop or within the framework of an environment that, inevitable changes notwithstanding, is experienced as a constant. This environmental constant is what normally ensures the connection between the different phases of our lives.

It is precisely this precondition, indispensable as it is if we are to experience life as *one*, that we were denied by being pushed from one environment to another. The notches between the different life phases are much deeper than is normally the case; so deep that we lose the sense that these phases belong to *one* life and that this fact becomes in itself objectively questionable. In a sense even the life of a butterfly, which, after its beginnings as a caterpillar, has hibernated as a larva and is now flitting around, may be *one*; but not in the same sense as the life of a dog is *one*.

However, not having had a "life" does not mean that the lives we did lead were lacking in substance. If I could assemble all the incarnations I walked around in at some time or who carried me on their shoulders across space and time to this here and now; if I could heap up in front of me all the *faits divers* that happened to me—in terms of numbers and mass they would suffice to fill even an unusually rich life. But they do not add up to a "vita." Only to "vitae." Only to lives in the plural.

I said "only." Since all this is taking place outside the remit of arithmetic, several *vitae* are not necessarily more than a single *vita*. Conversely, it often seems to us who have been condemned to plurality as if we had no life to look back on at all or, at best, only the latest installment of a life. As a single whole, our life eludes us. The loss of our ability to comprehend and summarize long stretches of time makes us comparable to those musical illiterates [*Musik-*

1   Günther Anders' "Der Emigrant" was first published in *Merkur* 16 (July 1962): 601–622; Otmar Binder, Vienna, translated this essay from German into English.

banausen] who are reduced to giving the finale of the symphony that has just been played (or the last few bars, which might just as well have served other symphonies as a finale) that hand of applause that it so peremptorily demands. There is a difference however. In our case the atrophy of that ability is easier to justify. What was played to us was not a symphonic whole; it was a haphazard succession of phases or, at best, a suite with many movements.

This brings me to where I wanted you all along.

Assuming (as you do) that a suite is as easy to remember as a symphony or, dispensing with metaphors: that our memory could—or even must—function equally well no matter what kinds of life we have led is simply a preconceived idea. The visibility of a physical object depends not only on the light radiating from it and the observer's acuity of vision but also on the nature and structure of the medium it inhabits. Similarly the rememberability [*Erinner-barkeit*] of a memory object does not depend exclusively on its radiance or the rememberer's power of recall but also on the structure of the life it is part of. For the generations before the outbreak of the new mass migration, for our grandparents, who lived wherever they happened to live out their (*one*) life, the world resembled a *forest of mnemonic signs*, each referring to one day or one hour of their lives. Active recall of any details was hardly required of them, everything reminded them of those details; they were largely spared the initiative and the labor of *memoria*. The things of the world effectively acted as cues for them. All the same, the assertion that the act of recall *then* was fundamentally different from the same act *now* will probably strike you as preposterous. You have, after all, studied with psychologists who accept only one type of memory that is allegedly impervious to history; who have no inkling therefore that there is, in analogy to the history of ideas, also a history of the development of the psyche's capacities and achievements over time that would oblige psychology to give itself a new charter as an historical discipline. However that may be, compared to the "recherches *des* temps perdu" that you have ill advisedly suggested I undertake, the "recherches *du* temps perdu" that our fathers were engaged on must, despite the considerable difficulties it involved even for them, have been child's play. And this was so not only because our fathers had solely their one *vita* to recapitulate or because their world contained in itself all the necessary pointers—whereas we have this multitude of *vitae* behind us and, in the absence of references to our earlier worlds, would have to conjure up these *vitae* by our own unaided efforts—: if the difference between the business of remembering then and now were only that between singular and plural, it might still be within our reach. But this is not so. That in our case we are dealing with several lives is not simply a matter of arithmetic; it is a function of the way we lived; one that makes remembering more difficult or even downright impossible. What I mean is that the course of life of someone who is forced to pass through several *vitae* differs from that of an average life roughly as the course of the Mosel differs from that of the Rhine: it is more sinuous, more meandering, at points downright labyrinthine.

To a certain extent this is true even of you. You told me only recently how amazed you were at how rarely your memory returns to your wartime experiences. This cannot be wholly explained—this was the interpretation we put on it at the time—by the fact that you are *unwilling* to recall those years; you are also *unable* to retrieve them by a linear route. Those years had branched off from the "trunk" of your life in an unforeseeable direction; they stuck out at an angle, as it were. An analogon: I met French remigrés who, after years in exile, returned to old and intact (at least compared to other places émigrés might return to) Paris, where their time in exile, which, while it lasted, had been a decisive part of their lives and was experienced with the utmost intensity, began to fade, even to shrink. And in some of these remigrés the wounds left by the intermezzo in exile have already healed without leaving any scars, which means that the time "in between" has indeed become a "temps perdu," a stretch of time that no "recherche" will ever be able to retrieve.

But remigrés are not the most significant cases, at least not (since the number of those who, like me, have in fact gone back is hardly worth mentioning) for us émigrés. What matters is not that our life has experienced an interruption by an (irretrievable) intermezzo but that its splintering into several lives has become irreversible; and this means that the second life sticks out at an angle from the first and the third from the second, causing a "bend in the road," a "folding," which makes looking back—I was tempted to say: physically—impossible.
"Branch-off," "angle," "folding"—all these terms obviously sound unusual when applied to "time."[2] We have all learnt that time may—no, must—be considered as a (one-dimensional and rectilinear) "river;" and having learnt that, the idea that the riverbed of time might resemble the Mosel rather than the Rhine would have struck us as perverse. Another preconceived idea. Because whenever the thread of a life is made to snap, no matter whether by a Damascus or a Night of Broken Glass, and whenever, as it plows on, that life is made to absorb completely new content, content with no reference whatsoever to the time "ante," the time that has gone before, then this stretch of time, saturated with new content as it is, will not be considered as a sequel to the time that had preceded it but as a new departure, a branching off at a more or less obtuse angle or even as a new organism altogether, the product of some kind of "calving," with its own head and its own tail.

In other words: as it fell to us to be hunted from one world in which we found ourselves beached to the next and as we were forced to soak up new content again and again, content that the previous one bore no relation to, these stretches of time, each linked to a different world, have now come to lie *across* each other. Each new folding made the life that had preceded it invisible. By the time I had reached my next destination, New York, Paris was no more than an indistinct memory; and since I moved to Vienna, the workshop I used to trudge to in Los Angeles is shrouded in impenetrable darkness. I cannot recall the name of even one of the people I worked with side by side there, I cannot conjure up a single face. Looking around a corner in time is even less feasible than looking around a corner in space; time periscopes have yet to be invented.

What is true of each segment of our life is doubly true of life as a whole. Its meandering design effectively forestalls experience; the multitude of foldings makes its course completely unplottable.

---

2   Even though these terms are borrowed from the language of space, the underlying process, the *change of direction*, precedes specificity. The possibility of changing direction or of being deflected from one's course is part of life itself, whether this process manifests itself as strength or as weakness. This is why the process can realize itself equally well as time and space.

A border-line case: when I met Herr K. again in California—we had been on bowing terms in Germany—he was seventy and had an odyssey behind him that had taken him from Berlin to Paris, on to Lisbon, on to Shanghai, on to Los Angeles. His state was as follows: the fact that he had already passed through several *vitae* was obviously not unknown to him but he was unable to recall any details. To questions about details he reacted vaguely and brusquely as if had been asked about the life of his father or grandfather. Since he had managed to cope with the imperative to break off again and again, since he had always fallen on his feet, he took his *palingenesis* for granted—it had become a matter of routine so that he now displayed an air of invulnerability, as if he had in his breast pocket an insurance policy that guaranteed him immortality. In clear moments he conceded that his conviction of being immortal was "pure rubbish," even adding on those occasions that this knowledge did not touch him in the least, that it made not the slightest difference to his attitude towards life, no, not even on the dispositions he had to make. In other words: the idea that the series of successful rebirths might not last forever, that, for better or worse, it might come to an end one of these days, was unthinkable for him. It is obvious that K.'s reaction to his multitude of *vitae* represents a crass, almost pathological border-line case. But it is border-line cases more than any others that throw light on normal cases. Cases such as mine.

Twenty years ago I saw a musical clown perform in Kansas. Pretending that his tuba was a telescope, he put the mouthpiece of the thrice folded instrument to his eye and pointed the bell at the moon. In ostensible despair he tried to catch sight of the moon through the curved tube. In the end, shrugging his shoulders, he informed the audience that it must be New Moon. If I were to accede to your request and make an effort to view the whole of my life, my pains would go similarly unrewarded.

Losing one's proof of existence

Each of us receives incontrovertible proof of their existence if that existence is put to use by others. As opposed to the Cartesian *Cogito ergo sum*, the proof of existence that is conclusive in real life should be formulated as *Cogitor ergo sum*—"people think of me, therefore I am." I said "should" because those who subscribe to this proposition (everyone, really) do not go to the length of explicitly formulating it. They do not do so because the truth of the proposition is too evident to warrant explicit formulation. Like many another truth, this one owes its universal acceptance to the fact that it has remained unknown.

*

People did not think of us in our exile. For a short time, it is true, an infernal variant of this proof of existence held sway: we had, after all, been persecuted. From "People are after me" there follows a "therefore I am;" in a way, even persecutors "think" of us—if only to ensure that people like us *cease* to exist. However, even that scandalous minimum of assurance was soon lost and in no time at all we wandered, wherever chance had deposited us, among millions who reckoned us no more than the air they breathed—so we *became* air. Each one of us, it is safe to say, stopped one day at some corner in whatever city he found himself in and realized that the shouts and noises of the world suddenly sounded as if they were meant only for others—in short, he experienced himself as *no longer* existent. The suicides of émigrés only put the last seal on that loss of existence. Those who hanged themselves or were run over and were then carted away as rubbish had each died already, long before the rope or the wheel did their work, of worldlessness [*Weltlosigkeit*] and social starvation.

No wonder then that most of us, unable to live without our daily ration of such a proof of existence, fell over ourselves to embrace a fresh instantiation as quickly as we could. Most of us therefore felt the craving to transmute the shore which chance had washed us up on into a fate given second *Heimat*, a second home country—the craving to allow ourselves to be "supported" by the new country, regardless of whether it was capable of providing support or not and, indeed, whether it showed the least inclination to do so or not. We needed to be recognized by that country. Instead of being counted as a superfluous fifth or five thousandth wheel by the immigration authorities we wanted to *count*—in short: most of us felt the burning desire to swap our émigré status as quickly as possible for that of *immigrant*. Dismissing those who were plagued by that desire as disloyal or sycophantic would be simply unjust. Only hardened ideologues expect average people to rise overnight to the demands of an overwhelming disaster and to carry on regardless. No one has it in them to last very long as a "*surplus*" entity. However deplorable or scandalous it may sound: even those who have been reduced to mere functionaries in some bureaucratic apparatus find life easier to bear than those who are forced to go on existing without any function at all.

*

But it is not about those starving souls that I want to talk to you here but about "professional émigrés," those who willingly shouldered the burden of "being surplus" and would have opted for it even if their country of exile had welcomed them with open arms.

Do not get me wrong. The people I have in mind are not simply the "politicos" who (whether in spite or because of its defeat) were rooted in their *cause*; and who, as both their cause and their hope were unaffected by geography, were neither compelled to put down new roots nor would they have been able to do so.

Nor am I speaking of those who were incapable of adaptation, who were insufficiently flexible or prevented from meeting the challenge of what was foreign by their provinciality and their philistine narrowness. The "socio-psychological problematic of emigration" (as the playful phrase in today's doctoral dissertations has it) was not that simple. Conversely, it was the "*Heilbronners*" (that was what we used to call them, I do not know after what genius of mimicry), the petit-bourgeois, the small-town guys among us, who threw themselves recklessly at what was still utterly foreign to them; who, after the first fortnight, had reinvented themselves as old Parisians or born New Yorkers; and had come to see "us" as meaning "us Parisians" or "us New Yorkers" rather than "us Berliners" or "us Viennese." My concern here is with a third group, the group whose members kept their distance even though as gifted linguists and seasoned travelers they had wide horizons and great mental agility. They did so because it seemed undignified to them to allow the indignity "over there" to coerce them into running around from one day to the next as would-be Frenchmen or would-be Americans. That many of these environmental ascetics now responded to the fact that they had fallen victim to a political catastrophe by becoming politicized themselves to a lesser or greater degree and by joining some group or other was only natural. This meant that they were not entirely in limbo any longer; they now belonged, if not to a country, at least to a community of fate. It does not mean that it was exclusively their politicization that made them tenaciously insist that they were émigrés and nothing else.

*

The advantage of again feeling supported, of being allowed to consider oneself part of a new environment, which was either denied altogether to the would-be parvenus or granted to them only after they had been kept waiting a humiliatingly long time, was not seen as an advantage by these ascetics and they threw it to the wind on their own accord. They continued to lead the lives of nobodies by choice and by choice they left the option unused of adopting the new world as their "environment." Again by choice, they missed out on the opportunity to make themselves at home in it, identify with it, prove their worth in it or acquire reputation, let alone authority in it.

Among the hundreds of environmental ascetics I came across in exile I do not remember a single one who mentioned what an exorbitant price he had to pay for his asceticism. Yet that price had to be paid by almost every one of them.

And what a price it was!

Posthumous Puberty and its vindication

The price of *adulthood*. Asceticism alone does not make you an adult. Neither strength of character nor biological maturity brings about adulthood by itself. Adulthood always has the additional component of *social status*, a status that is open only to those who belong to a specific world; who know the "ways" of that world; who enjoy a certain autonomy *in* that world; who are recognized as competent, experienced and trustworthy *by* that world and employed by it as such; and for whom, *on the basis* of the authority accorded to them, it has become a matter of course to feel responsible for those who grant them recognition.[3] What is true of

---

3   This is probably why "adulthood" as an educational ideal is generally in decline today. Presumably it cannot be disentangled from the historical concepts of "autarky" and "economic autonomy." The world as apparatus [die verapparatisierte Welt] demands unfailing attention and smooth adaptation to its operations. Conscience, taking a stand and unspecific competence are not in demand in this world. It follows that there is no place for grown-ups in it and that grown-ups are therefore undesirable. This applies as much to the totalitarian world as to our welfare world, the conformist world under the sway of "soft terror." "Grown-up cogs" or "grown-up pension receivers" are "square circles." – Just as it was unheard of in the old days to cite his "adulthood" in the praise of a private soldier, so it is unthinkable today to specify this quality in the character of a company employee. It goes without saying that non-adulthood of the sort *we* were condemned to differed from that generally on the advance today. If we failed to grow up, it was not due to our excessive integration as cogs or beneficiaries; it was because we were unwilling to integrate in the first place. There is, incidentally, one other reason for the decline

the "proof of existence" is also true of adulthood: we get it from other people; it cannot thrive without social partnership. Those who are not beholden to anyone—the stranger, the adventurer, the anarchist, the saint—are forever cut off from adulthood, as are those who are utterly dependent on others and never attain autonomy.

That this could not but apply with full force to us whose program consisted in retaining our status as strangers is easy to see. Again, do not misunderstand this. This is not simply an admission that this determination of ours was no virtue. Reaching a conclusion is no easy matter here. It is by no means certain that adulthood is a virtue regardless of circumstances. If we call those "adults" who are fully aware of the weaknesses and contingencies that beset us; who know the "ways of the world;" and who make that knowledge—this is arguably also part of adulthood—the basis of their actions and non-actions, the result is that these people will never demand the "impossible" either from themselves or from others. This means that nothing is more alien for them than adherence to principles, which in their eyes is always a symptom of stubbornness and childishness. Seeing those two, adulthood and unquestioning adherence to principle, ever thrive in the same soil is not something I recall.

*

It goes without saying that eschewing adulthood did not buy us everlasting youth. Only a handful of the most energetic and most enterprising of us succeeded in transforming the liability of foregoing adulthood into the asset of real youth. Rather than staying youthful we simply failed to grow up. Adolescents are *on the cusp of growing up*. We, on the other hand, were *stuck on the cusp of growing up* or, in the worst cases of biographical disorientation, we were *no longer grown-up*. Many faces assumed, at an equal and equally frightening pace, expressions at once senile and youthful; they gave the impression of forward and backward momentum struggling for precedence, with the outcome undecided; the expression "old boy" suddenly sounded meaningful. The facet of youthfulness we were stuck with was its least attractive one. Given that we lived in the furnished rooms of transitory existence; that we saw our everyday lives as nothing more than an intermezzo; that the life we lived today was only a stand-in for the life we were going to lead the day after tomorrow; that, as bohemians against our will, we lived from hand to mouth; and that we refused to recognize the reality that surrounded us as a world in its own right and to make a go for it in that world, we made do with a life that was, seen both from outside and inside, completely *invalid*; with a state that, on the basis of its similarity to the lifestyle of the as yet unformed, could be called "puberty"—with the only qualification that in our case this was a "prolonged puberty" or—as was most commonly the case—a regression to a kind of displaced puberty; or, finally, a "posthumous puberty," which could be observed in those who saw only their previous life as valid, dismissing their present existence as a kind of shadowy epilogue.

---

of the ideal of adulthood: the rapid change of our world or, more precisely, of our modes of production, production models and types of demand. As a consequence of the rapidity of this change, younger workers, who are capable of updating themselves from day to day, have better access to information, are more "experienced" than their older colleagues, who are subject to regular panic attacks at the prospect of being cut off from experience altogether. The process of role change is already in full swing; it is no longer the exception for older generations to be able – and in many cases to be forced – to learn from their younger colleagues.

However plausible the term puberty may sound, its use demands the greatest caution and is justified only if it is followed immediately by the identification of those features of the regression it refers to that provide vindication. This is all the more urgent since the number of those who have led this kind of life and who can bear witness to it is dwindling day by day, increasing the risk of missing the last opportunities for rehabilitation. Conversely, the defamation of our existence at that time is becoming more and more popular as the years go by. It is not that rehabilitation is difficult in itself. It consists in a simple statement of facts: beyond the choice between obtrusive assimilation and the regression outlined above no third option was available to us. This meant that people who had just been appallingly humiliated and were in imminent danger of additionally humiliating themselves even more were at least in no doubt about what not to do. In other words: opting for "puberty" was the unseemly sacrifice that we had to make for our principles. Interpreting it as a symptom of collective immaturity would be nonsense. And it is a fact that we did not pay this high price in vain. The difference between us and those who were sensible enough to waste no time before launching the performance of the second or third "valid" act of their life, to make themselves at home in Paris, Shanghai, Oslo, Caracas or wherever else they had washed up was quite obvious. Whereas they ran the moral risk of succumbing to forgetfulness or of reclassifying the scandal as just one of those things, we "non-adults" were immune to such temptations. Instead of counting the rapidly passing years as valid, we observed the pause as a pause; we "marked time" at the point in time where "it" had happened; and, instead of joining the everyday conversation of our new environment, we preferred to keep up the howl of indignation we had set up on the very first day—no matter whether we were heard or not. Therefore we not only resisted the temptation to add to the humiliation we had already experienced by succumbing to forgetfulness or to accept the regime "over there" as an entity eligible for reconciliation, we were spared those temptations altogether.

(The Jews among us, including me, were treated to the even greater luxury of being spared the explicit effort to be moral. The possibilities of falling in line [*Gleichschaltung*] were excluded by our own exclusion [*Ausgeschaltetsein*] and entering into a pact with the enemy had been forestalled by that enemy himself. As virtue was not made nearly as difficult for us as life itself, we found ourselves, despite everything, in an abnormally advantageous situation.)

*

Hundreds of us were snatched by death from this "invalid" life, in places that were equally "invalid" for them, many of them grossly prematurely, which was inevitable in view of the precariousness of our existence. At least for a moment I want to think of these men and women. Not only because dying in the wrong place as someone who has been utterly defeated and is fully aware of his or her lack of validity is not a beautiful death;[4] nor only because the memory

---

4   In death, incidentally, we were real children of our time. If there is one dilemma that is characteristic of our epoch across the board it is this: millions (provided the place of their death can be identified) lie in the wrong graves, in graves in the wrong place, in graves to which their surviving relatives will never find their way. The woman who was cheated of her "valid death" and is buried in an out-of-the-way suburban cemetery in Paris; my father, whose ashes still await their homecoming in one of the tobacco cities in the American South; Walter Benjamin, who came to rest on his flight under a bush in the Pyrenees – they are all contemporaries of the American boys who rot away on jungle islands, the German youngsters who have become Caucasian soil and those Kyrgyz boys whose bodies have disintegrated beneath Wrocław's newly refurbished street surface.

of the eyewitnesses who were present at the time has been weakened (you know the reasons) or because those eyewitnesses have themselves died in the meantime. There is also the fact that many of these deaths were very strange. For many of the dying, dying was uncharacteristically, not to say humiliatingly easy. *"This one doesn't count,"* I heard one woman say about her imminent demise, as I stood by her mattress grave, *"this one's just for the stage."* Since there are no such things in exile as a deathbed audience, a funereal drama, flowery obituaries and the like the only thing she could have meant was: as this whole life is unreal even its end has been vitiated by the rust of unreality; this death is therefore not a "valid" death. In short, "we are even denied a valid death." For death to be real you have to die at home.

Absentees don't change

Occasionally the tenacity with which we clung to the provisional nature of our lives was motivated by what can only be called *magical thinking*. It seems to me as if, in the absence of genuine chances for action and for lack of any other option, we had hoped that we might produce some sort of *long-distance effect* simply by upholding the invalidity of our lives; that we might imprint the seal of impermanence and invalidity, which we had impressed on ourselves, also on the terror regime that raged over there; as if by consciously suspending our own existence we might succeed in suspending the power of the executioner on the other side. This effort at invalidation necessarily ended in self-deceit. I remember for instance a man in the room next to mine beneath the roof of a Quartier-Latin hotel, a formerly thoroughly grown-up trade unionist, who had escaped by the skin of his teeth in March '33. The man had lived next to me for over a year at the time of the Roehm putsch; during that entire period he had never wholly unpacked his pitiful valise (or, like Penelope, had returned it again and again to that pristine state that would enable him to leave at a moment's notice); he would have felt shame, he would even have considered it an act of treason if he had hung up his bits and pieces in the wardrobe and pushed his empty valise under his bed, thereby creating a symbolic point of no return. He could not read French either so he had only a sketchy idea about what was going on over there. Time more or less stood still for him.

And then the news of the Roehm putsch broke. A man had shouted the news into his den, running breathlessly from door to door and exaggerating the already immensely exaggerated radio report even more as he did so. Five minutes later my poor neighbor, his valise already (or still) packed in his hand, scarlet red in the face and not doubting in the least that the long overdue end of a provisional arrangement had now truly and finally come, stood in front of me and told me triumphantly that "the time had now come," that he was going "to pick up the thread again," and did I want to come with him? He reacted to my skepticism by shaking his head: I was being obstinate and defeatist as usual. For him the matter was beyond question. He was firmly convinced that he was now going to return to that day when his "valid" life had been torn apart. Clearly he had to stay put, clearly he *did* stay put. And it was equally clear that he would avoid my room from that day. Whenever we met in the hall by chance his hostile glance told me that he would never forgive me for having "sabotaged his return" (for this must have been what it looked like in his eyes). (His enmity has dissolved into thin air long since; he met his end two and a half years later somewhere in Spain, where he was granted a chance to "pick up the thread" by coming face to face once more with his nemesis—at least in his hour of death. Honor to his memory and to the symbol of his loyalty: his never fully unpacked valise.)

*

Let us beware of being unjust. Classifying my neighbor's behavior as simply immature or bizarre would be a mistake. We can only do justice to the man (and at the same time to ourselves) if we make allowance for the fact that, psychologically, *those who are absent* differ radically from those who are present (in their world); that longing (even the longing for old duties) has its own relationship to time. In the (un-seeing) eyes of the absent what is absent is *immutable*, it successfully resists change and is not subject to time; "the greater the distance that separates us from a friend, the more slowly he will age" (a "Molussian"[5] adage); and it may well be that even our idea of immortality results from absence—the absence of the dead. However that may be: what those who are absent, those who hope for an opportunity to return, have in mind or anticipate is never simply the return to a point in space but always a return to a point in time, even though that has passed away long since. That this is true for those who are conservative by temperament goes without saying. I met German-Americans in the States, immigrants from the time around 1900, who gave in to their homesickness and revisited the old country for the first time in the late twenties; on arrival they realized to their rising consternation that this was not the Wilhelmine Germany they had—in spite of what they had read in the papers and what they "knew"—expected. As if cheated of what was rightfully theirs, they dashed quick as they could back to America, cured of their homesickness, I may add, for good. Against such a delusion we, the "enemies of the other side," were no more immune. This was true even of those who, like my neighbor, had cursed the epoch in which they lived, had hoped for its abolition and had helped prepare for the leap into a new future. This leap into a new future, which they kept envisioning as still lying before them, presupposed, at least in the role of a *spring board*, that same execrable good old time whose abolition they had toiled for all their lives. And just as they remained loyal to their hope for the new future and kept "returning" to it, they remained loyal to their old spring board that was supposed to ease their leap to the new; they found themselves unable to do without it; they longed to return to it and thought it was possible to do so. Parting with an inveterate hope; admitting that a "future can lie behind you" and conceding that a new present may necessitate the design of a *new* "new future" and a new spring board on the way to that new future demands not only intelligence but also courage: the courage to admit that you have been wrong; the courage to enter decades of toil and risk (and therefore, in a certain sense, yourself) into the ledger as wasted; the courage to allow yourself to be labeled a coward or traitor; or, at best, the courage to live with a worldlessness that became ever more complete. Living all your life as a dissident and swimming against the current is already difficult enough; but swimming neither with the current nor with those swimming against it and avoiding becoming indolent or a turncoat is something hardly anyone is capable of. We should not be surprised that, of those who found it in them to take the leap, some did so extremely clumsily; even though they had

---

5   Molussia, a fictional country under totalitarian rule, puts in its most extended appearance in Anders' anti-fascist novel *Die molussische Katakombe* [The Molussian Catacomb], written in the 1930s. From then onward, Molussia served Anders as a private myth which he freely drew on whenever it suited his purpose. (TN)

the strength to launch themselves they were already much too exhausted for the further shore and landed instead in an abyss of melancholy or suicide; or else they stumbled into the camp of some oppositional group, where their right to stay was contingent on the payment of an extortionate fee: allowing themselves to be used as propaganda instruments. There were those who were not deterred by this, presumably because it let them enjoy a minimum of continuity or at least the semblance of such a minimum: the possibility of retaining, against all odds, the old devotion to their cause, despite the momentous changes that had taken place.

Maintaining one's dignity was hard, as you can see. Unbalanced to start with, we were treading a narrow path where each step threatened to bring us crashing down. Once you accept the impossibility of our situation you will understand how difficult it is for us today to hold our tongues when Hinz and Kunz[6] voice are trotting out their critiques of our lives as émigrés. In fact it seems to become increasingly common today for Hinz and Kunz, who never even dreamt of taking decisions themselves, least of all in the Hitler era, to set themselves up in moral judgment over our lives at that time—and for them to feel qualified for the office of judge not despite having connived at every organized stupidity but rather because they had: they had, in their own words, "only ever connived" at those stupidities. It is the word "only" that they love to insist upon; and what makes them think they are beyond reproach is the fact that they had always been clever enough to avoid taking any personal responsibility for stupidities.

Our own actions have often been mistaken, stupid and hurtful, falling a long way short of the ideal standard of a rational being. But we retained at least some of our human dignity: our stupidities were our own; they arose from scruples that we had conceived ourselves and we knew that we would have to bear the consequences ourselves. Even though this was in vain, it is still worth underscoring—given that a government minister was good enough not long ago to say in public, when discussing a prominent émigré, that it was common knowledge what those who had stayed put in the Hitler era had done but that it would be interesting to find out how émigrés had lived during that time. If the minister has the stomach for it, he can find some information here.

Ignominy

I said that the misery of our "regression to puberty" did not worry us, that we did not recognize it for what it was. How was that?

There were three causes.

First, a mechanical cause: even abstention from habit and an improvised life become habitual before long and, as with all habits, the speed with which they form ruts is such that we do not become aware of the process.

Second, a moral cause: it would have appeared inappropriate and an unjustifiable waste of energy to focus attention on ourselves and, even more objectionably, on a delicate psychological problem such as our "second puberty." With a positive twist, this meant that we had other worries, greater, more congenial, more dignified ones—worries that did not relate to our own

---

6   The German counterparts of Tom, Dick and Harry (TN).

person. For no matter what concern we were pursuing and no matter where we were, in waiting rooms, prefectures or in search of accommodation, these were never *our* concerns. Our mind was always somewhere else. It was on what was going on at home, on those who were perhaps attempting to escape at that very moment, who were making a Gestapo cellar reverberate with their screams or had already been slain and were lying on the floor unheeded. Last but not least, our mind was also on the breath-stopping possibility that the catastrophe that had befallen human rights, which we felt had seized us as its first victims, might engulf the entire globe.

*

Is that how it really was? Or was there something different?

Well, there was. This brings me to my last cause. There was, after all, a third worry. And this third worry was made of different stuff. It could not be swept from the table with the same casual, grandiose gesture as the "delicate" psychological problems.

I am now referring to the mundane worry about how to stay alive. Each of us (the exceptions from this rule are hardly worth mentioning) had, first of all, to hunt down the bare essentials, such as a bed, ration stamps, illegal employment, and, above all, a *life permit* (a.k.a. work permit). And the hunt for this life permit (mostly spent waiting in corridors) held out hardly any hope at all. We had exchanged rain not for fair weather but for another bout of rain (by moving from one world of unemployment to another world of unemployment). In some cases this took a particularly sinister turn: the hunt itself became a punishable offense, carrying a deadly penalty (being transported back to the border). This meant that we were officially forced to evade the law by accepting illegal employment; without illegal employment we would have lacked not only the small change that you need to live from hand to mouth but also the big notes required for the work permit. In other words: the state demanded payment of sums of money whose acquisition that same state had made a punishable offense.[7] The upshot of this situation: this mundane worry was, at least in the initial stages of emigration, so overwhelming and so nerve-racking that it frequently ran out winner by several lengths in the worry stakes.

And that made us blind not only to "delicate" problems but also quite frequently to real, more deserving ones; it forced us to sideline even those last as a luxury we could not afford. It often happened to people like us that, exhausted from hunting around, we found ourselves *deprived* not of sleep but *of sleeplessness*, of that sleeplessness that we would have needed to give adequate consideration to our real worries. "Too tired for the furies," as the Molussian phrase goes.

"Too tired for the furies"—that describes the lowest low of our humiliation. Anyone who does not have the time and the strength to allow themselves to be pursued by their real worries and to suffer from them is deprived even of the *right to their worries* and the *right to their suffering*—and at this point the deprivation of rights tilts into downright ignominy—which of course says nothing at all against those who had to live with this ignominy, given that

---

7   That thousands of us managed to achieve and/or to shoulder the impossible defies comprehension today. At the time, every success was certainly considered to be *the* exception. But there must have been countless such successes: Kafka would probably have suspected that breaking the rule was itself the administratively preordained rule and he would have been right.

ignominy is hardly ever the consequence of guilt.[8] However that may be, I witnessed scenes in which to my intense sadness co-sufferers of mine became fellows in misplaced suffering, for instance by having a break-down because they were unable to get hold of papers that were both idiotic and indispensable or by suddenly clowning around noisily because some coincidence had dropped those papers in their lap—scenes, in short, where we reacted to our trivial plight as if we had no other worries, as if we had never caught wind of the atrocities on the other side or had never noticed the formation of the storm clouds of World War Two.

Under the title of "Die falschen Tränen" [The wrong tears] (and told with unmistakable *schadenfreude*, raising the suspicion that this is all about a cleverly executed sleight-of-hand), the Molussian chronicle tells the story of prisoner Mo; awaiting beheading, Mo felt such hellish pain from a nail in his shoe that his fear of death took second place; freed of this torture at last, he smiled, they say, as he bowed his neck under the sword.

In a certain sense this ignominious story was ours. When we really ought to have been worrying about other things, we too were often driving ourselves mad with worry over the "nail in our shoe" and crying our eyes out for all the wrong reasons. This is because nothing demands stricter discipline and keener discernment than coping with the task of *emotional schizophrenia*. Suffering from two sources of pain that, even though they coincided in time, belonged to different types and were utterly different in terms of rank, we tried to "cope" by simultaneously being mindful of both while keeping them separate nevertheless. Where, when, and from whom could we possibly have learnt that? The number of those who were up to that task, who could for example school themselves to partition the pain, keeping one type for the daytime, the other for the night—I am going to say something about those in a moment—that number was very small indeed.

*

And yet it is precisely the ignominious experience of "begrudged suffering" that I would not want to do without today, for the simple reason that it *was* ignominious. To those who are interested in their own experiences only in so far as they believe they are entitled to attribute general validity to them today; who mobilize their memories and push their self-analysis to the point where they hope discoveries about today's world will become possible; and who perceive a lack of solidarity in turning their back to the chief moral dilemmas humanity is facing today—to those at least the experience of this ignominy is simply indispensable.

Those who have never realized to their horror that, in the midst of a global catastrophe, they were prevented from attending to what was happening and were condemned instead to eating their utterly private bread with utterly private tears do not know today's hellish powers;[9] they have failed to take in today's main scandal. This scandal systematically prevents us—and by us I mean the millions that make up humankind—from participating emotion-

---

8   Real ignominy was for those who were thrown into the concentration camps like so much trash to live out their last days waiting for their extermination. Compared with such ignominy our woes amounted to sheer privilege. Those who are still here today experience the undeservedness of this privilege as even deeper ignominy; and there is such a thing as the shame-filled community of those who happen not to have been gassed.

9   This is an allusion to the harp-player's song from Goethe's *Wilhelm Meisters Lehrjahre*: "Wer nie sein Brot in Tränen aß / Wer nie die kummervollen Nächte / Auf seinem Bette weinend saß, / Der kennt euch nicht, ihr himmlischen Mächte!" ["Who never ate with tears his bread / Who never through night's heavy hours / Sat weeping on his lonely bed, – / He knows you not, ye heavenly powers." Translator unknown] (TN).

ally in the chief dilemmas of our world; it forces us to shed "wrong tears," tears spilled over insignificant, trivial matters; and it deprives us of the time, the strength and the right to shed tears over what does have a claim, if not the sole claim, to them. A hundred years ago Marx reacted with gloom to the ignominy of "false consciousness." How humane the ignominy of a false worldview appears compared with today's false emotions!

It goes without saying that not having experienced this ignominy confers no more ignominy on anyone than having had bodily experience of it constitutes a claim to merit or virtue. However, as this ignominy is now an essential part of humanity's predicament the rule applies that whoever was lucky enough not to be touched by it is thereby precluded from making pronouncements about those millions; conversely, that right (including the infinitesimally small chance of being able to speak on behalf of humanity) may be claimed only by those who have experienced in person the ignominy of being totally stripped of all rights. To that extent this experience can perhaps prove useful: note the "can" and the "perhaps."[10]

Stammering along

Inevitably the consequences of this way of life find their way into our *speech*. In fact it can only be said with a certain reservation that the general definition of man (λόγον ἔχειν) applied to émigrés. Anyone who has to start from scratch in a new world, a world they may well feel to be invalid, let alone anyone who has to start from scratch several times over, is not only a castaway in a succession of countries but also in a succession of different languages. And this means both for those who are happy to join the general chatter and for the linguistically independent[11] that they are suddenly condemned to interact with their environment at a level

---

10 Even though there is nothing more repugnant to us than ignominy, no experience may be as entitled to the appellation "experience" as the experience of ignominy; this is because – my initial "even though" was misconceived – experience is the more *real* the less congenial to us is *what* we experience. The point I chiefly want to make is this: not only does the positive usually remain invisible (the way our health, being congenial to us, is invisible as opposed to our sickness) but – this is where the "calamity of happiness" comes in – those things and circumstances that fit us perfectly or that we have tailored to fit us perfectly deprive us of the opportunity to encounter the world, which is, after all, what we mean when we say we experience something. The made-to-measure shoe cheats our foot of the experience of root and stone. Genuine experiences do not come into being as *adaequatio* (of *res* and *intellectus* or of sun and "sun-like eye" or of an easeful world and humanity) but on the basis of *inadaequatio*, as their *collisio*, in which the unknown asserts *qua* unknown its totally uncongenial power and reality. With regard to experience the rule applies: *The false is the true.* Nothing would therefore be less justified than to think that thanks to technology we live in an age of nature and world experience. On the contrary: since technology, however much experience of nature it may presuppose, aims eudaimonistically to make the world more comfortable for us—and by the same token to make it conform to us—and to reduce friction between ourselves and the world to a minimum, it transforms us into people who are short of experience, who lack experience, who are incapable of experience. As all this applies equally to the moral sphere, the experience of what is morally least congenial to us—ignominy—may be considered to be the most valid of all experiences.

11 It was remarkable that those who had succeeded in mastering an unmistakable idiom and had acquired an indisputable linguistic prowess felt much more inhibited by foreign languages, at least by spoken foreign languages, than those—including those writers—who had never known anything but middle-of-the-road complicity with other speakers or writers. While the latter, boasting the advantageous character defect known as "talent," were able sooner or later to go with the flow of conversation in their second or third language, men like Thomas Mann or Brecht were exceedingly unwilling to make do with a low level of proficiency and least of all to mangle a foreign language. It is equally remarkable that the lucky masters of the *international* language —musicians—quickly

several storeys below their real level and that this primitivization proves to be a boomerang: the people the stammerer is in contact with, who have neither the time to think about what causes his stammering nor the inclination to make allowances for it, now relegate him to a level in keeping with the poor quality of his speech. This is not only painful nor is it only humiliating, it is a disaster. No one can live for years exclusively in languages that he has no command of and that he is capable at best of parroting imperfectly and not fall victim to his linguistic incapacity. How we express ourselves is decisive for who we become. Distinctions that we are incapable of making as speakers (no longer or not yet) soon cease to be relevant for us as sensuous or moral beings. This applied to us émigrés as much as to anyone else who finds himself in this situation. The moment we arrived safe in our place of exile we found ourselves surrounded by a new danger, the danger of dropping to a lower level of speech and of becoming stammerers. And stammerers is what many of us did become, even bilingual stammerers. While we had not yet mastered our French, English or Spanish, our German was already starting to crumble away, so secretly and incrementally in most cases that we did not notice the loss any more than we had noticed the loss of our adulthood. And those of us who had the misfortune to be stranded abroad as solitary specimens were even deprived of the possibility of realizing that their own language was no longer intact since they had no opportunity of speaking it in the first place.

And yet—I am now reverting to those who were indeed capable of deliberate schizophrenia—there were a few who were aware of this danger, a few who made despairing efforts to defend themselves against it, who immersed themselves fanatically in their mother tongue, which was being denied them both here and over there, and who made it a matter of habit to snatch the least moment in which to write in German or even to try and do so for the very first time. And those who did so were not motivated only by their clumsiness in foreign languages or only by the possibility that writing in German afforded them of assuaging even a little their longing for home [Heimweh]; nor were they motivated only (even if this "only" is perfectly legitimate) by the fact that *what* they wrote was exclusively intended for those over there, at least for the tomorrow of those others there—but also because they could not bear the indignity of leading a stammering life; because language was the only tool they had to help them stave off, if not physical extinction, at least the final stages of degradation; and because language is the only inalienable good, the only piece of home that, provided they were prepared to defend it, was still at their command even in a state of unqualified degradation and that would always testify (if only to themselves) to where they really belonged. As is well known, there were writers, even writers of poetry in the camps who, before they fell victim to those mercenaries and torturers who were also torturers of the German language, tried to write verses on scraps of newspapers or on the back of their number tags, verses that could not possibly—from what those writers knew—find a way into the open at some stage. We were the brothers of these people, even if we were unspeakably more privileged.

There may never have been any lovers of language and writers who were stranger than they were. Nor has there ever been a life style that less resembled the one we expect from men of

---

felt at home wherever they were and that only few of them are still stubborn enough to cling to their "professional émigré" status as writers like us, who remain wedded in the most obsolete manner to our provincial dialect.

letters. They too were inevitably forced to spend their days hunting down the basics necessary for survival; they too peddled (provided they had been graced with the requisite documents) soap or salami from door to door, an enterprise in which their only hope of being understood rested on fortuitously knocking at the door of fellow sufferers, who, subsisting as they did on giving German lessons or selling homemade jam, hardly qualified as customers. This is what poets' conferences looked like in those days. Time to pore over words was never available unless we cut back on sleep, unless we made the change from day to night coincide with a change from daytime language to night-time language. The use of our night-time language then enabled us to safeguard the continuum of our lives until the hectic daytime hours seemed to be no more than holes in the fabric in our lives.

These were the circumstances that formed some into writers perhaps not without merit. Even though more often than not we wrote on our knees rather than at a desk; always for no one or for tomorrow's people rather than for impatient editors; always for the drawer or the valise, never for the bookcase, what an apprenticeship those years afforded us! For something that had barely gone beyond planning to be snatched from our hand was completely unheard of and the questions of who was going to come up with what comment on it in what medium, whether the piece would be completed "on schedule" (what schedule?) and would then "catch on" (catch on where?)—such questions never occurred to us. Still, what an opportunity to ask yourself whether the piece of writing you were engaged on was really needed and who you were writing it for. What an opportunity to excise what was only partially successful, to throw away what had got bogged down and to so create room in your backpack for boots and bread! What happiness to get rid of a misconceived piece by accidentally leaving it behind in a handbag or by having it idiotically requisitioned by some authority—and to get rid of it so irrevocably that its need for revision could never again importune us. It goes without saying that much was lost in the dilemma we were caught in, including much that could not have been bettered, and many of us have sunk by the wayside. Some however, as chance would have it, did not sink by the wayside and did eventually make their way back. If three or four of those who were accidentally spared are now capable of "wielding a pen," as the phrase goes; if they have learnt to find that tone for the ears they want to reach that actually penetrates to them; that word for the point they want to hit that only hits that point; and the syntax for the context they believe is necessary to depict that depicts only that context—then they owe the mastery of their trade to the opportunity of a long apprenticeship utterly devoid of opportunities. In the meantime we have dedicated our work to the memory of some of these men. But there is no one who has a claim to our dedication as valid as that staked by our teacher: the fruitful misery of exile.

Günther Anders

Theses for the Atomic Age[*]

1. Hiroshima as World Condition: On August 6, 1945, the Day of Hiroshima, a New Age began: the age in which at any given moment we have the power to transform any given place on our planet, and even our planet itself, into a Hiroshima. On that day we became, at least "modo negativo," omnipotent; but since, on the other hand, we can be wiped out at any given moment, we also became totally impotent. However long this age may last, even if it should last forever, it is "The Last Age": for there is no possibility that its "differentia specifica," the possibility of our self-extinction, can ever end—but by the end itself.

2. The Time of the End Versus the End of Time: Thus, by its very nature, this age is a "respite," and our "mode of being" in this age must be defined as "not yet being non-existing," "not quite yet being non-existing." Thus the basic moral question of former times must be radically reformulated: instead of asking *"How* should we live?", we now must ask *"Will* we live?" For us, who are "not yet non-existing" in this Age of Respite, there is but one answer: although at any moment The Time of the End could turn into The End of Time, we must do everything in our power to make The End Time endless. Since we believe in the possibility of The End of Time, we are Apocalyptics, but since we fight against this man-made Apocalypse, we are— and this has never existed before—"Anti-Apocalyptics."

3. Not Atomic Weapons in the Political Situation, but Political Actions in the Atomic Situation: Although it sounds absolutely plausible, it is misleading to say that atomic weapons exist in our political situation. This statement has to be turned upside down in order to become true. As the situation today is determined and defined exclusively by the existence of "atomic weapons," we have to state: political actions and developments are taking place within the atomic situation.

4. Not Weapon, but Enemy: What we are fighting is not this or that enemy who could be attacked or liquidated by atomic means, but the atomic situation as such. Since this enemy is the enemy of all people, those who, up to now, had considered each other to be enemies, have now to become allies against the common menace.—Peace actions from which we exclude those with whom we wish to live in peace amount to hypocrisy, self-righteousness and a waste of time.

---

[*]   In February, 1959 at the Free University of Berlin, Günther Anders conducted a two-day seminar on "The Moral Implications of the Atomic Age." At its conclusion, the students asked Anders for a short text which could serve them as a basis for further discussion. Anders dictated these "theses," which later appeared as "Thesen zum Atomzeitalter," *Berliner Hefte* (1960), 16–22. The translation here printed in the *Massachusetts Review*, Vol. 3, No. 3 (Spring 1962): 493–505 is by Mr. Anders; the *Massachusetts Review* has granted permission to reprint Anders' essay.

5. To Threaten with Atomic Weapons Is Totalitarian: A pet theory broad enough to be embraced by subtle philosophers as well as by brutal politicians, by Jaspers as well as by Strauss, runs: "If it were not for our ability to threaten with total annihilation, we would be unable to hold the totalitarian menace in check." This is a sham argument for the following reasons: 1) The atom bomb *has* been used, although those who used it were not in danger of falling victim to a totalitarian power. 2) This argument is a fossil from the "ancient" days of atomic monopoly and has become suicidal today. 3) The catchword "totalitarian" is taken from a political situation which not only *has* already fundamentally changed, but will continue to change; atomic war, on the other hand, excludes all chance of such a change. 4) By threatening with atomic war, thus with liquidation, we cannot help being totalitarian; for this threat amounts to blackmail and transforms our globe into one vast concentration camp from which there is no way out. Thus, whoever bases the legitimacy of this extreme deprivation of freedom upon the alleged interests of freedom is a hypocrite.

6. Expansion of Our Horizon: Since radioactive clouds do not bother about milestones, national boundaries or curtains, distances are abolished. Thus in this Time of the End everybody is in deadly reach of everybody else. If we do not wish to lag behind the effects of our products—to do so we would be not only a deadly shame but a shameful death—we have to try to widen our horizon of responsibility until it equals that horizon within which we can destroy everybody and be destroyed by everybody—in short, till it becomes global. Any distinction between near and far, neighbors or foreigners, has become invalid; today we are all "proximi."

7. "The United Generations": Not only our horizon of space must be widened, but also that of time. Since acts committed today (test explosions, for instance) affect future generations just as perniciously as our own, the future belongs within the scope of our present. "The future has already begun"[1]—since tomorrow's thunder belongs to today's lightning. The distinction between the generations of today and of tomorrow has become meaningless; we can even speak of a *League of Generations* to which our grandchildren belong, just as automatically as we ourselves. They are our *"neighbors in time."* By setting fire to *our* house, we cannot help but make the flames leap over into the cities of the future, and the not-yet-built homes of the not-yet-born generations will fall to ashes together with our homes. Even our ancestors are full-fledged members of this League: for by dying we would make them die, too—a second time, so to speak; and after this second death everything would be as if they had never been.

8. Nothingness—the Effect of the Not-Imagined Nothingness: The apocalyptic danger is all the more menacing because we are unable to picture the immensity of such a catastrophe. It is difficult enough to visualize someone as not-being, a beloved friend as dead; but compared with the task our fantasy has to fulfil now, it is child's play. For what we have to visualize today is not the not-being of something particular within a framework, the existence of which can be taken for granted, but the nonexistence of this framework itself, of the world as a whole, at least of the world as mankind. Such "total abstraction" (which, as a mental performance, would correspond to our performance of total destruction) surpasses the capacity of our natural power of imagination: "Transcendence of the Negative." But since, as "homines fabri," we

---

1   This formula is taken from the title of Robert Jungk's book, *Die Zukunft hat schon begonnen.*

are capable of actually producing nothingness, we cannot surrender to the fact of our limited capacity of imagination: the attempt, at least, must be made to visualize this nothingness.

9. *"We Are Inverted Utopians":* The basic dilemma of our age is that "We are smaller than ourselves," incapable of mentally realizing the realities which we ourselves have produced. Therefore we might call ourselves "inverted Utopians": while ordinary Utopians are unable to actually produce what they are able to visualize, we are unable to visualize what we are actually producing.

10. *"The Promethean Discrepancy"²:* This inverted Utopianism is not simply one fact among many, but the outstanding one, for it defines the moral situation of man today. The dualism to which we are sentenced is no longer that of spirit against flesh or of duty against inclination, is neither Christian nor Kantian, but that of our capacity to produce as opposed to our power to imagine.

11. *The Supra-Liminal:* Not only has imagination ceased to live up to production, but feeling has ceased to live up to responsibility. It may still be possible to imagine or to repent the murdering of one fellow man, or even to shoulder responsibility for it; but to picture the liquidation of one hundred thousand fellow men definitely surpasses our power of imagination. The greater the possible effect of our actions, the less are we able to visualize it, to repent of it or to feel responsible for it; the wider the gap, the weaker the brake-mechanism. To do away with one hundred thousand people by pressing a button is incomparably easier than to slay one individual. The "sub-liminal," the stimulus too small to produce any reaction, is recognized in psychology; more significant, however, though never seen, let alone analyzed, is the "supra-liminal": the stimulus too big to produce any reaction or to activate any brake-mechanism.

12. *Senses Distort Sense. Fantasy Is Realistic:* Since our pragmatic life horizon (sec. 6), the one within which we can reach and be reached, has become limitless, we must try to visualize this limitlessness, although by trying to do so we would evidently violate the "natural narrowness" of our imagination. Although insufficient by its very nature, there is nothing other than imagination which could be considered as an organon of truth. Certainly not perception. Perception is a "false witness," in a far more radical sense than Greek philosophy meant when warning against it. For the senses are myopic, their horizon is "senselessly" narrow. It is not in the wide land of imagination that escapists of today like to hide, but in the ivory tower of perception.³

13. *The Courage To Fear:* When speaking of the "imagining of nothingness," the act meant is not identical with what psychology imagines to be imagination for I speak of fear, which *is* the imagining of nothingness "in concreto." Therefore we can improve the formulations of the last paragraphs by saying: it is our capacity to fear which is too small and which does not

---

2   The elaboration of this category is given in the author's *Die Antiquiertheit des Menschen*, 3ʳᵈ ed. (Munich: C. H. Beck, 1961), 21–95.

3   No wonder that we feel uneasy in front of those normal pictures which are painted according to the conventional rules of perspective. Though realistic in the ordinary sense of the word, they are actually utterly unrealistic since they ignore the limitless horizon of today's world.

correspond to the magnitude of today's danger. As a matter of fact, nothing is more deceitful than to say, "We live in the Age of Anxiety anyway." This slogan is not a statement but a tool manufactured by the fellow travellers of those who wish to prevent us from becoming really afraid, of those who are afraid that we once may produce the fear commensurate to the magnitude of the real danger. On the contrary, we are living in the Age of Inability to Fear. Our imperative: "Expand the capacity of your imagination," means, in concreto: "Increase your capacity of fear." Therefore: don't fear fear, have the courage to be frightened,[4] and to frighten others, too. Frighten thy neighbor as thyself. This fear, of course, must be of a special kind: 1) a fearless fear, since it excludes fearing those who might deride us as cowards, 2) a stirring fear, since it should drive us into the streets instead of under cover, 3) a loving fear, not fear *of* the danger ahead but *for* the generations to come.

14. Productive Frustration: Time and again our efforts to comply with the imperative, "Widen your capacity to fear and make it commensurate with the immensity of the effects of your activities," will be frustrated. It is even possible that our efforts will make no progress whatsoever. But even this failure should not intimidate us; repeated frustration does not refute the need for repeating the effort. On the contrary, every new failure bears fruit, for it makes us vigilant against our initiating further actions whose effects transcend our capacity to fear.

15. "Displaced Distance": If we combine our statement about the abolition of distances (sec. 6) with that about the Promethean discrepancy (sec. 10)—and only this combination makes the picture of our situation complete—we reach the following result: the "abolition" of time and space distances does not amount to abolition of distances altogether, for today we are confronted with the daily increasing distance between production and imagination.

16. End of the Comparative: Our products and their effects surpass not only the maximum size of what we are able to visualize or to feel, but even the size of what we are able to *use*. It is common knowledge that our production and supply often exceed our demand and produce the need for the production of new needs and new demands. But this is not all: today we have reached the situation in which products are manufactured which simply contradict the very concept of need, products which simply *cannot* be needed, which are too big in an absolute sense. In this stage our own products are being domesticated as if they were forces of nature. Today's efforts to produce so-called "clean weapons" are attempts of a unique kind: for what man is now trying is to increase the quality of his products by decreasing their effects.
If the number and the possible performance of the already existing stock of weapons are sufficient to reach the absurd aim of the annihilation of mankind, then today's increase in production is even more absurd and proves that the producers do not understand at all what they are actually doing. The comparative, the principle of progress and competition, has lost its sense. *Death is the boundary line of the comparative: one cannot be deader than dead and one cannot be made deader than dead.*

17. Appeal to Competence Proves Moral Incompetence: We have no reason to presuppose (as, for instance, Jaspers does) that those in power are better able to imagine the immensity of the

---

4   It is not Roosevelt's "Freedom *from* Fear" for which we have to strive, but the Freedom *to* Fear.

danger or that they realize the imperatives of the atomic age better than we ordinary "morituri." This presupposition is even irresponsible. And it would be far more justified to suspect them of having not even the slightest inkling of what is at stake. We have only to think of Adenauer, who dared to berate eighteen of the greatest physicists of today, telling them that they are incompetent in the "field of atomic armament and atomic weapons questions," and that they should talk shop instead and not "meddle" with those issues. It is precisely by using these vocables that he and his kind demonstrate their moral incompetence. For there is no more final and no more fatal proof of moral blindness than to deal with the Apocalypse as if it were a "special field," and to believe that rank is identical with the monopoly to decide the "to be or not to be" of mankind. Some of those who stress competence are doing so solely in order to disguise the anti-democratic elements of their monopoly. By no means should we be taken in by this camouflage. After all, we are living in allegedly democratic states. If the word "Democracy" has any sense at all, then it means that precisely the province *beyond* our professional competence should concern us, that we are not only entitled, but obliged —not as specialists but as citizens and human beings—to participate in deciding about the affairs of the "res publica." Since, after all, we *are* the "res publica," the reproach that we are "meddling" amounts to the ridiculous accusation that we are interfering with our own business. There has never been and will never be an affair more "publica" than today's decision about our survival. By renouncing "interference," we not only fail to fulfill our democratic duties, but we risk our collective suicide.

18. *Abolition of "Action"*: The possible annihilation of mankind seems to be an "action." Therefore those who contribute to it seem to be "acting." They are not. Why not? Because there is hardly anything left which, by a behaviorist, could be classified as "acting." For activities which formerly had occurred as actions and were meant and understood as such by the acting subjects themselves, now have been replaced by other variants of activity: 1) by working, 2) by "triggering."

1) WORK: SUBSTITUTE FOR ACTION: The employees in Hitler's death factories did, so to speak, "nothing," thought they had done nothing, because they had done "nothing but work." By "nothing but work" I mean that kind of performance (generally considered to be the natural and only type of operation today) in which the *eidos* of the end-product remains invisible to the operator—no, does not even matter to him—no, is not even supposed to matter to him—no, ultimately is not even permitted to matter to him. Typical of today's work is its seeming moral neutrality; *non olet*; no work-goal, however evil, can defile the worker. Nearly all jobs assigned to and performed by man today now are understood as belonging to this universally accepted and monocratic type of operation. Work—the camouflaged form of action. This camouflage exempts even the mass murderer from his guilt, since, according to today's standards, the Worker is not only "freed" from responsibility for his work, but he simply *cannot* be made guilty by his work.
Consequence: once we have realized that today's fatal equation runs, "All action is work," we have to have the courage to invert it and to formulate: *"All work is action."*

2) "TRIGGERING"—SUBSTITUE FOR WORK: What is true of work applies even more to "triggering," for in triggering, the specific characteristics of work—effort and consciousness

of effort—are diminished, if not nullified. Triggering—the camouflaged form of work. As a matter of fact, there exists hardly anything today which cannot be achieved through triggering. It can even happen that one first push of a button sets in motion a whole chain of secondary triggerings—till the end-result—never intended, never imagined, by the first button pusher—consists of millions of corpses. Seen behavioristically, such a manipulation would be considered neither work nor action. Although seemingly no one would have done anything, this "doing nothing" would actually produce annihilation and nothingness. No button-pusher (if such a minimum-operator is still required at all) feels *that* he is acting. And since the scene of the act and the scene of the suffering no longer coincide, since cause and effect are torn apart, no one can perceive what he is doing—*"schizotopia"* by analogy with "schizophrenia." Evident again (see above): only he who continuously tries to visualize the effect of his doings, however far away in space or in time the scene of his effects may be, has the chance of truth; perception "falls short."

This variant of camouflage is unique. While formerly it had always been the aim of camouflaging to prevent the prospective victim from recognizing the danger, or to protect the doer from the enemy, now camouflaging is meant to prevent the doer himself from recognizing what he is doing. Therefore today's doer is also a victim. Eatherly[5] belongs to those whom he has destroyed.

19. The Deceitful Form of Today's Lie: The examples of camouflage teach us something about the present-day type of lie. For today the lie no longer needs to dress itself in the costume of an assertion; ideologies are no longer required. Victorious today is that type of lie which prevents us from even suspecting that it *could* be a lie; and this victory has become possible because today lying no longer needs to assume the disguise of assertions. For whereas until now, in "honest hypocrisy," lies had pretended to be truths, they now are camouflaging themselves in a completely different costume.

1) Instead of appearing in the form of assertions, they now appear in that of naked *individual words* which, although seemingly saying nothing, secretly already contain their deceitful predicate. Example: since the term "atomic weapon" makes us believe that what it designates may be classified as a weapon, it already is an assertion, and as such, a lie.[6]

2) Instead of appearing in the form of false assertions, they appear in that of *falsified reality.* Example: once an action appears in the disguise of "work," its action-character becomes invisible; and so much so that it no longer reveals, not even to the doer himself, that ultimately he is acting; and thus the worker, although working conscientiously, enjoys the chance of renouncing conscience with a clean conscience.

3) Instead of appearing in the form of false assertions, lies appear in that of *things.* In the last example it is still man who is active, although he misinterprets his acting as working. But even

---

5   See *Burning Conscience, The Case of the Hiroshima Pilot, Claude Eatherly, Told in His Letters to Günther Anders* (New York: Monthly Review, 1962).

6   For a discussion of why the atomic bomb cannot be classified as a weapon, see the author's *Die Antiquiertheit des Menschen,* 247 ff., *Der Mann auf der Brücke* (Munich: C. H. Beck, 1959), 95 ff., and *Off limits für das Gewissen* (Rowohlt, 1961), 30 (English edition: London: Weidenfeld and Nicolson, 1962, p. 15). The main argument runs: a weapon is a means. Means are defined by dissolving in their ends, ends by their surviving the means. This cannot be applied to atomic weapons, since there is no end which could survive the use of those weapons and no end conceivable which could justify such an absurd means.

this minimum can disappear—and this, the supreme triumph of lying, has already begun. For during the last decade action has shifted (of course through human action) from the province of man to another region: to that of machines and instruments. These have become, so to speak, "incarnated" or "reified actions." Example: through the mere fact of its existence, the atom bomb is an uninterrupted blackmailing—and that blackmailing has to be classified as an "action" is, after all, indisputable. Since we have shifted our activities and responsibilities to the system of our products, we believe ourselves able to keep our hands clean, to remain "decent people." But it is, of course, just this surrender of responsibility that is the climax of irresponsibility.

This, then, is our absurd situation: in the very moment in which we have become capable of the most monstrous action, the destruction of the world, "actions" seem to have disappeared. Since the mere existence of our products already proves to be action, the trivial question, how we should use our products for action (whether, for instance, for deterrence), is an almost fraudulent one, since this question obscures the fact that the products, by their mere existence, already *have* acted.

20. Not Reification but Pseudo-Personalization: One cannot adequately interpret the phenomenon by giving it the Marxian label of "reification," for this term designates exclusively the fact that man is reduced to a thing-function. We are stressing, however, the fact that the qualities and functions taken away from man by his reification are now becoming qualities and functions of the products themselves, that they transform themselves into pseudo-persons, since, through their mere existence, they are acting. This second phenomenon has been ignored by philosophy, although it is impossible to understand our situation without seeing both sides of the process simultaneously.

21. The Maxims of Pseudo-Persons: These pseudo-persons have rigid principles of their own. The principle of "atomic weapons," for example, is pure nihilism, because, if they could speak, they would say: "Whatever we destroy, it's all the same to us." In them, nihilism has reached its climax and has become naked "Annihilism."[7]

Since action has shifted from man to work and products, examination of our conscience today cannot confine itself to listening to the voice of our heart. It is far more important to listen to the mute voice of our products in order to know their principles and maxims—in other words, the "shift" has to be reversed and revoked. Therefore, today's imperative runs: have and use only those things, the inherent maxims of which could become your own maxims and thus the maxims of a general law.

22. Macabre Abolition of Hatred: If (sec. 18) the scene of action and the scene of suffering are torn apart—if the suffering does not occur at the place of the act, if acting becomes acting without visible effect, if suffering becomes suffering without identifiable cause—hatred disappears, although in a totally delusive way.

---

7   Even this climax of nihilism has been surpassed, for the principle of the neutron bomb would run: "Whomever we destroy, it's all the same to us. The world of objects, however, has to remain sacrosanct. *Products should not kill other products.*" As a matter of fact, this is the most radical perversion of moral principles which has ever existed.

Atomic war will be waged with less hatred than any war before: attacker and victims will not hate each other since they will not see each other. There is nothing more macabre than this disappearance of hatred which, of course, has nothing to do with peacefulness or love. It is striking how rarely, and with how little hatred, Hiroshima victims mention those who have caused their suffering. This, however, does not mean that hatred will play no part in the next war: since it will be considered indispensable for psychological warfare, the production of hatred will, no doubt, be organized. In order to nourish what a perverted age calls "morale," identifiable and visible objects of hatred will be exhibited, in emergency cases invented—"Jews" of all kinds. Since hatred can bloom only if the objects of hatred are visible and can fall into the hater's hand, it will be the domestic scene from which one will choose scapegoats. Since the targets of this artificially manufactured hatred and the target of the military attacks will be totally different, the war mentality will become actually schizophrenic.

I HAVE PUBLISHED THESE WORDS in order to prevent them from becoming true. If we do not stubbornly keep in mind the strong probability of the disaster, and if we do not act accordingly, we will be unable to find a way out. There is nothing more frightful than to be right.—And if some, paralyzed by the gloomy likelihood of the catastrophe, have already lost courage, they still have a chance to prove their love of man by heeding the cynical maxim: "Let's go on working as though we had the right to hope. Our despair is none of our business."

Selected Bibliography

Books by Günther Anders (or published under Günther Stern)

Über das Haben: Sieben Kapitel zur Ontologie der Erkenntnis. Bonn 1928.

Kafka-Pro und Contra: Die Prozess-Unterlagen. Munich 1951.

Die Antiquiertheit des Menschen. Volume I. Über die Seele im Zeitalter der zweiten industriellen Revolution. Munich 1956.

Der Mann auf der Brücke: Tagebuch aus Hiroshima und Nagasaki. Munich 1959.

(and Claude Eatherly) Burning Conscience: The Case of the Hiroshima Pilot. New York 1962.

Wir Eichmannsöhne: Offener Brief an Klaus Eichmann. Munich 1964.

Die Blick vom Turm: Fabeln. Munich 1968.

Visit Beautiful Vietnam: ABC der Aggressionen heute. Cologne 1968.

Der Blick vom Mond: Reflexionen über Weltraumflüge. Munich 1970.

Endzeit und Zeitenende: Gedanken über die atomare Situation. Munich 1972.

Besuch im Hades. Munich 1979.

Die Antiquiertheit des Menschen. Volume II. Über die Zerstörung des Lebens im Zeitalter der dritten industriellen Revolution. Munich 1980.

Hiroshima ist überall. Munich 1982.

Ketzereien. Munich 1982.

Mensch ohne Welt: Schriften zur Kunst und Literatur. Munich 1984.

Tagebücher und Gedichte. Munich 1985.

Lieben gestern: Notizen zur Geschichte des Fühlens. Munich 1986.

Gewalt-ja oder nein: Eine notwendige Diskussion. Edited by Manfred Bissinger. Munich 1987.

Die molussische Katakombe: Roman. 2nd Edition. Munich 2012.

Über Heidegger. Edited by Gerhard Oberschlick in association with Werner Reimann as translator. Munich 2001.

Die Kirschenschlacht: Dialoge mit Hannah Arendt und ein akademisches Nachwort. Edited by Gerhard Oberschlick. Munich 2011.

Published Articles and Book Chapters by Anders

Zur Phänomenologie des Zuhörens. Zeitschrift für Musikwissenschaft 9 (1927): 610–619.

Über die sog. 'Seinsverbundenheit' des Bewusstseins: Anlässlich Karl Mannheim 'Ideologie und Utopie.' Archiv für Sozialwissenschaft und Sozialpolitik no. 64 (1930): 492–509.

Spuk und Radio. Anbruch XII, no. 2 (1930): 65–66.

(co-authored with Hannah Arendt) Rilkes 'Duineser Elegien.' Neue Schweizer Rundschau 23, no. 11 (1930): 855–871.

Une interprétation de l'a posteriori. Translated by Emmanuel Levinas. Recherches philosophiques 4 (1934–1935): 65–80.

Pathologie de la liberté: Essai sur la nonidentification. Translated by P.-A. Stéphanopoli. Recherches philosophiques 6 (1936–1937): 22–54.

Nihilismus und Existenz. Die Neue Rundschau 5 (October 1946): 48–76.

On the Pseudo-Concreteness of Heidegger's Philosophy. Philosophy and Phenomenological Research 8, no. 3 (March 1948): 337–371.

Der Emigrant. Merkur 16, no.7 (July 1962): 601–622.

Zur Kuba-Krise. Blätter für deutsche und internationale Politik no. 11 (1962): 834–836.

Mein Judentum. In: Hans Jürgen Schultz, ed. Mein Judentum. Stuttgart 1978.

Die Antiquiertheit des Hassens. In: Renate Kahle/Heiner Menzner/Gerhard Vinnai, eds. Hass: Die Macht eines unerwünschten Gefühls. Reinbek bei Hamburg 1985.

Die Antiquiertheit des Proletariats. Forum no. 462–464 (July-September 1992): 7–11.

Secondary Sources on Anders

Althaus, Gabriele. Leben zwischen Sein und Nichts: Drei Studien zu Günther Anders. Berlin 1989.

Babich, Babette. O Superman! Or Being Towards Transhumanism: Martin Heidegger, Günther Anders, and Media Aesthetics. Divinatio 36 (Autumn-Winter 2012–2013): 41–99.

Bahr, Raimund, ed. Urlaub vom Nichts: Dokumentation des gleichnamigen Symposiums zum 100. Geburtstag von Günther Anders im Juni 2002 in Wien. St. Wolfgang 2004.

_____. Günther Anders: Leben und Denken im Wort. St. Wolfgang 2010.

Brumlik, Micha. Günther Anders: Zur Existenzialontologie der Emigration. In: Dan Diner, ed. Zivilisationsbruch: Denken nach Auschwitz. Frankfurt am Main 1988.

Dawsey, Jason. Where Hitler's Name is Never Spoken: Günther Anders in 1950s Vienna. In: Günter Bischof/Fritz Plasser/Eva Maltschnig, eds. Austrian Lives (CAS=21). New Orleans/Innsbruck 2012.

_____. The Limits of the Human in the Age of Technological Revolution: Günther Anders, Post-Marxism, and the Emergence of Technology Critique. Phil. Diss. University of Chicago 2013.

Dries, Christian. Günther Anders. Paderborn 2009.

_____. Die Welt als Vernichtungslager: Eine kritische Theorie der Moderne im Anschluss an Günther Anders, Hannah Arendt und Hans Jonas. Bielefeld 2012.

Ellensohn, Reinhard. Der andere Anders: Günther Anders als Musikphilosoph. Frankfurt am Main 2008.

Fetz, Bernhard, ed. Dossier Günther Anders. In: Klaus Kastberger/Konrad Paul Liessmann, eds. Die Dichter und das Denken: Wechselspiele zwischen Literatur und Philosophie. Vienna 2004.

_____. Günther Anders' literarische Moral der Philosophie. In: Bernhard Fetz, Das unmögliche Ganze: Zur literarischen Kritik der Kultur. Munich 2009.

_____. Anthropologie im Exil: Das Archiv des Schriftstellers und Philosophen Günther Anders. In: Stéphanie Cudré-Maroux/Irmgard Wirtz, eds. Literaturarchiv—Literarisches Archiv: Zur Poetik literarischer Archive. Göttingen 2013.

Liessmann, Konrad Paul. Günther Anders zur Einführung. Hamburg 1988.

_____, ed. Günther Anders kontrovers. Munich 1992.

_____. Hot Potatoes: Zum Briefwechsel zwischen Günther Anders und Theodor W. Adorno. Zeitschrift für kritische Philosophie 6, no. 98 (1998): 29–38.

_____. Verzweiflung und Verantwortung: Koinzidenz und Differenz im Denken von Hans Jonas und Günther Anders. In: Christian Wiese/Eric Jacobson, eds. Weiterwohnlichkeit der Welt: Zur Aktualität von Jonas. Berlin 2003.

Lohmann, Margret. Philosophieren in der Endzeit: Zur Gegenwartsanalyse von Günther Anders. Munich 1996.

Lütkehaus, Ludger. Philosophieren nach Hiroshima: Über Günther Anders. Frankfurt am Main 1992.

Müller, Marcel. Von der Weltfremdheit zur Antiquiertheit: Philosophische Anthropologie bei Günther Anders. Marburg 2012.

Palandt, Sabine. Die Kunst der Vorausschau: Günther Anders' methodische und psychologische Ansätze zur Technikkritik. Berlin 1999.

Pollmann, Ann-Kathrin. Ein offener Brief: Günther Anders schreibt Klaus Eichmann. In: Werner Renz, ed. Interessen um Eichmann: Israelische Justiz, deutsche Strafverfolgung und alte Kameradschaften. Frankfurt am Main 2012.

Reimann, Werner. Verweigerte Versöhnung: Zur Philosophie von Günther Anders. Vienna 1990.

Schraube, Ernst. 'Torturing Things Until They Confess': Günther Anders' Critique of Technology. Science as Culture 14, no. 1 (2005): 77–85.

Schubert, Elke. Günther Anders. Reinbek bei Hamburg 1992.

Van Dijk, Paul. Anthropology in the Age of Technology: The Philosophical Contribution of Günther Anders. Translated by Frans Kooymans. Atlanta 2000.

Wiesenberger, Berthold. Enzyklopädie der apokalyptischen Welt: Kulturphilosophie, Gesellschaftstheorie und Zeitdiagnose bei Günther Anders und Theodor W. Adorno. Munich 2003.

Wittulski, Eckhard. Kein Ort, Nirgends: Zur Gesellschaftskritik Günther Anders'. Frankfurt am Main 1989.

List of Contributors

Günter Bischof is a native of Austria and has taught at UNO for more than 20 years. He studied English and History at the Universities of Innsbruck, Vienna, New Orleans and holds a PhD in American History from Harvard University. He is the Marshall Plan Professor of History and the Director of Center Austria at the University of New Orleans; he was appointed a University Research Professor in June 2011. He served as a visiting professor at the Universities of Munich, Innsbruck, Salzburg, Vienna, the *Wirtschaftsuniversität Wien*, VSE in Prague, and the RGGU in Moscow, as well the "Post-Katrina" Visiting Professor at LSU. He is the author of *Austria in the First Cold War, 1945/55: The Leverage of the* Weak (1999), coeditor of *Contemporary Austrian Studies* (23 vols) and the co-editor of another 20 books on topics of international contemporary history (esp. World War II and the Cold War in Central Europe), among them with Barbara Stelzl-Marx and Stefan Karner *The Vienna Summit of 1961* (2014), with Stephen E. Ambrose, *Facts against Falsehood: Eisenhower and the German P.O.W.'s* (1992), *Eisenhower: A Centenary Assessment* (1995), and with Saki Dockrill, *Cold War Respite: The Geneva Summit of 1955* (2000). He serves as a "Presidential Counselor" at the National World War II Museum in New Orleans and on the board of the Botstiber Institute for Austrian-American Studies.

Jason Dawsey teaches history at the University of Southern Mississippi. He received his PhD in Modern European history from the University of Chicago. His dissertation is titled "The Limits of the Human in the Age of Technological Revolution: Günther Anders, Post-Marxism, and the Emergence of Technology Critique." His dissertation draws on materials from the *Anders Nachlass* at the Literature Archives in Vienna. He is the author of "Where Hitler's Name is Never Spoken: Günther Anders in 1950s Vienna," which appeared in Volume XXI of *Contemporary Austrian Studies*, ed. Günter Bischof, Fritz Plasser, and Eva Maltschnig (New Orleans and Innsbruck, 2012) and of the forthcoming "After Hiroshima: Günther Anders and the History of Anti-Nuclear Critique," in *Unthinking the Imaginary War: Intellectual Reflections on the Nuclear Age, 1945–1990*, ed. Benjamin Ziemann and Holger Nehring (Stanford UP, in preparation). His broader research interests include critiques of modern technology, the history of Western Marxism, and the emergence of Holocaust awareness.

Jean-Pierre Dupuy is Professor Emeritus of Social and Political Philosophy, Ecole Polytechnique, Paris and Professor of Political Science, Stanford University. He is a member of the French Academy of Technology and of the Conseil Général des Mines, the French High Magistracy that oversees and regulates industry, energy and the environment. He chairs the Ethics Committee of the French High Authority on Nuclear Safety and Security. He is the Director of the Research Program of Imitatio, a new foundation devoted to the dissemination and discussion of René Girard's mimetic theory. His most recent work has dealt with the topic of catastrophe, and is being translated and collected in a volume to be published by Stanford University Press. Among his most recent publications: *The Mechanization of the*

Mind (Princeton University Press, 2000); *Pour un catastrophisme éclairé* (Paris, Seuil, 2002); *Avions-nous oublié le mal? Penser la politique après le 11 septembre* (Paris, Bayard, 2002); *Petite métaphysique des tsunamis* (Paris, Seuil, 2005); *Retour de Tchernobyl: Journal d'un homme en colère* (Paris, Seuil, 2006) ; *On the Origins of Cognitive Science* (The MIT Press, 2009) ; *La Marque du sacré* (Paris, Carnets Nord, 2009); *Dans l'œil du cyclone* (Carnets Nord, 2009); *L'Avenir de l'économie* (Flammarion, 2012).

Reinhard Ellensohn studied Philosophy and History at the University of Vienna and holds MA degrees in Philosophy (Mag. phil.) and in Library and Information Studies (MSc). In 2008 he published a monograph about Günther Anders' philosophy of music entitled *Der andere Anders: Günther Anders als Musikphilosoph* (Frankfurt/Main 2008). Currently he is engaged in the preparation of an edition of Anders' early writings on the Philosophy of Music from his literary estate, within the context of a scientific project financed by the Austrian Science Fund (FWF) and under direction of Konrad Paul Liessmann and Bernhard Fetz, entitled "Günther Anders: Editing and Contextualisation of Selected Writings from the Estate."

Bernhard Fetz is director of the *Literaturarchiv der Österreichischen Nationalbibliothek* and associate professor of German Studies at the University of Vienna. He has played a leading role in collaborative work on major research projects, for example with the *Ludwig Boltzmann Institut für Geschichte und Theorie der Biographie*. First Hermann Broch Fellow at the Beinecke Library/Yale University in 1998; he serves as a literary critic for Radio Austria, *Die Presse*, and the *Neue Zürcher Zeitung*. He has published extensively on twentieth-century literary and cultural history and is co-editor of the ten-volume edition of the works of Albert Drach, as well as co-editor of the book series "Profile". Other recent publication are *Das unmögliche Ganze: Zur literarischen Kritik der Kultur* (Munich, 2009); *Die Biographie—Zur Grundlegung ihrer Theorie* (ed., Berlin, 2009); *Die Ernst Jandl Show* (ed., with Hannes Schweiger, Salzburg, 2010); *Theorie der Biographie. Grundlagentexte und Kommentar* (ed. with Wilhelm Hemecker, Berlin, 2011).

Konrad Paul Liessmann is professor for Teaching Methods in the Fields of Philosophy and Ethics at the Department of Philosophy, University of Vienna. He holds an MA Degree in German Language and Literature and PhD Degree in Philosophy. Since 1997 he has been the Academic Director of the annual international symposium *"Philosophicum Lech"* and Editor of the book series of the same name, from 2004–2008 he was Director of the Studies Program at the Faculty for Philosophy and Educational Science, University of Vienna, from 2008–2012 he was Vice Dean of the Faculty for Philosophy and Educational Science, University of Vienna. Research fields: Aesthetics, philosophy of the 19th and 20th centuries (Marx, Kierkegaard, Nietzsche, Adorno, Anders); theory of education, philosophy of culture. He is the author of over 20 books, some have been translated into languages such as Dutch, Spanish, Czech, Russian, Croatian, and Chinese. Among his most recent publications: *Philosophie der modernen Kunst,* 5th ed. (2000), *Die großen Philosophen und ihre Probleme,* 5th ed. (2001); *Philosophie des verbotenen Wissens: Friedrich Nietzsche und die schwarzen Seiten des Denkens* (2000/2010); *Günther Anders: Philosophieren im Zeitalter der technologischen Revolutionen* (2002); *Ästhetik der Verführung: Kierkegaards Konstruktion der Erotik aus dem Geiste der*

Kunst (2005); *Theorie der Unbildung: Die Irrtümer der Wissensgesellschaft*, 17th ed. (2010); *Reiz und Rührung. Über ästhetische Empfindungen* (2008); *Schönheit* (2009); *Das Universum der Dinge: Zur Ästhetik des Alltäglichen* (2010); *Lob der Grenze: Kritik der politischen Unterscheidungskraft* (2012).

Berthold Molden works on the global intellectual history of the Cold War, with regional focusses on Europe and Latin America; he is the 2012/2013 Marshall Plan Chair of Austrian and European Studies at the University of New Orleans and taught as a Mellon Visiting Scholar at the University of Chicago during the spring of 2011. In 2010 he was a Visiting Professor of Global History at the University of Vienna, where he also serves on the faculties of the Erasmus Mundus MA program "Global Studies: A European Perspective" and the MA degree program in "Higher Latin American Studies." From 2005 to 2010, he directed an international research project on European Cold War memory at the Ludwig Boltzmann Institute for European History and Public Sphere, of which he was a founding member. He is co-editor of *Polyphonic Pasts: Politics of History in Latin America* (2009), and of *Friedrich Katz: Essays on the Life and Work of a Transnational Historian* (2012).

Andreas Oberprantacher is Assistant Professor at the Department of Philosophy, University of Innsbruck; Core Faculty Member at the UNESCO Chair for Peace Studies, University of Innsbruck; senior lecturer for Philosophy, Sociology as well as for Peace and Conflict Studies in Bangkok, Thailand, and Puducherry, India. He is the secretary general of the Austrian Society of Philosophy. Recent Publications in English include: "Who is we? On the Excessive Use of a Political Pronoun," *L'Excès. L'hypermodernitè, entre droit et politique*, Pascal Mbongo, ed. (Paris: mare & martin, 2012); "Off Limits: Elastic Border Regimes and the (Visual) Politics of Making Things Public," *Activist Media and Biopolitics: Critical Media Intervention in the Age of Biopower*, Wolfgang Sützl and Theo Hug, eds. (Innsbruck: Innsbruck University Press, 2011); with Marie-Luisa Frick: "Shared is not yet Sharing, Or: What Makes Social Networking Services Public?" *IRIE: International Review of Information Ethics* 15 (2011); "Culture Jammed. The Art of Subverting Violence." *Medienimpulse. Beiträge zur Medienpädagogik* 2 (2011); "Beyond Rivalry? Rethinking Community in View of Apocalyptical Violence," *Contagion: Journal of Violence, Mimesis and Culture* 17/1 (2010); with Marie-Luisa Frick, eds., *Power and Justice in International Relations: Interdisciplinary Approaches to Global Challenges* (Farnham: Ashgate, 2009).

Wolfgang Palaver is Professor of Catholic social thought and Dean of the Faculty of Catholic Theology at the University of Innsbruck, Austria. From 2007 to 2011 he served as president of the Colloquium on Violence and Religion (COV&R). He has written articles and books on Thomas Hobbes, Carl Schmitt, René Girard and on the relationship between religion and violence. His most recent books are: *René Girard's Mimetic Theory* (2013); *Passions in Economy, Politics, and the Media* (ed. with P. Steinmair-Pösel; 2005); *Aufgeklärte Apokalyptik: Religion, Gewalt und Frieden im Zeitalter der Globalisierung* (ed. with A. Exenberger and K. Stoeckl); *Politische Philosophie versus Politische Theologie? Die Frage der Gewalt im Spannungsfeld von Politik und Religion* (ed. with A. Oberprantacher and D. Regensburger; 2011); *Gewalt und Religion: Ursache oder Wirkung?* (with René Girard; 2010).

Kerstin Putz is a student of German Studies and Philosophy at the University of Vienna (Mag.ª phil.). She is specializing in literary and cultural theory, aesthetics, interrelationships between literature and philosophy with a particular focus on the *Frankfurter Schule*. Her MA thesis dealt with the concept of realism in the works of Alexander Kluge. In 2011 she received a dissertation research grant from the University of Vienna for the preparation of her thesis on the theory of the anecdote in Cultural Sciences, as well as on anecdotes in Günther Anders' interdisciplinary writings between literature and philosophy. Since 2012 she has served as a researcher in the project "Günther Anders: Editing and Contextualisation of Selected Writings from the Estate" (direction: Konrad Paul Liessmann, Bernhard Fetz). This project is funded by the Austrian Science Fund (FWF) and is being hosted by the Literature Archives of the Austrian National Library; she is working on the preparation of an edition of Anders' correspondences.

Elisabeth Röhrlich is researcher and lecturer in contemporary history at the University of Vienna. She holds a PhD in contemporary history from Tübingen University, Germany. Her dissertation dealt with Bruno Kreisky's foreign policy and was published as her first book in 2009. In 2010, the book was awarded the Bruno Kreisky Prize for the Political Book (Recognition Award). In 2011 Röhrlich was short-time visiting research fellow at the German Historical Institute in Washington, D.C. Her current research activities focus on the early history of the International Atomic Energy Agency (IAEA), the origins of the nuclear nonproliferation regime as well as on Europe's nuclear history. In 2011, together with Oliver Rathkolb, she was cofounder of the research project "The Early History of the IAEA" (funded by a research grant of the Austrian Central Bank). She is partner of the Nuclear Proliferation International History Project (NPIHP) at the Woodrow Wilson International Center for Scholars. She was also one of the coordinators of the EU Erasmus Intensive Program "Atomic Energy, the Threat of Nuclear Warfare, and the History of European Integration" (ATEU), 2012–2013.